The 16th edition
London Baby Directory

C000319725

20

78

LONDON BABY DIRECTORY
BABY AWARDS 2012

92

80

96

The 16th edition
London Baby Directory

contents

The
Baby Directory Website

www.babydirectory.com

The site includes

Product reviews   Health Clinic

What's on calendar   Doorstep favourites

As well as competitions, news, views and events

welcome

Welcome to The 16th edition London Baby Directory

photograph: Robin Farquhar-Thomson

Clare, Georgia, Max and the office mutt

Congratulations if you are expecting your first baby in this Jubilee and London 2012 Olympic year. There will be a lot to take in over the next few months as you prepare to welcome your first born into the world. Where to have the baby? Which pushchair or car seat? Do you need a moses basket - and can you find a mattress to fit?

For parents with toddlers and preschool children the decisions don't get easier, if anything they are more plentiful. When do I potty train? What nursery or school? Where can we go on holiday? Which is the best toddler activity for my child? Who is the best baby photographer? How can I help my children learn to read?

In this guide we provide answers to your questions, allay your fears and anxieties and line you up with the best companies or people who can help you in and around London. You will be the most sorted mum in town.

Our website www.babydirectory.com also offers you information at your fingertips so, do register for our monthly e-newsletter which keeps you in touch with What's On and What's New around town.

London continues to be a great place to raise a family, so much to see and do: great baby and toddler activities, excellent shopping and loving nursery schools catering for the busiest of working mums. However, if we have left anything out which deserves a slot then do let me know at editor@babydirectory.com.

Clare Flawn-Thomas

Clare Flawn-Thomas Editor

Don't forget to like and follow us...
facebook.com/babydirectory
twitter.com/babydirectory
londonbabydirectory.blogspot.co.uk

Edited, designed and published by Brockwell Publishing

Tel: +44 (0)20 7733 0088
editor@babydirectory.com

www.babydirectory.com

Editor	Clare Flawn-Thomas
Designer	Caroline Mills
Contributors	Laura Lee Davies
	Emma Perry
	Livia Pizzichini
Advertising	Patricia Bellotti
	Geeta Chamdal

pregnancy and birth

Choosing a preferred path early in pregnancy can help get you the best suited antenatal care.

Now that almost all NHS midwifery is organised in 'teams', it is likely you will see more than one midwife during check-ups, quite possibly having never met the midwife who is going to deliver your baby. There is no reason why this should be a problem, but some people feel the 'continuity of care' from one person or a small familiar team is worth ensuring by 'going private'.

Private care and birth

Full **private hospital** maternity care includes antenatal check-ups, tests and scans carried out by the team who will then deliver your baby. Alternatively, it is possible to hire your own **independent midwife** who will carry out all your check-ups, be present at the birth and oversee the early days of post-natal care. If you have to transfer to an NHS hospital before or during labour, your midwife will either continue the delivery but more commonly act as your birthing partner while the hospital team delivers your baby. It is also possible to hire a **doula** to offer practical and emotional support in pregnancy, birth and early parenthood. A doula is a not a qualified health professional so during medical procedures would act as a 'birth partner' while you receive NHS or private medical attention.

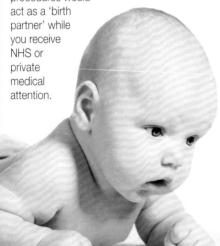

NHS options

Although services vary from area to area, generally your NHS options will be to give birth at a **hospital**, at a **birth centre** (a smaller clinic dedicated to maternity care) or at **home**. When your GP confirms your pregnancy you will be assigned a midwife team either attached to the surgery or a specific hospital. However, it's worth noting that you can change your intended place to give birth, so do ask for details of your options and visit the different places if you want to explore all alternatives.

What to consider

Your budget, where you live and your health are key factors.

If consistent one-to-one care is important to you, you might want to choose a private option. These days delivery choices like water or home birth are more commonly offered through NHS teams so the chosen manner of birth has become less of an issue.

Bear in mind you will have to attend scans, check-ups and potentially getting to the labour rooms in a hurry, so keeping the location accessible to you will be a good idea.

Lastly, if you have specific health concerns you might opt for a specialist obstetrician who can oversee all your antenatal and labour care. However, in some cases, specific NHS maternity units may offer the best resources for particular medical needs and potential emergencies.

Both private and NHS services should be able to accommodate your birth plan preferences if you are, for example, hoping to use a birthing pool or 'active birth' techniques (movement and massage during labour to relieve pain and aid birth) or even a planned caesarean.

pregnancy & birth

ante natal classes

HYPNOBIRTHING CLASSES

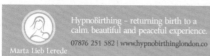

HypnoBirthing – returning birth to a calm, beautiful and peaceful experience.
Marta Lieb Lerede
07876 251 582 | www.hypnobirthinglondon.co

Hypnobirthing London   **07876 251 582**
www.hypnobirthinglondon.co
What if giving birth made you feel Calm, Powerful, Connected and Blissful? HypnoBirthing® antenatal classes provide you with all the tools to achieve that. We will teach you how to reconnect with your body so you can enjoy all the benefits that nature has in store for you and your baby.

NCT CLASSES

National Childbirth Trust   **0300 330 0770**
www.nct.org.uk
The NCT has over 40 years experience of providing ante-natal and post-natal courses across the UK. There are couples courses, women-only courses, 8 week courses practising different positions for labour as well as information on pain relief, life with a new baby and postnatal care. NCT classes cost between £190-£300 per course depending on where you live.

NHS CLASSES

National Health Service   **0845 4647**
If you have chosen a hospital birth you may be offered NHS ante-natal classes (or parentcraft classes) at the hospital or at a midwife-led clinic. The ante-natal teachers are midwives who will cover waterbirth (if available at the hospital), breastfeeding, labour and pain relief available, complications in labour and Caesareans. You can also just go on a hospital tour to see where you need to come when in labour.

E8

Bridget Baker   **020 7249 3224**
Bridget Baker taught with the NCT for over 35 years but now runs independent birth preparation classes, groups and individual sessions in Hackney, Islington and the City.

N10

Plus Baby   **07961 363 833**
www.plusbaby.co.uk
Much more than just antenatal classes - Plus Baby supports parents through the birth and beyond with professional, practical, personal advice. Their antenatal classes are taught by trained healthcare professionals and cover all the options for labour, birth and feeding. They also give practical support for six months post birth with access to our local knowledge bank and help and advice if and when you decide to return to work. Classes are in Crouch End, East Finchley, Hampstead, Highgate, Muswell Hill, and the surrounding areas.

The Baby Moon   **07767 348 462**
www.thebabymoon.co.uk
Set up by Mars Lord and Rebecca Stewart, Baby Moon offers private antenatal classes on a one-to-one basis for couples and/or mums-to-be in Muswell Hill, N10. Postnatally they also offer breastfeeding support and sleep counselling.

N14

Jill Benjoya Miller   **020 8445 1159**
Jill Benjoya Miller offers Active Birth pregnancy yoga classes, and a birth preparation workshop in venues around in North Finchley, N12. She is also a Doula and can provide ante and postnatal support to new mothers.

Karen Patrick   **020 8882 5996**
karen.patrick@mac.com
Active birth teacher with weekly classes held in Watford and Children's centers in Hertfordshire. You can start from the 18th week of your pregnancy right up until the baby arrives. There is also weekend course run with Sarah Bearman, a midwife from Watford ABC, for couples. Classes are very popular so book as soon as you know you are pregnant. Karen also offers 6 week postnatal classes with baby massage (and a class for Dads as well).

N16

Jessica James   **020 8806 4820**
www.jessicabirthclasses.co.uk
Jessica offers weekly pregnancy yoga classes in Stoke Newington and during your last trimester she runs a couples birth preparation class. She originally trained with the NCT and Active Birth Centre but now operates independently. Postnatally Jessica offers groups baby yoga, talking, sharing experiences and how to manage life with a new baby.

Yogahome   **020 7249 2425**
11 Allen Road, Stoke Newington, N16 8SB
www.yogahome.com
Yogahome offers a variety of classes for mums-to-be including pregnancy yoga and birth preparation courses taught by Kirsty Gallacher. It's a great venue to connect and meet other local mothers, prepare for birth and get back into shape afterwards (postnatal Pilates). There are a range of mother and baby classes to enjoy too including baby yoga, music and movement for babies and toddlers and baby gym. Acupuncture, reflexology, cranial osteopathy are offered by complementary therapists to trouble shoot pregnancy aches and pains or unsettled babies.

N19

Active Birth Centre   **020 7281 6760**
25 Bickerton Road, Archway, N19 5JT
www.activebirthcentre.com
The Active Birth Centre based in Archway was set up and is run by the renowned childbirth educator Janet Balaskas. She offers Active Birth pregnancy yoga classes, an Active Birth preparation course (2-day over a weekend), hypnobirthing

and Active water birth courses. Postnatally, you can attend Baby & Me classes to help you adjust to new motherhood, get breastfeeding support, learn baby massage and first aid techniques.

Lynn Murphy   020 7281 7059
www.activebirthcentre.com

Lynn runs Active Birth classes at the Active Birth Centre and locally in N19. She also offers post natal yoga, mother and baby yoga and baby massage classes.

NW3

Yvonne Moore   020 7794 2056
www.yvonnemooreyogabirth.com

Yvonne Moore is an established childbirth educator and a member of YogaBirth. She teaches ante and postnatal yoga and birth preparation courses in North London. She has day-time, evening and weekend groups and also teaches privately. The areas she covers include: NW3 (Hampstead /Belsize Park); NW1 (Primrose Hill/Swiss Cottage); N19 (Archway); and N7 (Tuffnell Park, Kentish Town and Camden).

Gilly Keith   07968 566 396
www.antenatalclasslondon.co.uk

Gilly Keith is a qualified midwife offering group and private antenatal classes from her home in Primrose Hill, NW3.

NW6

Julie Krausz   020 8459 2903
www.juliekrausz.co.uk

For the last 15 years Julie has run yoga for pregnancy, Active Birth classes, postnatal yoga classes, breastfeeding and massage workshops in NW6.

NW7

Madeleine Moss   07957 216 112
www.bumptobirthandbeyond.co.uk

Madeleine Moss offers private antenatal classes in Mill Hill and Swiss Cottage in north west London. The course prepares couples and mums-to-be with advice and information in a non-judgemental way. Madeleine also runs a specialist courses for mums wishing for a normal birth following a caesarean section.

NW8

Gentle Birth Method   020 8530 1146
Viveka, 27a Queen's Terrace, NW8 6EA
www.gentlebirthmethod.com

Gentle Birth Method antenatal classes are offered at Viveka in north west London. The courses are held weekly in the evenings with a "trial" class to let you see if this is the right course for you. Gentle birth, developed by Gowri Motha, prepares you both mentally and physically to be "birth fit" based around a combination of self-hypnosis and visualisation techniques. A book accompanies the series for those who cannot make the classes.

SE22

Verona Hall   07946 093 094
www.veronahall.co.uk

Verona is a south London gem, offering small group and private antenatal classes, postnatal and breastfeeding support for south east London mums. Classes are held at the Family Natural Health Centre in Lordship Lane, SE22 or in your own home. Postnatally she also runs workshops covering baby massage, breastfeeding (she's a lactation consultant) and other new-parenthood challenges. Visit her excellent website to see time/dates of classes.

Need to Know: Antenatal Tests

All tests are optional and you will be given detailed information about what they are before taking them.

- **Blood tests**: Between 8 and 12 weeks you will have a first detailed appointment with a midwife. Blood tests are taken to check for conditions or infections to en sure you do not need further medical care or treatment. You might be offered an optional test to check the fetus for conditions like Down's Syndrome.

- **Urine tests**: At each antenatal appoint-ment you will be asked to give a urine sample. This is a quick, easy and important way to check for signs of pre-eclampsia, which affects 1 in 10 pregnancies and is safely treatable if detected.

- **Blood pressure**: This is also taken at each antenatal appointment as a general health precaution.

If your doctor or midwife have any concerns you might be asked to take extra tests later on in your pregnancy, just to ensure you are still in good health.

pregnancy & birth

Prepare4birth   07949 951 769
www.prepare4birth.co.uk
Swedish born Nina Thorstensson Nwese is a registered nurse, nurturing birth trained doula, baby massage teacher, certified life coach, and complementary health practitioner with experience in pre and post pregnancy. She offers 1-day intensive antenatal workshop in your own home or in small group classes.

SW3

Heather Guerrini   020 7352 0245
www.wellmums.co.uk
Heather teaches "Early Bird" classes for mothers in their 1st and 2nd trimesters in Chelsea, SW3. She also offer 1-2-1 private classes. She is a gentle birth method practitioner incorporating massage and reflexology.

SW6

New Baby Company Fulham   020 8785 3528
Babylist, The Broomhouse, 50 Sulivan Road, Fulham, SW6 3DX
www.newbabycompany.com
Established in 2002, New Baby Company runs regular antenatal courses in Fulham called "Birth and Beyond" which prepares mums and dads for the birth and up to 3 months after baby is born.

Stacia Smales Hill   020 7385 7417
Stacia holds weekly Birthlight yoga classes from her home in Fulham and towards the end of your pregnancy you can book onto a birth preparation course (NCT/Birthing from Within).

SW11

Nadia Raafat   07771 687 128
www.hypnoyoga.co.uk
Nadia Raafat offers weekly or drop-in pregnancy yoga classes and birth preparation classes in 5 south west London venues in Battersea and Clapham. She can also teach small groups of partners in her home. Nadia is trained in Sivananda Hatha yoga and is trained in Birthligh, and is a doula - as well as a being a mum of two. There is lots of useful information about pregnancy and birth on the website and her blog.

Lesley-Anne Kerr   020 7564 3316
www.expecting.info   07871 528 309
Independent pregnancy yoga classes and Active Birth preparation classes held in SW1 and SW11. She also runs post-natal classes for mothers and babies incorporating massage, Pilates and breastfeeding consultations.

SW13 and SW15

Natalie Meddings   0797 6261542
www.activebirthlondon.co.uk
Natalie Meddings is an Active Birth pregnancy yoga teacher and London doula. She holds pregnancy yoga classes in Barnes and Putney, and also offers a one-day birth preparation workshops for couples and early parenting workshops to help you adjust to life with a new baby. She is also behind a free website www.TellMeAGoodBirthStory.com which connects parents who have had a good birth experience with those who have yet to give birth.

SW16

Kathleen Beegan   020 8769 3613
Kathleen Beegan offers weekly pregnancy yoga classes (Yogabirth), postnatal yoga classes with baby massage as well as postnatal yoga recovery and baby massage courses from her home studio in Streatham. She is also a birth Doula in London and offers a one day birth preparation workshop for couples at the weekends.

SW19

Vicki Scott   020 8785 3528
www.newbabycompany.com
Vicki Scott is an established midwife and antenatal teacher. She runs "Birth and Beyond" private antenatal classes in London for parents living in South West and West London, with classes taking place in Fulham and Wimbledon. In addition Vicki offers "First Aid", and a "Starting Solids" course for parents looking for weaning support at 4-6 months.

SW20

Sue Lewis   020 8946 8561
www.suelewisantenatal.co.uk
Sue Lewis has been running independent antenatal birth preparation classes, postnatal exercise classes (Pilates based) and a range of baby confidence classes for over 20 years in Wimbledon. She has small and personalised groups which help new parents meet others with a similar due date. She has a post-graduate training in Pilates and is also a postnatal physiotherapist helping mums with postnatal gynaecological problems.

W1

Zita West   020 7224 0017
37 Manchester Street, W1U 7LT
www.zitawest.com
One-to-one antenatal birth and parenting workshops for couples plus hypnobirthing, breastfeeding and twins classes.

The Portland Hospital   020 7390 6553
for Women and Children
234 Great Portland Street, W1W 5QT
www.theportlandhospital.com
The Portland Hospital offers a wide range of practical and informative antenatal classes including Child Birth Preparation Classes, Breastfeeding Workshops and First Aid and Safety Classes, available either on a one-to-one class basis, group courses or Saturday workshop. Antenatal classes are available to expectant parents regardless of whether they will be delivering at the hospital.

FUTURE HEALTH
CORD BLOOD CELLS

FUTURE HEALTH
CORD TISSUE CELLS

Because...

... you deserve a long, healthy life.

... you're the best thing that's happened to us and we want nothing but the best for you.

... chances like this only come around once in a lifetime.

... we decided to store your umbilical cord stem cells the same day we decided on your name.

... we've found someone who can save your stem cells from your cord tissue as well as your cord blood.

... finally the whole idea of collecting your stem cells doesn't seem scary or confusing any more.

... it's better to have your stem cells and not need them, than need them and not have them.

In addition we also offer

FUTURE HEALTH
TOOTH CELLS

... we don't want to hide your future health under your pillow.

... we know someone even better than the tooth fairy.

... we've chosen to prepare for what the future may hold.

... we've found someone who cares for your health just as much as we do.

... your toothy grin is our peace of mind.

... your little tooth could be a big help in the future.

Because we want you to have the facts simply explained, about why you should have your cord blood and cord tissue or tooth stem cells collected and preserved, we'd like to send you our Information Pack. To request it, simply call our Customer Care Team on 0800 954 5335, email custcare@fhbb.com quoting London Baby Directory or visit our website at www.fhbb.com.

pregnancy & birth

W2

The Lindo Wing   **020 3312 6224**
St Mary's Hospital, South Wharf Road, W2 1NY
www.imperial.nhs.uk/privatehealthcare
From 2012 The Lindo Wing will be offering practical and
comprehensive antenatal classes, either on a group or a one
to one basis.

W4

Christine Hill   **020 8994 4349**
78 Grove Park Road, Chiswick, W4 3QA
www.christine-hill-associates.com
Christine Hill runs well-established birth preparation classes in
Chiswick.

W8

Lynda Leach   **01707 660 318**
The Life Centre, 15 Edge St, Kensington, W8 7PN
www.lyndaleach.co.uk
Ante-natal classes designed for couples (although women
may attend on their own). Courses last for 5 weeks and are
held on Wednesday evenings in Kensington W8. All classes
are led by Lynda, who is a practising midwife and lactation
consultant. Classes have an informal atmosphere and are
interactive; they do not focus solely on information-giving and
they are designed to help prospective parents develop coping
strategies for labour and the transition to parenthood.

Need to Know: Cord Blood

The collection of cord blood is from the
placenta and umbilical cord and is totally
painless. The blood, which contains stem
cells, is stored for any potential medical
treatments in the future, such as blood,
immune and metabolic diseases.

You must ask your hospital about its policy
towards cord blood collection as, under
current NHS guidelines, it is not possible for
your midwife or consultant to collect the
cord blood on your behalf. Instead, your
birth support partner collects the cord
blood or your independent midwife.

There is some very helpful information
published by the Royal College of
Gynaecologists on cord blood collection
under Patient Information. You might also
consider donating cord blood to one of
the UK's public cord blood banks.

www.rcog.org.uk

Bookings at approximately 20 weeks gestation. Also available
are one-to-one sessions (including refresher) in client's home.

W12

Sarah Johnson   **020 8743 4995**
www.sarahjohnson.co.uk   **/07747 075340**
Sarah Johnson, a mother of four, offers specialist group
hypnobirthing classes from her home in Shepherd's Bush
(just 4 couples) and NCT classes in the Kite Studios or St
Saviour's Church. She's also a birth doula offering ante and
post-natal care in your own home.

W13

Ella Van Meelis   **020 8567 1599**
Ella Van Meelis is an Active Birth pregnancy yoga teacher in
Ealing, W13. She also offer postnatal yoga classes
incorporating baby massage.

cord blood banking

Future Health BIOBANK   **0800 954 5335**
www.fhbb.com
Future Health BIOBANK are one of the UK & Europe's top
private cord blood and cord tissue stem cell banks, now also
offering clients tooth stem cell banking.

antenatal scanning

N4

The Hendon Clinic   **020 8732 8777**
234 Hendon Way, Hendon, NW4 3NE
www.thehendonclinic.co.uk

N6

Women's Ultrasound Centre   **020 8341 4182**
17-19 View Road, Highgate, N6 4DJ

N8

Clinical Diagnostic Services   **020 7483 3611**
27a Queen's Terrace, St John's Wood, NW8 6EA

SW10

Women's Wellness Centre   **020 7751 4488**
204 Fulham Road, Chelsea, SW10 9PJ
www.womenswellnesscentre.com

SW19

Women's Ultrasound Centre   **020 8971 8026**
53 Parkside, Wimbledon, SW19 5NX
www.womensultrasound.co.uk

W1

Baby Premier   **0845 345 7262**
142-146 Harley Street, W1G 7JQ
www.babypremier.co.uk

Foetal Medical Centre   020 7486 0476
137 Harley Street, W1G 6BG
www.fetalmedicine.com

Women's Ultrasound Centre   020 7636 6765
86 Harley Street, W1G 7HB
www.womensultrasound.co.uk

The Portland Hospital   **020 7390 6350**
for Women and Children
212 Great Portland Street, W1W 5QN
www.theportlandhospital.com
The Portland Hospitals Maternal and Fetal Wellbeing Centre offers state of the art ultrasound technology, offering a wide range of scans and associated services including early pregnancy scans, anatomy scans and 3D and 4D scanning, as well as a team of fetal medicine consultants if necessary.

baby planning

The Baby Planners   **07512 179 239**
www.thebabyplanners.com
info@thebabyplanners.co.uk
The Baby Planners are a London based baby planning and maternity concierge company dedicated to providing support and guidance to new and expectant parents. The Baby Planners along with their team of professional consultants ensure that you have a happy, healthy, worry free pregnancy.

gynaecologists and obstetricians

Dr Paul Armstrong   020 7580 5754
www.drpaularmstrong.co.uk
Dr Paul Armstrong is an obstetrician specialising in miscarriage, keyhole surgery and general gynaecological care. His consulting rooms are based at The Portland Hospital in the West End and the Lister Hospital in Chelsea. Patients can also be seen at The Lindo Wing of St Mary's Hospital, Paddington and The Cromwell Hospital, Kensington.

Professor Phillip Bennett   020 7594 2141
Queens Charlotte's Hospital, Du Cane Rd, W12 0HS
Consultant obstetrician at Queen Charlotte's, Professor Bennett provides antenatal care as well as delivering. He specialises in recurrent miscarriages as well as normal deliveries, favouring waterbirths.

Miss Shohreh Beski   020 7272 5752
St Bartholomew, West Smithfield, EC1A 7BE
Heading up the high-risk obstetric clinic at St Barts, Miss Beski deals regularly with high-risk pregnancies and deliveries. She has been a consultant obstetrician and gynaecologist at Barts and the London NHS Trust for over 5 years, as well as seeing private patients at the Portland, the London Independent Hospital and the Clementine Churchill Hospital. She has a specialist interest in acupuncture.

Dr Maggie Blott   020 7034 8969
Consulting Rooms, 78 Harley Street, W1G 7HJ
Consultant Obstetrician and University College Hospital and The Portland Hospital. Maggie Blott has over 10 years experience dealing with high risk pregnancies. She takes private consultation in Harley Street and delivers privately at The Portland.

Mr Carl Chow   07917 835 812
The London Clinic, 5 Devonshire Place, W1G 6BW
A busy private obstetrician/gynaecologist, trained in central London with a NHS practice in Kingston. He provides ante-natal care to both high and low-risk women at The Portland Hospital with an emphasis on informed decision-making and normal birth.

Need to Know: Scans

Unless there are specific concerns or medical reasons, you will usually have just two regular ultrasound scans in pregnancy.
- **Dating scan**: This is taken at 10 to 14 weeks to measure the size of your baby and to more accurately predict a 'due date' for the birth.
- **Nuchal scan**: You might also be offered a nuchal scan to check for signs of chromosomal conditions like Down's Syndrome. This is optional and tends more commonly to be offered to older pregnant women.
- **20-23 week scan**: Around this time you will have a scan to check for the general health of your baby's major organs, skeleton, and growth. Abnormalities can also be checked for. If there is any concern about your baby's growth or position in the womb, you may be offered a scan closer to your due date, as a precaution.

Mr Colin Davis   020 7034 5000
Albert House, 47 Nottingham Place, W1U 5LZ
www.gynaecologyspecialistcentre.com
A highly recommended consultant obstetrician and gynaecologist at Barts, Mr Davis specialises in the area of infertility due to polycystic ovaries and endometriosis. He consults privately at Nottingham Place and delivers around 50 babies a year at the Portland. He offers support through pregnancy and afterwards and favours a holistic approach to childbirth and delivery.

Dr Keith Robert Duncan   020 7349 5204
Chelsea & Westminster Hospital, 369 Fulham Road, SW10 9NH
Dr Keith Duncan is a consultant obstetrician and fetal medicine specialist and also the Service Director of the Kensington Wing at the Chelsea & Westminster Hospital. His specialty is multiple pregnancies and he delivers at the Chelsea & Westminster and also the Portland.

Ms Friedericke Eben   020 7390 8089
Consulting Rooms, 212-214 Great Portland Street, W1W 5QN
Over the last 15yrs, Eben has been a consultant obstetrician and gynaecologist at the Portland Hospital dealing with high-risk pregnancies and particularly women with fibroids which may affect fertility. She consults private on Wednesday at the Consulting Rooms in W1, but delivers at the Portland.

Ms Katrina Erskine   020 7390 8079
Consulting Rooms, 212-214 Great Portland Street, W1W 5QN
Consultant obstetrician and gynaecologist at the Homerton, Erskine deals with high-risk pregnancies (diabetes or other medical problems) and those with abnormal smears. She consults privately on Thursdays at the Consulting Rooms.

Mr Kevin Francis Harrington   020 7387 0022
212 Great Portland Street, W1W 5QN
www.womenshealthcare.eu
Highly regarded consultant specialising in endometriosis as well as maternal and fetal medicine. Mr Harrington delivers at the Portland and the Hospital of St John & Elizabeth.

Dr Kumar Kunde   07856 813 806
/01892 521 715
www.londonpregnancycare.com
Mr Kumar Kunde is a senior consultant obstetrician and gynaecologist at St Thomas' Hospital where the Lansdell Maternity Suite is based. Highly recommended for his services, he provides private consultant led care in pregnancy and childbirth at the Lansdell Suite and the Portland Hospital. He also specialises in key hole surgery and has a special interest in treatment of miscarriages, fibroids and endometriosis.

Mr Karl Murphy   020 7390 6327
The London Maternity Centre, 212 Great Portland Street, W1W 5QN

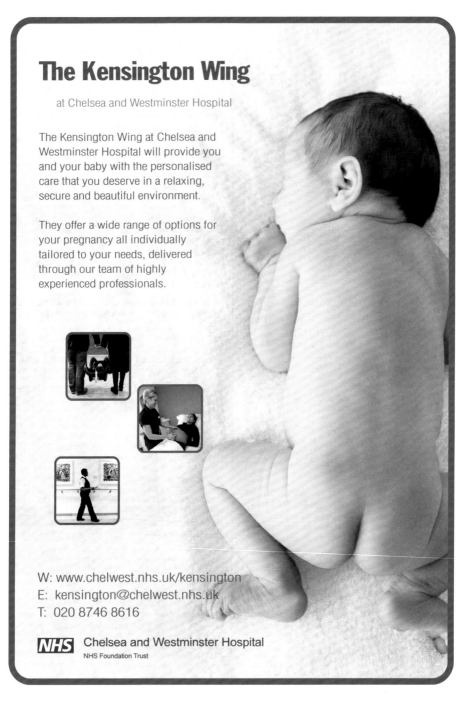

The Kensington Wing

at Chelsea and Westminster Hospital

The Kensington Wing at Chelsea and Westminster Hospital will provide you and your baby with the personalised care that you deserve in a relaxing, secure and beautiful environment.

They offer a wide range of options for your pregnancy all individually tailored to your needs, delivered through our team of highly experienced professionals.

W: www.chelwest.nhs.uk/kensington
E: kensington@chelwest.nhs.uk
T: 020 8746 8616

NHS Chelsea and Westminster Hospital
NHS Foundation Trust

pregnancy & birth

Murphy is a senior consultant at St Mary's Lindo wing, and is a foetal-maternal specialist. He sees mothers right from the start of their pregnancy, delivers at the Lindo Wing and the Portland Hospital and provides support for six weeks postnally.

Mr Nicolas H Morris   020 7390 8041
The Portland Hospital, 205-209 Great Portland Street, W1W 5AH
www.rapidaccessgynaecology.co.uk
Nick Morris runs 4 clinics, at Hospital of St John and St Elizabeth, The Portland Hospital, BUPA Cromwell Hospital and The Wellington Diagnostics Centre. He carries out elective Caesarean sections at both Hospitals.

Patrick O'Brien   020 7034 8969
Consulting Rooms, 78 Harley Street, W1G 7HJ
www.hscfw.co.uk
Patrick O'Brien is a consultant in Obstetrics and Gynaecology at University College London and the Portland Hospital, with over 10 years' experience in high risk pregnancies.

Mr Tiong Teoh   020 7886 2388
Lindo Wing, St Mary, W2 1NY
If you are considering an elective caesarian consider Mr Teoh. He delivers at the Kensington Wing, Chelsea & Westminster, and The Portland as well as St Mary's Lindo Wing.

Mr Guy Thorpe-Beeston   020 7224 4460
148 Harley Street, Marylebone, W1G 7LG
Mr Thorpe-Beeston has a specialist interest in high-risk pregnancies where the mother has additional medical complications such as high-blood pressure. He delivers at St Mary's Lindo Wing, the Portland and Chelsea & Westminster.

Mr Charles Wright   020 7935 0023
144 Harley Street, Marylebone, W1G 7LD
Mr Wright is a senior consultant obstetrician at the Hillingdon Hospital, as well as a general gynaecologist. He sees private patients at St Mary's Lindo Wing, the Portland Hospital and the London Medical Centre. His specialist areas of interest are high-risk obstetrics such as pre-eclampsia as well as on-cology.

Miss Yoon   020 7730 2383
The Lister Hospital, Chelsea Bridge Rd, SW1W 8RH
Miss Yoon is a Consultant Obstetrician and Gynaecologist. Her NHS practice is at The Homerton Hospital. Her specialist interests are polycystic ovarian disease, menstrual disorders, PMT, problems with the menopause and contraception.

private hospitals and clinics

The Kensington Wing   020 8746 8616
Chelsea & Westminster Hospital, Fulham, SW10
The Kensington Wing offers a wide range of options for the various stages of your pregnancy, from antenatal care to childbirth through to postnatal care. The service is delivered by a team of highly experienced professionals, ensuring the highest quality care for you and your baby.

The Lansdell Maternity Suite   020 7188 3457

St Thomas' Hospital, North Wing, Westminster Bridge Road, SE1 7EH
The Lansdell Suite offers access to consultant obstetricians and private ante-natal scans alongside private midwife led care for pregnancy, labour and birth, using the facilities of one of the UK's top teaching hospitals. There is breastfeeding support given as and when necessary and continuous post-natal care.

The Portland Hospital for Women and Children   020 7390 6068
205-209 Great Portland Street, London, W1W 5AH
www.theportlandhospital.com
The Portland Hospital provides a safe and clean environment for mother and baby to ensure a memorable birthing experience. For expectant mothers a range of midwifery and consultant led care packages are available. As well as water birth facilities there is an emergency operating theatre adjacent to the delivery suites and the added reassurance of an onsite adult high dependency unit, all supported by a 24/7 resident obstetric anaesthetist. A Neonatal Intensive Care Unit and Special Care Baby Unit gives Portland babies the best possible start in life, offering parents peace of mind and invaluable advice. To arrange a hospital tour of the maternity facilities or for further information please call 020 7390 6068.

St Mary's Lindo Wing   020 3312 1465
St Mary's Hospital, South Wharf Road, Paddington, W2 1NY
Following extensive refurbishment, St Mary's Lindo Wing reopened in May 2012. It provides first-class obstetric care for both straightforward and complex pregnancies, birthing facilities and a paediatric services for families.

Sir Stanley Clayton Ward   020 8383 3569
Queen Charlotte's Hospital, Du Cane Road, Shepherd's Bush, London, W12 0HS
Sir Stanley Clayton Ward has eight private rooms with en-suit facilities. Care is led by a team of consultant obstetricians (including Mr Douglas Keith Edmonds, Professor Philip Bennett, Mr Sailesh Kumar, Mr Andrew McCarthy, Mr Ruwan Wimalasundera) as well as dedicated midwives who provide one-on-one care throughout your pregnancy, delivery and postnatally. The ward also has a dedicated baby nursery.

tens hire

Maternity Tens   01332 812 825
www.maternitytens.com
Maternity Tens was set up by Kerry Greenland and offers Tens machines to hire from £19.99 for a six week period, or purchase from £34.95. They offer two models, the Babycare TENS and TENS care which NCT approved and highly recommended. Kerry offers an efficient and flexible service, delivering anywhere within the UK. Her website has a number of other really useful ideas, such as the Widgey nursing pillow from PHP Baby.

Babycare Tens   020 8532 9595
www.babycaretens.com
Babycare TENS is the worldwide market leading provide of

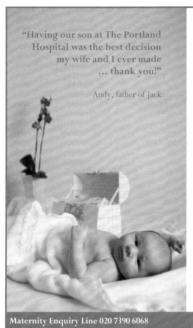

pregnancy & birth

Obstetric TENS machines for hire or purchase. The award winning Elle TENS is the premier obstetrics TENS machine on the market today.

Mama Tens　　　　　　　　　**0845 230 4647**
www.mama-tens.info
Easy to use, drug-free pain relief during labour, allowing you to stay in control and keep mobile. 4 week hire starts from £29.99 inc p&p, available for an extra 2 weeks if needed.

waterbirth pool hire

Probably about half the maternity units in the UK have birth pools. If you plan to use water during labour and your local unit does not have a pool, or you are going to give birth at home, then you will need to hire your own pool. See below for reliable pool hire companies:

Birthworks　　　　　　　　　**03332 409 710**
www.birthworks.co.uk
For over 25 years Birthworks have been hiring their luxurious and high quality pools to pregnant women all over the country. Prices start as low as £60 to £445 (depending on the duration of the hire). There are three styles to choose from which also affect the price of the hire, they are a rectangle, hexagonal or an octagonal shaped tub. There is also an extra fee added for any extra length of time needed for hire.

Made in Water (La Bassine)　　　**01442 506 330**
www.madeinwater.co.uk
Made in Water manufacture and sell La Bassine, a popular inflatable water birth pool in the UK. The pool is supplied with a number of essential accessories as well as bath thermometres, electric pumps and liners. The website also offers pregnancy pillows, TENS machines to hire or buy, birthing balls and books.

The Baby Show　　　　　　　**0871 231 0844**
www.thebabyshow.co.uk
These are the UK's biggest baby shows for mums, dads, babies, toddlers and grandparents too. Taking place four times a year in London's Excel Centre (February), at the NEC in Birmingham (May), Manchester's EventCity (Aug/Sept) and London's Earls Court (October).

Need to Know: Milk Banking

At the heart of every milk bank is the gift of breastmilk that mothers donate to help feed sick and premature babies. The **UKAMB** advises mothers interested in donating some of their breastmilk and will put them in contact with their closest milk bank. Supporters of the charity are also very welcome to make contact.

There are 4 Milk Banks in London collecting screened and heat treated breast milk from healthy mothers who have a plentiful supply. Donors express and then freeze their milk which will either be collected by the Milk Bank's delivery service or the donor will deliver it to the bank themselves.

- St George's Hospital, SW17 0QT - *Contact Theresa Alexander*　　**020 8725 1936**
- Guy's and St Thomas' NHSFT, SE1 7EH - *Contact Camilla Kingdon*　　**020 7188 4030**
- Queen Charlotte's and Chelsea Hospital, W12 0HS - *Contact Gillian Weave*　　**020 8383 3559**
- The Newborn Unit, King's College Hospital, SE5 9RS - *Contact Paula Blanchette*　　**020 7346 3038**

Contact the UKAMB on 020 8383 3559 or via info@ukamb.org
www.ukamb.org

health and wellbeing

Ways in which you can get back to your old self and enjoy wellbeing in the demanding days of early parenthood.

In the first few days after the birth of your child, you will receive home visits from your midwife to check you and your baby are progressing well. However, after this and a six-week check for you and your baby at your GP's surgery, your main contact might be with health visitors based at your local Children's Centre. While this contact can be useful, there are other ways you can start to physically and mentally rebuild your wellbeing.

Getting back in shape

Yoga and **Pilates** are useful ways to help build your body's strength back up after the birth, and offer you valuable time to focus your mind on something other than washing, feeding and sleeping. Many local studios have sessions where you can bring your baby along or you can consult **specialist trainers** such as Chrissie at LAPF (*lapf.co.uk*). If you are returning to your usual **gym**, make sure you consult with the trainers, telling them how recently you gave birth so they can advise you on safe exercising - especially if you had a caesarean section. Or you could join a local **new-mums fitness group**. These are sessions where you get to do low-level fitness routines without leaving your pushchair (and baby) at home - for example groups like Jelly Belly (*jellybellypt.com* - also specialists in post- caesarean fitness) design informal but lively sessions where new mums can exercise at the park with movements that incorporate your pram. This can

also be a really positive way to get out and meet other women going through the same experiences as you.

Alternative therapies

Many of the relaxing therapies you can enjoy in pregnancy - like **acupuncture**, aromatherapy massage and reflexology - are useful ways to give yourself a postnatal boost, too. Always tell the practitioner if you have specific postnatal problems and if you are breastfeeding, but unlike pregnancy, you will find a lot more treatments are safe now. **Reflexology** and **aromatherapy** can really help reduce aches and stress which not only helps you enjoy parent-hood more but can even help with better breastmilk production.
Cranial osteopathy is a popular choice in the early weeks after birth. You and your baby can enjoy the benefits during one session. This gentle therapy can be useful for relieving back pains for mothers and is used to relieve problems like colic and sleeplessness in babies.

Postnatal health

Although it's no surprise that new parenthood is tiring, you will recover over time. Try not to rush around and achieve too much, especially in the first six weeks but even in the first three months, as this can affect how your body heals and how it deals with new demands like broken sleep and breastfeeding. If you have specific health problems it's important to get them checked out by your GP as soon as possible. These include: headaches, heavier than usual postnatal bleeding, persistent backache, breastfeeding problems and extreme fatigue.

health & wellbeing

Baby Safe Homes   **0207 559 1491**
www.babysafehomes.co.uk
Baby Safe Homes offers free assessments, equipment and same-day installations, sending in a qualified team to fix stair gates, cabinet latches and other safety equipment to protect little ones from household hazards. Baby Safe Homes is a must for parents who want to save time and money whilst avoiding the pitfalls of DIY baby proofing.

acupuncture

Natural Mother   **0800 008 6844**
www.naturalmother.co.uk
Expert pregnancy, postnatal and fertility treatments in the comfort of your home. 5 week birth preparation course. Specialised overdue and breech service. **See our ad in Complementary Health**. No travel, no stress. London wide.

breastfeeding specialists

Clare Byam-Cook   **020 8788 8179**
Clare is a leading breastfeeding consultant covering London with years of hands-on experience. If you attend Christine Hill's ante-natal classes you'll come across her excellent feeding talks. She's also a published author of many breast-feeding books.

Geraldine Miskin   **07947 741 415**
www.breastfeedingexperience.com

Geraldine Miskin provides invaluable support and advice and in home consultations on all breastfeeding matters.

Juliet Albert   **07730 970 738**
www.midwifeonline.co.uk
Juliet Albert is a midwife and mum offering help with breast-feeding problems such as sore nipples, poor weight gain, attachment problems, engorgement and what to do for reflux/colic and settled babies.

Lynda Leach   **01707 660 318**
The Life Centre, 15 Edge St, Kensington, W8 7PN
www.lyndaleach.co.uk
Lynch Leach offers breastfeeding classes and support to mums in central London via the Life Centre or at home.

National Childbirth Trust   **0300 330 0771**
www.nct.org.uk
The NCT provides trained consultants who are available via their breastfeeding helpline (8am-10pm). There is also a register for mothers and babies with special challenges eg multiple births, feeding a toddler and a newborn at the same time or feeding after breast surgery.

Rachel Garcia Breastfeeding Support 07780 677 602
Rachel offers breastfeeding support and routine guidance for mothers via home visits or over the telephone. She can also advise on potty training, weaning, moving from breast to bottle and baby sleep advice. She covers London, home counties, south west and abroad. Specialist in multiples.

Need to Know: Safety around the Home

Preventing accidents is not about restricting children or wrapping them in cotton wool. Instead it's about creating safer environments in the home and garden to enable children to lead a healthy and active life.

- **Latches:** put safety latches on doors and cupboards that shouldn't be opened by curious tots, but can be by adults.

- **TVs/Furniture:** large screen plazma TVs have been responsible for a sudden increase in admissions to hospital. Secure with straps to the wall or shelving. Other large pieces of furniture such as bookshelves or chests of drawers should also be secured. Move sofas away from windows, and chairs from balconies.

- **Curtain/Blind cords:** make sure all tie-backs and blind cords are tied out of reach and don't become a choking hazard.

- **Coffee table corners:** put corner protec tors on sharp edges to protect wobbly toddlers from unavoidable falls.

- **In the garden:** fill in ponds or convert them into sandpits, and consider covers for containers that collect rainwater. Supervise paddling and swimming pools all the time.

For peace of mind, organisations such as **Baby Safe Homes** provide in-house consultations – and will come with tools at the ready to install stairgates, latches and straps. **www.babysafehomes.co.uk**

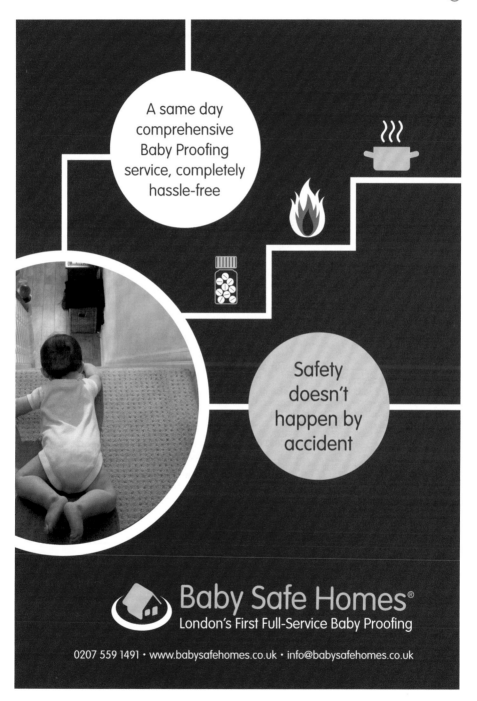

health & wellbeing

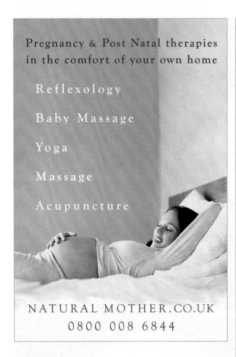

Pregnancy & Post Natal therapies in the comfort of your own home

Reflexology

Baby Massage

Yoga

Massage

Acupuncture

NATURAL MOTHER.CO.UK

0800 008 6844

The Maris Practice　　　020 8891 3400
www.themarispractice.com
The Maris Practice offers specialist breastfeeding support from highly qualified, experienced breastfeeding consultants - Joanna Knap, Anna Page, Geraldine Chew and Liz Lambourn. All are NCT trained.

Verona Hall　　　07946 093 094
www.veronahall.co.uk
Verona is a London lactation consultant, offering breastfeeding support for south east London mums.

Vicki Scott - Baby Confidence　　　07960 611 987
www.babyconfidence.co.uk
Experienced midwife Vicki Scott offers up-to-date practical help and advice with breastfeeding at her home in Earlsfield, SW18 as well as telephone and email support for clients further a field. Her Baby Confidence classes start in the last trimester of your pregnancy and run post-nataly (with a free crèche/teas & coffee). They offer mums an opportunity to discuss concerns they have in the early weeks with a new baby and really get you off to a good start, followed by sleeping, general routines and weaning. She has a maximum of 6 couples per course.

Zita West　　　020 7224 0017
37 Manchester Street, Marylebone, W1U 7LT
www.zitawest.com
Zita West offers one-to-one breastfeeding support from her clinic in Marylebone.

chiropractors

Barnes Chiropractic　　　020 8878 7887
43 Barnes High Street, Barnes, SW13 9LN
www.barnes-chiropractic.co.uk
Along with a range of complementary therapies for adults including pregnancy massage, this clinic offers services for children. Julian Keel is a Doctor of Chiropractic who uses chiropractic and cranial techniques.

Body Matters Belsize Village　　　020 7419 7900
1 McCrone Mews, Belsize Village, NW3 5BG
www.bodymattersclinic.co.uk
Body Matters Health and Beauty Clinic offers holistic therapies that are suitable for young children including: acupuncture, cranial osteopathy and reflexology, from practitioners of the highest standard.

Dulwich Therapy Rooms　　　020 8299 4232
47 Lordship Lane, East Dulwich, SE22 8EP
www.dulwichtherapyrooms.co.uk
Dulwich Therapy Rooms have a team of 45 independent therapists, instructors and advisors, who are offering support and treatment for many health conditions. Their range of therapies and services include complementary and conventional therapies, such as acupuncture, chiropractic, osteopathy, massage, counselling (couples & individuals), hypnotherapy, reflexology, ayurvedic medicine, medical herbalism and homeopathy.

Hampstead Chiropractic Clinic　　　020 7433 3323
Esporta, O2 Centre, 255 Finchley Road, NW3 6LU
www.hampsteadchiropractic.co.uk
Treatments include baby and child chiropractic as a safe and effective therapy. They have a discounted rate for babies and under-13's, and offer a free spinal check to all children whose parents are receiving chiropractic care with them.

complementary health centres

Natural Mother　　　0800 008 6844
www.naturalmother.co.uk
An expert service bringing pregnancy and postnatal therapies to the comfort of your home. Reflexology, Massage, Acupuncture, one to one Baby Massage and Yoga. No travel, no stress. London wide.

The Awareness Centre　　　020 8673 4545
41 Abbeville Road, Clapham South, SW4 9JX
www.theawarenesscentre.com
A mother and baby clinic and private GP services are widely used by local families. There are also complementary health treatments from massage and reflexology to Pilates and cranial osteopathy.

Blossom Health　　　020 8293 9371
5 Ferndale Court, Blackheath, SE3 7QU
www.blossomhealth.com
Treatments at Blossom Health include five-element acupuncture, osteopathy, cranial osteopathy, naturopathy

COCO
N A I L B A R

The venue

The cocktails

The experience

The treatment

Mummy & Baby Mornings

Champagne, Wine & Cocktails

Latest Essie & OPI colours in stock
Shellac, Artistic & Axxium Gels
Fish Spa, Massage Chairs, Threading, & much more..

Coco Nail Bar, 267 Portobello Road, London W11 1LR   0207 243 1113   www.coconailbar.com

As recommended by   VOGUE   TATLER   DAILY CANDY   TimeOut   Spa Secrets   Red

Follow us on Twitter & Facebook   for weekly deals

health & wellbeing

and food intolerance testing.

The Chaim Centre **020 8452 0900**
10a Station Parade, Willesden Green, NW2 4NH
www.chaimcentre.com
This is a well-established thereapy centre offering a wide range of natural treatments for fertility, pregnancy, mother and baby. Treatments include acupuncture, reflexology, homeopathy, cranial osteopathy/craniosacral therapy, reflexology, pregnancy massage, hypnotherapy, ante-natal yoga, mum and baby yoga and baby massage courses.

Evolve Yoga and Wellness Centre **020 7581 4090**
10 Kendrick Mews, South Kensington, SW7 3HG
www.evolvewellnesscentre.com
The Evolve and Wellness Centre in the heart of South Kensington offers yoga and pilates classes, holistic treatments, innovative workshops and a variety of courses on the body, mind and spirit. It is also the leading centre for fertility, Grinberg Method and Yoga Therapy in London.

Family Natural Health Centre **020 8693 5515**
106 Lordship Lane, East Dulwich, SE22 8HF
The Family Natural Health Centre (above Soup Dragon, 106 Lordship Lane) has lots of complementary therapies on offer including cranial osteopathy, reiki, acupuncture, and pregnancy yoga.

Greenwich Natural Health Centre **020 8691 5408**
70 Royal Hill, Greenwich, SE10 8RF
www.greenwichnaturalhealth.co.uk
The centre offers a variety of treatments including reflexology, cranial osteopathy and pregnancy massage.

Healthy Living Centre **020 7704 6900**
282-284 St Pauls Road, N1 2LH
www.thehealthylivingcentre.co.uk
Complimentary Health practice as well as a drop-in homeopathic clinic Mon-Sat pms. A natural solution for teething, colds, gummy eyes, digestive upsets and sleep problems.

The Life Centre Notting Hill **020 7221 4602**
15 Edge Street, Kensington, W8 7PN
www.thelifecentre.com
This is a hub of natural healthcare for all things mother and child related. You can have a range of holistic natural health treatments with leading specialists for fertility, pregnancy and postnatally including: osteopathy, homeopathy, acupuncture, massage, reflexology and kinesiology.

Living Centre Clinic **020 8946 2331**
32 Durham Road, Raynes Park, SW20 0TW
www.livingcentreclinic.com
Services include osteopathy, homeopathy and other therapies for babies, children and mothers. They also offer allergy/sensitivity testing.

Neal's Yard Remedies **0845 262 3145**
www.nealsyardremedies.com
Branches of Neal's Yard in London stock the full range of Mother and Baby products and gifts as well as offering complementary antenatal and postnatal treatments during pregnancy and with your new baby, such as: aromatherapy, homeopathy, ante and postnatal pregnancy massage, baby massage, cranial osteopathy and reflexology. There are now 21 branches across London including: Notting Hill, Covent Garden, Marylebone, St John's Wood, Chelsea, Wimbledon, Clapham, Richmond, Westfield, Westfield Stratford, Islington, Camden, Bromley, Borough and Blackheath

The Organic Pharmacy Chelsea **0844 800 8399**
www.theorganicpharmacy.com
This is a registered herbal dispensary with qualified homeopaths and pharmacists to consult and advise on herbal and homeopathic medicine. Branches are: Chelsea, Kensington, Covent Garden, Hampstead and Richmond.

Osteopathic Centre for Children **020 8875 5290**
22a Point Pleasant, Wandsworth, SW18 1GG
www.occ.uk.com
The Osteopathic Centre for Children opened in these purpose built premises in order to expand its service to pregnant women and new mothers. As a charity, the OCC is reliant on public donations to maintain the provision of osteopathic treatment to ante and postnatal mothers and children, regardless of their ability to pay. Open Mon-Fri 9.30am-5.30pm.

Putney Bridge Clinic **020 8789 2548**
265 Putney Bridge Road, Putney, SW15 2PT
www.putneybridgeclinic.co.uk
Midwife trained in fertility, ante and post-natal therapies, babies and children's treatments.

The Vale Practice **020 8299 9798**
64 Grove Vale, East Dulwich, SE22 8DT
www.thevalepractice.co.uk
Established for over 10 years in East Dulwich, SE22, The Vale Practice offers an integrated approach to health, offering complete natural healthcare in a relaxing and professional environment.

The Vitality Centre **020 8871 4677**
155 Merton Road, Wimbledon, SW18 5EQ
www.vitality-centre.com
Lots of services for the pregant mum ranging from massage to acupuncture. Ante and postnatal pilates and yoga classes are also held in the centre.

Viveka **020 7483 0099**
27a Queen's Terrace, St John's Wood, NW8 6EA
www.viveka.co.uk
The Viveka team of highly qualified doctors and complementary therapists offers you a choice of specialties. Choose from one-to-one consultations, integrated clinics and workshops for adults, children and babies.

Willows Complementary Centre **020 8523 2669**
3 The Broadway, Chingford, E4 9LQ
www.willowshealth.com
Treatments include; homeopathy, infant massage, osteopathy and cranial osteopathy and a special children's clinic.

dentists

The Family Dental Practice   020 8654 1434
262 Portland Road, South Norwood, SE25 4SL
www.family-dental.co.uk
Dr Angelica Khera is the principal dentist here, leading a team of friendly dentists. There are also hygienist services at this is long established practice, which has been treating patients for over 70 years. They understand the importance of sympathic dental care for small children and welcome new patients.

Toothbeary   020 8831 6870
358A Richmond Road, East Twickenham, TW1 2DU
1 Farm Yard, Windsor, Berkshire, SL4 1QL
www.toothbeary.co.uk
Toothbeary is a dedicated children only practice, providing top quality paediatric dentistry exclusively for children aged 0-18 years. The exquisite building is designed for children in mind, and the specially trained team encourage children to have positive first experiences of going to the dentist that will in turn influence the way they care for their teeth and the way they feel about going to the dentist throughout their life. New branch open in Windsor (tel: 01753 257 230).

Weymouth Street Paediatric   020 7580 5370
Dental Practice
32 Weymouth Street, W1G 7BY
www.paediatric-dentistry.co.uk
Established 1973, Weymouth Street Paediatric Dentistry is a leading private practice dedicated to children and adolescents. The emphasis is on total oral care in a happy, friendly environment where they welcome healthy, medically compromised or anxious children, and those with dental trauma.

exercise

London Academy of   020 8647 4787
Personal Fitness
www.lapf.co.uk
London's top motivational instructors. Complete ante- and post-natal programmes including yoga and pilates.

first aid

Safe and Sound   020 8445 8998
www.safeandsound.uk.net
Paediatric first aid training for parents and child carers. Courses can be run in your home, business or nursery. Alternatively you can attend one of our monthly courses at venues across London. Our trainers work in paediatric nursing and the emergency services and this, combined with their teaching experience, means they can confidently respond to any questions which may arise.

Toothcare for babies and toddlers

Get into good teeth-cleaning regimes with your baby even before the first tooth breaks through. Although first ('milk') teeth don't last forever, they are important because they affect early developments in eating and speaking. Looking after your child's oral health now sets up great habits for life, so we asked Dr Cheryl L Butz, from the children-only dental practice Toothbeary, to give us some useful tips and advice.

When should I start cleaning my child's teeth?

Good dental care is important even before your child is one year old. Streptococcus Mutans is one of about 3000 kinds of bacteria found in the mouth and it's one of the "bad guys" that is usually found in the mouths of infants by the age of two. The earlier and the more of this bacteria in the mouth, the greater risk of decay and problems later on.

How can parents keep a baby's first teeth cleaned when they are so tiny?

Firstly with infant oral care wipes, or clean face towels, then with special infant toothbrushes that are very soft. Xylitol can be used to clean the mouths of infants even before they have teeth, by using Xylitol wipes.

With a soft cloth or brush, use a pea-sized amount of fluoride toothpaste in very small amounts regularly (twice daily) from the first tooth on. Try Brushbaby's gentle applemint flavoured toothpaste with Xylitol and lower levels of fluoride.

Are there any golden rules to remember?

Discipline in health care in general is be an important one. Teethbrushing is not "natural" - a child will not automatically learn it. It has to be taught, practised and supervised for a long while (up to about the age of 10).

Just because a child is "able" to brush correctly doesn't mean he will do so. There are lots of ways to positively influence that and in my experience, it is the first few years which count the most. Often children will listen to the dental nurse or dentist better than the parents, so early contact with them is positive.

Visiting a dentist in the early years is a good experience for all children - getting used to the dental surgery as a familiar friendly place linked to oral health long before it becomes associated with fillings and drilling. Check-ups and dental hygiene advice can be fun and relaxed, especially if you visit a dentist which offers dedicated children's care.

Toothbeary are paediatric dental specialists, with a surgery in Richmond and one in Windsor. For more information visit **www.toothbeary.co.uk**

massage

Massage during pregnancy is a luxury everyone should treat themselves to. Easing tension and boosting energy levels are two of the benefits. Newborns and babies benefit mentally and physically from regular massage and it's a communicative experience for parents whilst helping baby settle prior to sleep.

Natural Mother   **0800 008 6844**
www.naturalmother.co.uk
Expert pregnancy and postnatal Full Body Massage in the comfort of your home. One to one Baby Massage; share the cost of Baby Massage with a small group of friends/Mums /NCT. **See our ad in Complementary Health**. No travel, no stress. London wide.

The Portland Hospital   **020 7390 6553**
for Women and Children
234 Great Portland Street, W1W 5QT
www.theportlandhospital.com
Offering a wide variety of massage services on both an inpatient and outpatient basis The Portland Hospital offers antenatal and postnatal massage and postnatal mother and baby workshop, where the technique of baby massage is taught.

medical services

Pebble UK   **01353 624 624**
www.pebbleuk.com
Uniquely designed, graduated compression maternity hosiery, to relieve and prevent swollen ankles, varicose veins, heavy feeling legs and leg fatigue. Socks, hold-ups, tights, footless tights and anti-cellulite shorts that enhance wellbeing, whilst supporting the pregnant figure with style and elegance.

The Portland Hospital   **020 7390 6068**
for Women and Children
205-209 Great Portland Street W1W 5AH
www.theportlandhospital.com
With world renowned consultants and leading medical professionals choosing to practice at The Portland Hospital we are delighted to offer private consultations spanning Children's Services, Maternity Services and Women's Health Services, supported by comprehensive diagnostic screening and state of the art inpatient facilities where required.

natural products

Forever Living Products   **07867 524 343**
www.shop-aloe.myflpbiz.com
Aloe Vera is a powerful natural health tonic. Containing over 75 different vitamins, minerals and amino acids, aloe balances the immune system, assists in healthy digestion, produces healthy, glowing skin, maintains healthy joints and helps the body balance itself. Contact Caroline Glassell for more information.

Need to Know: Vaccinations under 5 years

There is a programme of vaccinations offered free to all children during their early years, configured to reduce the risk of serious illnesses.

At two months:
- 5-in-1 (DTaP/IPV/Hib). A single injection to protect against diphtheria, tetanus, pertussis (whooping cough), polio and Haemophilus influenzae type b (Hib, a bacterial infection that can cause severe pneumonia or meningitis in young children).
- Pneumococcal infection (which can cause pneumonia, septicaemia and meningitis). Single injection.

At three months:
- 5-in-1, second dose (see above).
- Meningitis C (this vaccine protects against infection by meningococcal group C bacteria, which can cause meningitis and septicaemia). Single injection.

4 months:
- 5-in-1, third dose (see above).
- Pneumococcal infection, second dose (see above).
- Meningitis C, second dose (see above).

Between 12 and 13 months:
- Hib/Men C booster. One injection for meningitis C, third dose and Hib, fourth dose.
- MMR – measles, mumps and rubella (German measles). Single injections.
- Pneumococcal infection, third dose (see above).

3 years and 4 months:
- MMR second injection (see above).
- 4-in-1 pre-school booster (DtaP/IPV). Given as a single jab containing vaccines against diphtheria, tetanus, pertussis and polio.

health & wellbeing

osteopaths

Dulwich Osteopathic Clinic   020 8299 9798
at The Vale Practice
64 Grove Vale, East Dulwich, SE22 8DT
www.thevalepractice.co.uk
Established in 1997. SE London leading complementary health clinic offers a team of seven osteopaths with daily appointments specialising in pre and post natal care and cranial treatment for children and babies. Also offering pregnancy massage, nutrition, hypnotherapy, homeopathy, reflexology, and acupuncture.

Fulham Osteopaths   020 7384 1851
769 Fulham Road, Fulham, SW6 5HA
www.fulhamosteopaths.co.uk
One of the UK's premier osteopathic practices.11 friendly osteopaths trained in both cranial and traditional approaches for the whole family. Easy parking with ground floor access. Baby changing facilities available. Est.1989.

physiotherapy

The Portland Hospital   020 7390 6553
for Women and Children
234 Great Portland Street, W1W 5QT
www.theportlandhospital.com
Offering an extensive range of physiotherapy services for both women and children, ranging from antenatal and postnatal services to child services and rehabilitative services. With a newly built state of the art gym on site physiotherapy services at The Portland Hospital are available on both an inpatient and outpatient basis.

Kiki's Children's Clinic   020 7207 4234
124 Thurleigh Road, Balham, SW12 8TU
www.kikisclinic.com
Physiotherapy,occupational therapy, speech & language therapy, massage and craniosacral therapy for babies and children. Therapy at the clinic or at your home.

private gp services (24 hours)

Children's Doc Around   020 7390 8022
the Clock
234 Great Portland Street, London, W1W 5QT
www.theportlandhospital.com/childrensdo-caroundtheclock.asp
The Portland Hospital's 'Children's Doc Around the Clock' is an urgent medical appointment service for babies and children up to the age of 16. The service is available 24 hours a day, 7 days a week, 365 days a year. Call us on 020 7390 8022

private health services

The Richmond Practice   020 8940 5009
richmondpractice.co.uk
One of Londonís top private health clinics with multi-lingual doctors (consultations provided in English, French, German and Mandarin). Services include: private GPs, paediatricians, gynaecology and maternity care (including pregnancy scans). Conveniently located close to Richmond train and tube stations with parking close by.

private practitioners

Dr Katrin Bain   07981 456 470
www.katrinbain.co.uk
Dr Katrin Bain offers personal development and parenting workshops, talks and books to mothers who want to embrace motherhood without losing themselves. She understands that adjusting to motherhood is not always straightforward especially for mothers who established their identity and career first. Don't struggle alone. Get in touch.

reflexology

Reflexology is used to relieve tension and treat illness in the corresponding zones of the body. In pregnancy reflexology can alleviate morning sickness, constipation and rid the body of excess catarrah and stubborn colds. Post-natally, therapy is said to boost energy levels and increase breastmilk.

Natural Mother   0800 008 6844
www.naturalmother.co.uk
Expert pregnancy and postnatal treatments in the comfort of your home. **See our ad in Complementary Health**. No travel, no stress. London wide.

Association of Reflexologists   01823 351 010
www.aor.org.uk
Largest association of reflexologists in the UK. The website offers listings of members county by county.

Need to Know: Pampering

Feeling like the 'old you' is an important part of recovering from the birth and giving you the boost you need now to enjoy the challenges of parenthood.

- **Cup Cake Spa, SW6.** A fabulous place to book a beauty or body therapy. The setting is luxurious and there is an in-house crèche if you have your baby with you.
new.cupcakemum.com

- **Coco Nail Bar, W11.** Manicures, pedicures, fish spa therapy and massage all feature on a tempting pampering menu at this chic Portobello venue. A treat when you don't have the time or energy yet for a great night out!
www.coconailbar.com

- **ESPA at Corinthia Hotel, SW1.** ESPA offers fabulous antenatal therapies but also an 80 or 50-minute post-baby treatment.

Under-16s can use the spa daily 10-11.30am and 3-4.30pm.
www.espalifeatcorinthia.com

- **Organic Pharmacy, across London.** There are six branches of this excellent pharmacy where you can seek advice for issues around pregnancy or postnatal health, and pick up organic treats for 'me-time' at home.
www.theorganicpharmacy.com

- **Thai Square Spa, WC2.** As well as pregnancy treatments, this spa studio offers a 75-minute 'Post-birth restoration' treatment including relaxing massage and skin treatment.
www.thaisquarespa.com

health & wellbeing

yoga - pregnancy and baby

Natural Mother   **0800 008 6844**
www.naturalmother.co.uk
One to one pregnancy Yoga and Mother and baby Yoga in
the comfort of your home. Share the cost with a small group
of friends. **See our ad in Complementary Health**. No travel, no
stress. London wide.

The Special Yoga Centre
yoga for everyone

The Special Yoga Centre   **020 8968 1900**
2a Wrentham Avenue, Kensal Rise, NW10 3HA
www.specialyoga.org.uk
Come to The Special Yoga Centre with your children this
Spring! We offer a wide variety of kids, pregnancy and
mummy & baby yoga.

The Portland Hospital   **020 7390 6553**
for Women and Children
234 Great Portland Street, W1W 5QT
www.theportlandhospital.com
Yoga and Pilates classes, both antenatal and postnatal, are
available at The Portland Hospital on an outpatient basis,
along with a wide variety of antenatal and postnatal exercise
classes. Classes are available as a course booking or on a
per class basis.

spas

Coco Nail Bar   **020 7243 1113**
267 Portobello Road, London W11 1LR
www.coconailbar.com
For the best groomed nails in London, from skilled nail
technicians who care about your busy lifestyle (especially
busy mums), look no further. Coco Nail Bar offers nail
treatments in a blissful, contemporary spa. With late opening
hours, mummy-baby mornings and great amenities, including
cocktail bar, sit back and pamper! (See ad page 17).

Cupcake   **020 3326 4986**
11 Heathmans Road, Parsons Green, SW6 4TJ
10 Point Pleasant, Putney, SW18 1GG
www.cupcakemum.com
Cupake spas offer a range of spa treatments for men and
women and are open to members and non-members. They
specialise in massages and other treatments designed
specifically for pregnant women and new mothers. It was
awarded the "Specialist Spa of the Year" in 2010 by the
Professional Beauty Awards.

Need to Know: Parenting books & iphone apps

Many parents survive the early years without burying their heads in books. However, a
book or app that reflects your own instincts as a parent can become an invaluable
tool to allay those 2am worries or help you stick to a "problem-solving" plan.

• **Pregnancy:** FREE up to 12 weeks
then £1.95 (The Smiles Factory). Lots
of factual information including a
baby size visualiser and beautifully
crafted photos of your baby inutero,
pregnancy recipes (and foods to
avoid reminder), baby shopping lists,
top baby names by country and
personal diary - all fully integrated
with facebook and twitter.

• **Pocket Rescue Tantrums:** £1.95 (Dr
Katrin Bain) Amazon e-book. This bite-
sized ebook just solves one parenting
challenge - dealing with tantrums.
Practical tips, common-sense solutions
presented in the clear, non-preachy
voice of Dr Bain, a parenting guru.
Others in the series cover sleep and
family meals.
www.pocketrescue.co.uk

• **iBaby Feed Timer:** £1.49 (Fehners Soft
ware). Designed by breastfeeding
mothers who want to track when and
for how long their baby feeds, whether
from breast, bottle or expressed milk.

• **Annabel's Essential Guide:** £3.99
(Annabel Karmel). Weaning your baby
is handled easily with suggestions of
introducing first foods and cooking
videos to demonstrate Annabel's
handy cooking and preserving tips.

All apps available from **itunes.apple.com**

childcare

Finding the right childcare is a potential minefield and few parents can get away without paying for childcare at some point. If you want help or are returning to work and don't have family nearby then below are your options.

Maternity Nurses: Specialising in the care of newborns, maternity nurses stay with you for the first 2-4 weeks, caring for your baby and allowing you as much rest and recuperation as possible. They are also expert in establishing sleeping and feeding routines and allaying the anxieties of first-time parents.

Doulas: A doula is an experienced, non-medical assistant who can look after mothers post-natally. They come to your home and support the family by cooking for the mother, breastfeeding support, newborn care assistance, errands, light house-keeping, taking older children to school as well as many other things.

Nurseries: Many parents are more comfortable with the idea that their child is cared for by a number of adults than leave them in the sole care of a nanny. Nurseries are fully equipped with the latest toys and most have good outdoor space for running around in all weathers. They often prepare home-cooked meals and children develop an enviable social life. Some day nurseries can also offer extended hours care so that if you want to start work early you can still arrive at your desk by 9am. For a complete list of day nurseries in postcode order see our Education section.

Childminders: Professional childminders are trained and inspected by OFSTED and their local authority. They are registered for a "family-sized" number of children (currently 3) and usually being local can continue the after school care for your children when they reach reception age. Vacancies with childminders are held by the local authority. (See councils pg180).

Nannies: This is an expensive option, although equates to the same as having two children at a day nursery. It's infinitely more convenient plus the added bonus of someone keeping on top of things at home. Many nannies are happy doing a job share with another local family if you are looking for part-time help.

Mother's Helps/Au pairs: This is the cheapest way of getting some help with the children and at home. However, we do not recommend an au pair for sole charge of children under 5 - whatever their experience. Mother's helps are slightly older, more mature and tend to have good experience with families. But neither should be looking after your baby or toddler whilst you and your partner work a full day.

Full-time nanny, childminder, mother's help or au pair? Through word of mouth, via the web, small ad in the local paper or scribbled card in a shop window? While such methods of finding help my yield happy results, childcare is one area where you don't want to take risks. In this section we recommend professional agencies that will find you a nanny, maternity nurse or other carer with proper qualifications, experience and references.

childcare

A friendly, professional service providing excellent Maternity Nurses & Nannies

GREYCOAT
Childcare & Education
www.greycoatchildcare.co.uk
020 7233 9950

Do you wish you could find a great Maternity Nurse?

Our experienced maternity team supports families in the UK and overseas, offering tailor-made solutions for you & your baby.

We look forward to talking to you soon.

0845 128 4279   www.eden-nannies.co.uk

Maternity Solutions

We are dedicated in finding the highest calibre staff for you

8 Cromwell Place, London, SW7 2JN
Tel: 020 7225 1556 Fax: 020 7589 4966
Email: all@nannyworld.co.uk www.nannyworld.co.uk

babysitters

Like Minders   **0844 879 7189**
www.likeminders.co.uk   info@likeminders.co.uk
Like Minders provides babysitting and ad hoc daytime childcare in London and the surrounding areas. With over a decade of experience, we offer a trustworthy, flexible and reliable service for parents. We only use the very best CRB checked childcarers, all of whom are over 21 years old and screened through our very strict selection process.

maternity nurses

Eden Nannies & Maternity   0845 128 4279
www.eden-nannies.co.uk
Let us help you find the right nanny, nanny/housekeeper, maternity nurse or special needs carer for your family. We can source professionally qualified and/or experienced child carers for full-time, part-time or temporary assignments.

Greycoat Childcare   020 7233 9950
& Education
www.greycoatchildcare.co.uk
Our Maternity Nurses are well known to us, as we use them time and again for maternity placements. They are able to take the pressure off Mum, so she can enjoy her first precious weeks with the new baby.

Maternity Solutions   020 7225 1556
www.nannyworld.co.uk
We specialise in providing top quality care right from the start. Our professional Maternity Nurses are there for those vital early weeks of your baby's life.

Maternally Yours   020 7795 6299
www.maternally-yours.co.uk
Established in 1996 Maternally Yours is one of the UK's leading maternity nurse agencies.

nanny agencies

Eden Nannies & Maternity   0845 128 4279
www.eden-nannies.co.uk
Let us help you find the right nanny, nanny/housekeeper, maternity nurse or special needs carer for your family. We can source professionally qualified and/or experienced child carers for full-time, part-time or temporary assignments.

Greycoat Childcare   020 7233 9950
& Education
www.greycoatchildcare.co.uk
Choosing the right childcare does not have to be difficult. Greycoat Childcare & Education is dedicated to finding the very best childcare for your family. Our professional, no obligation service makes us one of the most trusted, leading London agencies.

Ideal Nannies   020 8150 9779
www.idealnannies.com
Ideal Nannies aims to supply you with staff carefully matched to your individual requirements. They will listen to your specific requests and will endeavour to find a match as close as possible to these needs. All nannies are personally interviewed and references checked to a very high standard.

Imperial Nannies   020 7795 6220
www.imperialstaff.com
Providing the very best for your children all over London and throughout the UK. Established in 1996 with offices in London and Bath.

ideal nannies

- UK and Overseas
- All staff personally interviewed
- Nannies, Nanny/Governess Nanny/Housekeepers, Mothers Helps & Maternity Nurses
- Live in & Live out
- Full time & Part time
- Permanent & temporary

Established 1988

1 Lyric Square, Hammersmith, London W6 0NB

Tel: **020 8150 9779**

info@idealnannies.com

www.idealnannies.com

Knightsbridge Nannies 020 7610 9232
www.knightsbridgenannies.com
Providing a personal childcare service in the UK and overseas
for professionals looking for high calibre nannies.

Mortimer Nannies 07793 502 483
www.mortimernannies.co.uk
Placing Nannies both internationally and Nationwide,
Mortimer Nannies provide an efficient, friendly and bespoke
service to both clients and candidates. Our candidates are of
the highest calibre, all having been personally interviewed,
reference and CRB checked.

Nannies of St James 020 7610 9218
www.nanniesofstjames.co.uk
The professional agency providing exceptional nannies and
maternity nurses.

Niche Nannies 0207 617 7543
www.nichenannies.co.uk
Being fully aware of the complex dynamics involved in forming a harmonious relationship between a nanny and a family,
they can help find you someone 'Perfectly Suited', a carefully
chosen, fully vetted Niche Nanny, maternity nurse or house-
keeper, genuinely interested in the wellbeing and development of your little ones and household.

North London Nannies 020 8444 4911
www.northlondonnannies.co.uk
Established over 20 years, North London Nannies is a leading
provider for all your childcare requirements. Permanent, temporary and emergency placements, very experienced agency,
understanding the needs of parents and their children's welfare and happiness. A very comprehensive programme of
Childcare training is available to include Paediatric First Aid,
OFSTED approved qualifications, Cache accredited Diploma
and Certificates levels 2,3,and 4. Funding possibly available.

Occasional & Permanent 020 7225 1555
Nannies
www.nannyworld.co.uk
Occasional and Permanent Nannies was founded over 55
years ago and has helped several generations of clients find
the most appropriate childcare support, whether that's a
nanny, housekeeper-nanny, or a governess with teaching
experience. They can also provide maternity nurses with
considerable experience both in the UK and abroad.

One World Nannies Ltd 07718 968 484
www.oneworldnannies.com
Providing a personal, friendly and efficient service and to
ensure you find the right nanny, or parent helper. We
specialise in qualified and experienced career nannies
seeking permanent live in or out positions plus teachers
looking for Nanny/tutor roles.

Parkside Nannies 07908 534 612
www.parksidenannies.co.uk
Parkside Nannies is a specialist childcare placement service
based in Richmond and surrounding areas.Whatever your
childcare needs we will endeavour to find a nanny who not

only meets those needs but is a good fit for your family to
encourage strong, long lasting relationships between families
and nannies.

Burlington Nannies 020 7821 9911
A team of professionals who seek out high calibre nannies,
governesses, maternity nurses and private tutors for families
in the South East, London and Overseas.

Taxing Nannies 020 8882 6847
A specialist payroll service for employers of nannies including
opening a PAYE scheme, calculating tax and national
insurance. They provide regular pay slips, advise on Sick and
Maternity pay and liaise with HM Revenue & Customs.

Have you heard about our very special childcare service?

We are dedicated to finding the very best childcare staff for your family, all thoroughly checked by our friendly, expert Consultants.

Maternity Nurses | Nannies | Nanny/Housekeepers
Nanny/PA's | Tutors & Governesses

To find out more call us on 020 7233 9950
or visit us at www.greycoatchildcare.co.uk

childcare

IMPERIAL NANNIES

Providing the very best for your children

As the UK's leading household staff agency, we specialise in placing qualified and experienced nannies and governesses with familics in London, the country and overseas. We aim to ease the difficult selection process by under-standing your family's needs and exactly what the job entails before sending you details of suitable candidates.

All of our candidates are fully reference checked with at least two years private household experience and are personally interviewed.

We provide an excellent selection of

DAILY NANNIES
Four to five days per week.
Candidates are available with years of excellent service.

LIVE-IN NANNIES
Flexible childcare based in the privacy of your own home.

OVERSEAS NANNIES
Experienced nannies looking for an exciting challenge.

NANNY/GOVERNESSES
Working towards developing the mind and skills of your children.

NANNY/HOUSEKEEPERS
Combining the abilities of childcare and domestic chores in the home.

Our dedicated team of consultants provide a confidential, discreet service which includes ongoing support from start to finish. Most of our clients come to us through recommendation.

17 RADLEY MEWS, KENSINGTON, LONDON W8 6JP
TEL: +44(0)20 7795 6220

19-20 CHARLES STREET, BATH, SOMERSET BA1 1HX
TEL: +44(0)1225 484222

Recruitment &
Employment
Confederation

WWW.IMPERIALNANNIES.COM

shopping

What parents really want right now and the bright ideas designers are coming up with for the next big thing.

Olli Ella has a lovely range of nursing chairs

On-trend shades

The fashion trends in 2012 reflected two key events in the British summer calendar – a zingy neon take on sportswear, and more classy cuts and muted, retro colours to bring a touch of royal class to trendy youthful design.

Bugaboo *(bugaboo.com)* can always been relied upon to pick up on the hot looks of the moment, and the coral, jade and electric blue colourway options certainly reflect this,

Olli Ella's baby bedding is far more muted, but their elegant nursing chairs *(olliella.com)* in turquoise, deep pink or purple certainly wouldn't have looked out of place at the Palace when Her Majesty was a young mum…

The **Mima Xari** *(mimakids.com)* might echo the simple baby-pod look of a few recent from-birth pushchairs (indeed, the M&P Joolz is getting a re-launch, *mamasandpapas.com*), but it's the detail in the Xari which has turned heads – a shell-like hood that looks like the Sydney Opera House, and sophisticated shiny metallic finishes.

And **Quinny**, whose compact pushchairs were instantly trendy on launch, also seem to be heading for the futuristic zone with a white option being revealed this year.

on-trend electric Bugaboo

There's an app for it

From pregnancy apps that update you on the progress of your baby's development and feature a kick-counter and even track your contractions, to apps to help remind you what time feeds and sleeps are due, your child can embrace the e-world long before he's old enough to drop your iPhone down the loo. If your children are older, don't miss out: for pre-schoolers there are shape sorting games, talking cats and first spelling and numeracy games.

Three-in-one

Not surprisingly, we live in times when we want our budgets to go further, so finding anything smart that has more than one purpose has to be a bonus.
The Rokka (rokkaplay.com) is a great-looking wooden unit that can be used as table, a see-saw 'row boat', then turned into a kitchen complete with cooker, sink etc.

Suitable from 1 to 5 years, the **Mini-Micro** 3in1 Scooter (micro-scooters.co.uk) can easily be recon-figured as a ride-on scoot-about toy for toddlers, then used as a small three-wheel scooter, and adjusted into a Mini-Micro as your child gets bigger.

The Mima Xari has a striking design

shopping

baby shops

independent stores - E5

Kiddi Centre   020 8809 4251
147 Clapton Common, E5 9AE
Friendly nursery goods store selling car seats (Maxi-Cosi), pushchairs (Baby Jogger, Stokke, My Child, Maclaren, Mountain Buggy, Mamas & Papas), nursery furniture (Mamas & Papas and East Coast) etc. They also offer a Maclaren pushchair repair service. Open Mon-Thurs 10am-6pm, Fri 10am-1pm, Sun 10.30am-2pm.

E15

Mamas & Papas   0845 268 2000
First Floor, Westfield Stratford City, E15 2JU

Mothercare Stratfield East   020 8534 5714
33-34 The Mall, E15 1XD

E20

Mothercare Stratford   020 3288 3930
Lower Ground Fl. Westfield Stratford City, E20 1EH

N1

Baby Concierge Islington 020 8964 5500
38 Pentonville Road, N1 9HF
www.babyconcierge.co.uk
Baby Concierge is a personalised shopping service by appointment only. Branch also in Ladbroke Grove.

N8

JoJo Maman Bebe Crouch End   020 8347 8139
47 The Broadway, N8 8DT

Rubadubdub   020 8342 9898
15 Park Road, Crouch End, N8 8TE
Rubadubdub has an eclectic selection of traditional wooden toys, Grobags, slings (Ergobaby) and changing bags (Skip Hop), pushchairs (Mountain Buggy, Bugaboo and Maclaren) and a range of organic baby toiletries (Earth Friendly Baby), Crocs, outdoor clothes (Bush Baby waterproofs/jackets), and Biodegradable nappies (Beaming baby and Bambo). Open Mon-Sat 10am-5.30pm, Sun 11.30am-4.30pm.

Soup Dragon   020 8348 0224
27 Topsfield Parade, Crouch End, N8 8PT
www.soup-dragon.co.uk
Not the largest selection of nursery goods, but well thought out selection for city families including the lightweight stroller from Micralite and the in-line pushchairs from Phil & Teds. They also stock buggy accessories (locks, sunshades and boards). Other nursery items include Babybjorn and Premaxx baby carriers, Sunshine Kids safety items, the Beaba Baby cook and a large range of traditional and wooden toys (ie Le Toy Van, Moulin Roty). Mon-Sat 9.30am-6pm, Sun 11am-5pm.

N11

Smyths Friern Barnet   020 8361 7345
4 Friern Barnet Retail Park, Southgate, N11 3PW
www.smythstoys.com
Smyths is a large warehouse style store selling value-brands alongisde the regulars such as Cosatto and Graco, toys (Lego, mini figures from TV/Films), bikes, scooters and games. Open Mon-Fri 10am-6pm, Sat 9am-6pm, Sun 11am-5pm.

N16

Born   020 7249 5069
168 Stoke Newington Church Street, N16 0JL
www.borndirect.com
Born offers a wide range of organic and natural baby products for green-minded families. They have an extensive range of real nappies from all corners of the world (dispensed with great advice). They are also stockists of Bugaboo, Stokke and Joolz pushchairs; organic toiletries, slings and baby carriers and other essential equipment. Open Tues-Fri 9.30-5pm, Sat 10am-6pm, Sun 12-5pm. On Mondays the store closes for workshops on breastfeeding, hypnobirthing and other mummy-relevant events.

N17

Totland   020 8808 3466
4 Bruce Grove, Tottenham, N17 6RA
Baby equipment stockist including cots (Mamas & Papas, East Coast), prams and pushchairs (Mamas & Papas, Quinny, Jane, Mutzy, Babystyle and Graco) as well as general baby goods. Free local delivery. Open Mon-Sat 9.30am-6.30pm.

N18

Mothercare Edmonton   020 8807 5518
Ravenside Retail Park, N18 3HA

N12

Mothercare Wood Green   020 8888 6920
38-40 High Road, N22 6BX

NW2

Babies R Us   020 8209 0019
Brent South Shopping Park, Tilling Road, NW2 1LP

Mamas & Papas   0845 268 2000
Brent South Shopping Park, Tilling Road, NW2 1LJ

NW3

Blue Daisy Hampstead   020 7681 4144
13 South End Road, NW3 2PT
www.blue-daisy.com
This little baby shop, handily located near the Royal Free Hospital, has everything for babies, toddlers and mums, including organic cotton, wooden toys, practical items such as prams, bottles and potties as well as the Mama Mio and

Green People organic skincare ranges. Open Mon-Fri 9.30am-5.30pm, Sat 10am-6pm, Sun 11am-5pm.

Huggle   020 7483 2826
8-10 Winchester Road, NW3 3NT
www.huggle.co.uk
Huggle has done the hard work so you don't have to! A unique nursery store offering a wide range of the best in stylish and modern baby products. From furniture and buggies to feeding and bathing, toys and gifts, Huggle has it covered!

NW4

John Lewis Brent Cross   020 8202 6535
Brent Cross Shopping Centre, NW4 3FL

NW6

Blue Daisy West Hampstead   020 7435 3100
190 West End Lane, NW6 1SG
www.blue-daisy.com
Everything for babies and toddlers, including organic cotton and merino clothing, wooden toys, practical items such as prams, bottles and potties as well as the Mama Mio and Green People organic skincare ranges. Open Mon-Fri 9.30am-6pm, Sat 10am-6pm, Sun 11.30am-5pm.

NW9

Just Kidding   020 8204 2233
501 Kingsbury, Kingsbury High Road, NW9 9HG
www.justkiddingonline.co.uk
Just Kidding is a friendly nursery goods store with pushchairs (including Bugagoo, Mamas & Papas, Graco and Maclaren), nursery furniture (East Coast, Izziwotnot, Boori), car seats (Maxi-Cosi, Kiddy and Britax) as well as a wide range of smaller nursery items. Open Mon-Sat 10am-6pm.

NW11

JoJo Maman Bebe Finchley   020 8731 8961
3 Ashbourne Parade, 1259 Finchley Rd, NW11 0AD

Yummy Kids   020 8201 8870
1-2 Russel Parade, Golders Green Rd, NW11 9NN
www.yummykids.co.uk
Yummy Kids stocks a wide range of nursery goods including nursery furniture (East Coast, Izziwotnot and Kub), pushchairs (Stokke, Bugaboo, Mutzy, Joolz and Baby Jogger) as well as car seats (Maxi-Cosi and Kiddy). Open Mon-Thurs 10am-6pm, Fri 10am-2pm, Sun 10.30am-3pm.

SE3

JoJo Maman Bebe Blackheath   020 8852 2058
21 Montpelier Vale, SE3 0TJ

shopping

SE9

Mothercare Eltham　　　020 8859 7957
146 High Street, SE9 1BJ

SE10

Greenwich Baby　　　020 8858 6690
52 Greenwich Church Street, Greenwich, SE10 9BL
Formerly Green Baby, this newly branded store sells baby equipment, eco-friendly clothing 0-8yrs including the Hatley range of boots raincoats and pyjamas, reusable nappies (Eco Bots, Bitti d'lish, and Beaming Baby biodegraable disposables), toys and gifts. Open Mon-Sat 9.30am-5.30pm, Sun 11am-5pm.

SE13

Mothercare Lewisham　　　020 8463 9960
Lewisham Retail Park, Lewisham, SE13 7RZ

SE15

Babies R Us　　　020 7732 7322
760 Old Kent Road, Peckham, SE15 1NJ

Mothercare
789-799 Old Kent Road, SE15 1NZ　020 7740 9200
Aylesham Centre, Rye Ln, SE15 5EN　　　020 7358 0093

Tommy's Wear and Cheer　　　020 7635 9252
160-162 Rye Lane, Peckham, SE15 4NB
www.tommyswearandcheer.com
A family run and long-established nursery shop selling the full range of top brand pushchairs (Stokke, Bugaboo, iCandy, Quinny), car seats and nursery furniture. They also have a simple website where you can order online. Open Mon-Sat 9am-6pm.

SE16

Mothercare Surrey Quays　　　020 7237 2025
Surrey Quays Shopping Centre, SE16 7LL

SE18

Mothercare Woolwich　　　020 8854 3540
62 Powis Street, Woolwich, SE18 6LQ

SE22

JoJo Maman Bebe Dulwich　　　020 8693 2123
6 Lordship Lane, SE22 8HN

SW1

Harrods　　　020 7730 1234
87-135 Brompton Road, Knightsbridge, SW1X 7XL
www.harrods.com
Head to the 4th floor where you will find the top of the range in nursery furniture, furnishings, fashion, toys, maternity wear,

collectables and a kids' hair dressing salon. Open Mon-Sat 10am-8pm, Sun 11.30am-6pm.

Peter Jones　　　020 7730 3434
Sloane Square, Chelsea, SW1W 8EL
www.johnlewis.com
Department store heaven for Chelsea mums, for everything you need prior to and after the birth, including expert advice from well-trained nursery advisors. A good range of car seats, puschairs and prams, nursery furniture and linens as well as highchairs and other necessary equipment (all never knowingly undersold, with full guarantees). Clothes, shoes and essential kit for mum, baby and older children. Their popular nursery advisory service (similar to their wedding list service) allows friends and family to buy things from your list. Open Mon, Tues, Thur, Fri, Sat 9.30am-7pm, Weds 9.30am-8pm, Sun 11am-5pm.

SW3

Blue Almonds　　　**020 7584 8038**
79 Walton Street, SW3 2HP
www.bluealmonds.co.uk
Blue Almonds does it beautifully. High quality bespoke furniture for babies and children, made from solid wood and painted in a choice of 2,000 different colours with optional hand-painted artwork or antique finish. Additionally, they offer a wide range of bespoke services and great gift ideas.

Bobo Kids　　　**020 7838 1020**
29 Elystan Street, SW3 3NT
www.bobokids.co.uk
Bobo Kids is an interior design shop for children. It specializes in furniture, linen, lamps, accessories, vintage pieces and art from nursery to teenagers. This unusual mix of modern, vintage and ethnicity will give a unique twist to your child's space! Interior design service available.

JoJo Maman Bebe　　　020 7589 9593
12 Cale Street, SW3 3QU

The Nursery Window　　　**020 7581 3358**
83 Walton Street, SW3 2HP
www.nurserywindow.co.uk
This delightful little shop in London's Walton Street has been a well kept secret for over 25 years. Treat your baby to the softest cashmere and luxurious cotton nursery and bed linens in The Nursery Window's own exclusive designs. Beautiful gift baskets can also be prepared for you and sent to anywhere in the world.

SW6

Babylist　　　**020 7371 5145**
The Broomhouse, 50 Sulivan Road, SW6 3DX
www.babylist.com
You can purchase all your nursery goods from Babylist, whether that's a cot, car seat, buggy or simply a babygro. And it's delivered direct to your home at a time convenient to you. You can try out many of the brands in their SW6 showroom and visit again when the baby is 6 months old to stock up on the next range of items required.

SW9

Mothercare Brixton   020 7733 1494
416 Brixton Road, SW9 7AY

SW10

Pure Baby   **020 7751 5544**
208 Fulham Road, West Brompton, SW10 9PJ
www.purebaby.co.uk
Luxury baby and toddler boutique with clothing for 0-3yrs,
conveniently situated opposite the Chelsea & Westminster
hospital. We stock a wide range of baby clothing, also in
cashmere, toys, gifts and a full range of nursery furniture.
Open Mon-Sat 10am-6.30pm, Thu 10am-7pm, Sun 11am-
5pm.

SW11

JoJo Maman Bebe Battersea   020 7228 0322
68 & 72 Northcote Road, SW11 6QL

Merino Kids   0800 917 7723
151 Northcote Road, SW11 6QB
www.merinokids.co.uk
Merino Kids opened a showroom last year in Clapham stocking their complete range of baby and toddler sleeping bags
and accessories. Open Tues-Fri 10.30am-4.30pm, Sat and
Sun 11.30am-4.30pm.

Peppermint Clapham   020 3393 3101
56 & 176 Northcote Road, SW11 1PA
www.peppermint.co.uk
These two Peppermint stores in Northcote Road have a
combination of Nursery goods (at 56 Northcote Road) and
Nursery furniture (at 176 Northcote Road). Pushchair brands
include Bugaboo, iCandy, Joolz, Phil & Teds and Maclaren.
Open Mon-Wed 10am-5.30pm, Thurs-Sat 10am-6pm, Sun
11am-5pm.

SW12

Twist   020 3538 6229
111 Balham High Road, SW12 9AP
www.twistkids.com
This Balham baby and children's independent nursery and
clothing shop sells a range of clothing (Bob & Blossom, Lily
and Sid, Toby Tiger, Splash About etc); urban pushchairs including Joolz, Stokke, Phil & Teds and Baby Jogger; toys and
games as well as cots. Open Mon-Sat 10am-6pm, Sun
11am-5pm.

SW15

JoJo Maman Bebe Putney   020 8780 5165
30 Putney Exchange, SW15 1TW

SW18

Mamas & Papas Colliers Wood   0845 268 2000
Tandem Shopping Centre, SW18 2NX

Bespoke & Cosy Rooms
for Your Little Ones

BLUE ALMONDS
79 Walton Street
London SW3 2HP
Tel: 020 7584 8038
www.bluealmonds.co.uk
iza.minkiewicz@bluealmonds.co.uk

Mothercare Wandsworth   020 7228 0391
Unit 59 Southside Shopping Centre, SW18 4TF

SW19

Mothercare Colliers Wood   020 8544 7750
2 Priory Retail Park, 131 High Street, SW19 2PP

Mothercare Wimbledon   020 8944 5296
Unit LSU4 Centre Court, SW19 8YE

W1

John Lewis Oxford Street   020 7629 7711
Oxford Street, W1A 1EX

Mamas & Papas   0845 268 2000
256-258 Regent Street, W1B 3AF
www.mamasandpapas.com
Mamas & Papas' flagship store and cafe is a spacious and
stylish environment with great services. Everything you'll ever
need for mother and child; fashionable maternity and babywear, nursery furniture and equipment, high chairs, car seats,
colourful prams and pushchairs, bathtime accessories, toys
and gifts. Open Mon-Fri 9am-5.30pm, Sat 9am-5pm, Sun
10am-5PM

shopping

Mothercare Oxford Street   **0845 365 0515**
461 Oxford Street, W1R 1DB**Selfridges**   **0800 123 400**

400 Oxford Street, W1A 1EX
www.selfridges.com
Snap up instore exclusives such as a Missoni Bugaboo or high-end baby fashion from Stella McCartney, Chloe, Ralph Lauren and Burberry. Open Mon-Sat 9.30am-9pm, Sun 12-6pm.

W2

JoJo Maman Bebe Notting Hill   **020 7727 3578**
101 Westbourne Grove, W2 4UW

W4

JoJo Maman Bebe Chiswick   **020 8994 0379**
80 Turnham Green Terrace, Chiswick, W4 1QN

Peppermint Chiswick   **020 8742 0637**
87-89 Chiswick High Road, Chiswick, W4 2EF
www.peppermint.co.uk
This branch of Peppermint in Chiswick is a nursery goods store specialising in prams, pushchairs, buggies, highchairs, cots, cot/bed, car seats and strollers including popular brands such as Bugaboo, Phil and Teds, Stokke, Quinny, Maxi Cosi, Kub, Micralite and Mountain Buggy. Their prices in store are as competitive as many online offerings, but with great service and support. Open Mon-Weds,10am-5.30 pm Thurs 10am-6pm, Sat 9.30am-6pm, Sun 11am-5pm.

W5

Baby e Ealing   **020 8840 8197**
20 The Green, W5 5DA
www.babye.co.uk
Boutique offering designer clothes for mum and baby aged 0-2, as well as shoes, toys by Steiff and Kaloo, pushchairs and highchairs, maternity and breastfeeding tops, christening and baby shower gifts. Open Mon-Sat 10am-5.30pm, Sun 12-4pm.

Mothercare Ealing   **020 8579 6181**
The Waterglade Centre, 1-8 The Broadway, W5 2ND

W6

Mothercare Hammersmith   **020 8741 0514**
26 Kings Mall Shopping Centre, W6 0PZ

W10

Baby Concierge   **020 8964 5500**
Studio 109, 300 Kensal Road, W10 5BE

W12

Mamas & Papas Westfield   **0845 268 000**
Unit 2004 Westfield, W12 7GF

HA

Baby Boom 2000   **01895 675 596**
4 New Pond Parade, West End Road, Ruislip Gardens, HA4 6LR
www.babyboom2000.co.uk
West London's premier nursery store and online shop offering next day delivery. Main stockist for all leading and specialist brands of cots, prams, pushchairs, highchairs, nursery furniture, car seats and accessories. Open 9.30am-5.30pm Mon-Sat.

large nursery chains

Babies R Us   **0800 038 8889**
www.babiesrus.co.uk
The Babies R Us chain offers just about everything you need from a complete set of nursery furniture to a packet of disposables. It's a similar range that you might find in Mothercare, but the products are generally less expensive. Worth visiting to try out the products if you live nearby. They have a catalogue and website which offers an even greater range than can be found in store. Open Mon-Sat 9am-10pm, Sun 11am-5pm. Branches are: Old Kent Road, Brent Cross, Ilford and Croydon.

John Lewis   **020 8202 6535**
www.johnlewis.com
The John Lewis stores offer a practical range of clothing, shoes, nursery equipment, toiletries as well as a good selection of prams, pushchairs, car seats, highchairs and nursery furniture, many of which are on display so you can test them out. The stores also offers a nursery advisory service, a bit like a wedding list, and it saves traipsing around yourself.

JoJo Maman Bebe   **0871 423 5656**
www.jojomamanbebe.co.uk
With 11 stores across London JoJo Maman Bebe has become a one-stop shop, catalogue and online store for maternity wear, baby and toddler clothing, toys and gifts - and now nursery products. For years they have avoided the competitive marketplace of prams, pushchairs and car seats, but customer demand has led them to join up with Silver Cross and offer a range of nursery furniture, car seats and pushchairs. However, there are hundreds of other brands across a range of practical and stylish nursery products. Free P&P on all UK mainland orders.

Mamas & Papas Brent Cross   **0845 268 2000**
www.mamasandpapas.com
Excellent one-stop shop with everything you'll ever need for mother and child - fashionable maternity and babywear, nursery furniture, feeding equipment, high chairs, car seats, prams and pushchairs, bathtime accessories, toys and gifts.

Mothercare   **0845 330 4070**
www.mothercare.com
More store closures expected as Mothercare switches its focus from high street retail to online and out of town shopping centres. But you'll find many of the top brands at competitive prices, as well as own label clothing.

shopping

baby shops online

Bobo Kids 020 7838 1020
29 Elystan Street, SW3 3NT
www.bobokids.co.uk
Bobo kids is an interior design shop for children. It specializes in furniture, linen, lamps, accessories, vintage pieces and art from nursery to teenagers. This unusual mix of modern, vintage and ethnicity will give a unique twist to your child's space! Interior design service available.

Custard & Crumble 020 7183 3799
www.custardandcrumble.co.uk
Create a stylish and inspiring nursery with the help of Custard & Crumble. This online boutique presents a beautiful handpicked selection of baby nursery furniture, accessories and gifts, many of which you won't find on the high street. They guarantee free UK mainland delivery and offer a gift list service.

JohnLewis.com 0845 604 9049
John Lewis remains competitive for all the major pushchairs, nursery furniture collections and essential baby items.

Kiddicare.com 08717 817 000
Based in an enormous warehouse outside Peterborough, Kiddicare is one of the UK's largest and most successful online baby goods retailers. Recently acquired by Morrisons, they have a state-of-the-art website with video reviews, real-time stock availability, and a 7 day purchase price match.

CUSTARD & CRUMBLE

BE INSPIRED...

CREATE A ROOM TO BE LOVED AND CHERISHED

www.custardandcrumble.co.uk

Oscar & Patch
TRADITIONAL LUXURIES FOR THE MODERN CHILD

www.oscarandpatch.co.uk
Exquisite clothing, furniture and toys for babies and children
Telephone 0845 838 0680

shopping

Piccalilly's gorgeous organic cotton playsuits feature a variety of designs including this Picadilly Circus inspired suit.

www.piccalilly.co.uk

Mothercare.com　　　　　0845 330 4070
With a choice of convenient delivery options (including worldwide) or collection from your local store, Mothercare remains very competitive across a wide range of brands and has a dedicated Price Match phone line open 7 days a week. You can also opt for an assembly service for flat-packed furniture (from £48).

Oscar and Patch　　　　0845 838 0680
www.oscarandpatch.co.uk
Oscar and Patch is a wonderful emporium of timeless traditional luxuries for babies and children, offering the finest clothing, alongside the most magical toys and exquisite hand crafted nursery furniture. Referred by many as the Harrods of the online children's world, it's a unique and exciting concept bringing back the best of British craftsmanship.

Pramcentreonline.co.uk　　　0141 552 3998
With a retail store under the name of the Glasgow Pram Centre, this online store is extremely competitive with a price match promise + 15% of the difference (on new orders which have not been dispatched).

Need to Know: Buying Online

Buying goods online with delivery to your home can be a convenient alternative to traipsing around stores. In fact you have more rights buying from a UK company than you do in store.

Under the Consumer Protection (Distance Selling) Regulations 2000 you can return goods up to seven days after delivery – even if you've just changed your mind.

sweetpea　　　　　　　0845 519 9154
www.shopatsweetpea.com
For simple, stylish, easy-to-wear, affordable designer fashion for boys and girls from 0-6 years look no further than sweetpea. This on-line boutique offers a real alternative to high street shopping with quality brands that don't lose their shape or shade and will happily take your little ones from the park to a party.

The Nursery Window　　　020 7581 3358
www.nurserywindow.co.uk
This delightful little shop in London's Walton Street has been a well kept secret for over 25 years. Treat your baby to the softest cashmere and luxurious cotton nursery and bed linens in The Nursery Window's own exclusive designs. Beautiful gift baskets can also be prepared for you and sent to anywhere in the world.

baby equipment advisory service

Babylist　　　　　　　020 7371 5145
The Broomhouse, 50 Sulivan Road, SW6 3DX
www.babylist.com
You might be wondering how much baby 'stuff' is really all that necessary. If so, then you need to book an appointment with Babylist, the longest running nursery advisory service in London. They will take you through their list of essentials, as well as the nice-to-haves in the comfort of their showroom. This is not an exclusive, A-list celebrity-only service (although they have had quite a few), but a thoroughly sensible way of tailoring your needs with the amazing range of products on offer.

baby equipment hire

Chelsea Baby Hire　　　　07802 846 742
www.chelseababyhire.com
A personal and reliable service offering top brand equipment for long- and short-term hire. Construction and collection anywhere within M25 and other regional locations.

baby shows

The Baby Show　　　　　0871 231 0844
www.thebabyshow.co.uk
These are the UK's biggest baby shows for mums, dads, babies, toddlers and grandparents too. Taking place four times a year in London's Excel Centre (February), at the NEC in Birmingham (May), Manchester's EventCity (Aug/Sept) and London's Earls Court (October). In addition to hundreds of exhibitors there are advice workshops on money matters, breastfeeding, nutrition with Annabel Karmel and much more. Ticket prices vary dependent upon time of booking, save by booking in advance online or by calling 0871 231 0844.

bobo kids
Online shop

Bed linen - Cushions - Wall stickers - Wallpaper - Lamps -
Decoration - Accessories - Toys

Interior Design service
29 Elystan Street London SW3 3NT - www.bobokids.co.uk

shopping

room to bloom
interior design for children

▾ nursery design
▾ kids' rooms
▾ playrooms

visit www.room-to-bloom.com or call Ursula on 0759 040 3997

nursery interior design

Koko Kids   **01273 626 347**
www.kokokids.co.uk
Koko Kids brings together a unique range of decor for rooms as individual as your children. Beautiful bedding, affordable art, innovative lighting and decorative accessories. Many of the designs are created exclusively by Koko Kids including personalised art, wall murals, fabric wall stickers, grow charts and handmade lampshades.

Room to Bloom   **07590 403 997**
Interiors for Children
www.room-to-bloom.com
Room to Bloom specialises in the interior design of children's spaces, including nurseries, children's rooms and playrooms. Home consultations, e-decoration and full interior design &

installation services available. Visit www.room-to-bloom.com to book a consultation or contact Ursula Wesselingh on 07590 403 997.

nursery furniture

Babylist   **020 7371 5145**
The Broomhouse, 50 Sulivan Road, SW6 3DX
www.babylist.com
Established over 10yrs ago, the Babylist is a tailored service for parents wanting to find quality furniture for their children - without the hassle of traipsing around London at 6 months pregnant. Their furniture range includes all UK brands plus many more sourced all over the world. You need to book an appointment, but parents come from all over London to have their every need catered for.

Aspace   **020 8994 5814**
140 Chiswick High Road, Chiswick, W4 1PU
www.aspaceuk.com
A full range of children's beds (not cots), wardrobes, chests of drawers, etc, with bedding to match. Also available online.

Bebe Bisou   **020 8740 9434**
Westfield Shopping Centre, Unit 1083, Ariel Way, Shepherd's Bush, W12 7GB
Luxury boutique catering for all your child's needs from newborn to 6yrs. Ranges include Baby Dior, Ralph Lauren, D&G Junior and Jean-Paul Gaultier. Timeless nursery furniture from Europe, bedding and accessories, prams by Aprica for Fendi and Roberto Cavalli, collections of soft toys from Kaloo and unique bikes and cars.

Need to Know: Places to swap or buy second-hand

If you're buying, selling or giving away nursery goods, always make sure they come with any relevant original safety instructions.

- **Gumtree:** Useful website for buying and selling items locally. **www.gumtree.com**

- **Mum2Mum Market:** Well-run nearly new sales to shop at or book a stall at. New sellers are given lots of useful advice. Events in London (and south west England). **www.mum2mummarket.co.uk**

- **NCT:** The National Childbirth Trust run locally-organised nearly new sales. **www.nct.org.uk**

- **Baby Swap or Shop:** Online selling and swapping system where you can link to people local to you, choosing how far

away you're prepared to travel to deliver or collect from. **babyswaporshop.co.uk**

- **Fara Kids:** As well as Fara's regular charity shops, there are 12 branches in and around London that are dedicated to selling brand new and secondhand donated kids' clothes, nursery goods and toys. **www.faracharityshops.org**

- **Freecycle UK:** A great way to pass on items you no longer need by giving them away locally via this website. **freecycle.org**

Blue Almonds 020 7584 8038
79 Walton Street, SW3 2HP
www.bluealmonds.co.uk
Blue Almonds does it beautifully. High quality bespoke furniture for babies and children, made from solid wood and painted in a choice of 2,000 different colours with optional hand-painted artwork or antique finish. Additionally, they offer a wide range of bespoke services and great gift ideas.

Bobo Kids 020 7838 1020
29 Elystan Street, SW3 3NT
www.bobokids.co.uk
Bobo kids is an interior design shop for children. It specializes in furniture, linen, lamps, accessories, vintage pieces and art from nursery to teenagers. This unusual mix of modern, vintage and ethnicity will give a unique twist to your child's space! Interior design service available.

Chic Shack 020 8785 7777
77 Lower Richmond Road, Putney, SW15 1ET
www.chicshack.net
French and Swedish style nursery furniture and cots (cot-beds) in painted finishes. Open 9.30am-6pm Mon-Sat.

Coco & Co 028 9266 9595
www.cocoand.co.uk
Our beautiful made to measure roman blinds are handmade using special blackout lining to help your baby sleep. With 36 different styles, our blinds have safety devices as standard, are easy to install, great quality and reasonably priced. Established 2000.

shopping

Custard & Crumble   020 7183 3799
www.custardandcrumble.co.uk
Create a stylish and inspiring nursery with the help of Custard & Crumble. This online boutique presents a beautiful handpicked selection of baby nursery furniture, accessories and gifts, many of which you won't find on the high street. They guarantee free UK mainland delivery and offer a gift list service.

Dragons of Walton Street   020 7589 3795
23 Walton Street, SW3 2HX
www.dragonsofwaltonstreet.com
Fine hand-painted children's furniture, fabrics and interior design.

Huggle   020 7483 2826
8-10 Winchester Road, NW3 3NT
www.huggle.co.uk
Huggle has done the hard work so you don't have to! A unique nursery store offering a wide range of the best in stylish and modern baby products. From furniture and buggies to feeding and bathing, toys and gifts, Huggle has it covered!

Ikea
Brent Cross, Lakeside, Croydon, Edmonton and Wembley
Ikea offers three good cot bed ranges: the Sundvik £60, the Somnat £45 and the Hensvik £60 - all of which come with matching wardrobes, storage furniture and changing tables. Mattresses are offered in varying quality for an additional £35-£100. Check out the Ikea Family Card which offers special discounts, events in store, a free quarterly magazine and 5% off any assembly required.

John Lewis Stores
Sloane Square, SW1W   020 7730 3434
Oxford Street, W1A 1EX   020 7629 7711
www.johnlewis.com
John Lewis have a wide range to suit all budgets including an exclusive and contemporary range from Bloom, East Coast, Boori and Kidsmill.

Kidsen   020 8969 7565
111 Chamberlayne Road, Kensal Rise, NW10 3NS
www.kidsen.co.uk
Great Scandinavian kids' store with two excellent cot beds, the A Series from £299, and the Kily from £699 – both transform from cots, to toddler beds and then into stylish sofas. Open Mon-Fri 10am-5.30pm, Sat 10am-5pm.

Mamas & Papas Westfield   0845 268 2000
256-258 Regents Street, W1B 3AF
Brent Cross Shopping Park, NW2 1LJ
Westfield Shopping Centre, W12 7GF
Purley Way Centre, Croydon, CR0 4XU
Tandem Shopping Ctre, Colliers Wood, SW19 2NX
www.mamasandpapas.com
Excellent one-stop shop with everything you'll ever need for mother and child - fashionable maternity and babywear, nursery furniture, feeding equipment, high chairs, car seats, colourful prams and pushchairs, bathtime accessories, toys and gifts. Personal shopping, fashion advisors, and award-winning Baby Bump fitting service to help you visualize your changing shape. Open Mon-Wed 10am-9pm, Thur-Fri 10am-10pm, Sat 9am-9pm, Sun 12noon-6pm.

naturalmat®
Mattresses made by hand in Devon

Naturalmat   020 7985 0474
99 Talbot Road, Notting Hill, W11 2AT
www.naturalmat.co.uk
Although specializing in high-quality mattresses Natural mat also offer an exclusive range of Leander cotbeds (www.leander.com) from Holland, Stokke, Oeuf and Troll.

Olli Ella   020 7713 8668
www.olliella.com
Olli Ella, a British brand celebrated for its modern nursing chairs, has a range of gliders and ottomans that will be the centrepiece of any nursery. Every piece is made by hand in England and upholstered in a stain-resistant microsuede (in a bevy of colours). Customising is offered too.

Oscar and Patch   0845 838 0680
www.oscarandpatch.co.uk
Oscar and Patch is a wonderful emporium of timeless traditional luxuries for babies and children, offering the finest clothing, alongside the most magical toys and exquisite hand crafted nursery furniture. Referred by many as the Harrods of the online children's world, it's a unique and exciting concept bringing back the best of British craftsmanship.

Peppermint Clapham   020 3393 3101
176 Northcote Road, Clapham, SW11 1PA
www.peppermint.co.uk
Nursery furniture includes ranges from Kidsmill, Boori, Stokke and Europe Baby. Open 9.30am-6pm Mon-Sat, 9.30am - 7pm Thurs, 11am-4pm Sun. Online shop also.

Punkin Patch Interiors   020 3371 7530
www.punkinpatch.co.uk
Patch Interiors supplies luxury furnishings for babies and children like cots, beds, decor items including personalised and commissioned art. Many items are bespoke and are made to the client's specifications. Other services we provide are wall mural painting, interior design and made to order soft furnishings.

STYLISH ACCESSORIES FOR THE MODERN NURSERY

LONDON

Lovingly made in England

WWW.OLLIELLA.COM

Pure Baby   **020 7751 5544**
208 Fulham Road, SW10 9PJ
www.purebaby.co.uk
Baby and toddler boutique conveniently situated opposite the Chelsea & Westminster hospital. In addition to a range of baby clothing, cashmere, toys, gifts they have a beautiful range of cot beds and nursery furniture from Belgium. Open Mon-Sat 10am-6.30pm, Thu 10am-7pm, Sun 11am-5pm.

Room to Bloom   **07590 403 997**
Interiors for Children
www.room-to-bloom.com
Room to Bloom specialises in the interior design of children's spaces, including nurseries, children's rooms and playrooms. Home consultations, e-decoration and full interior design & installation services available. Visit www.room-to-bloom.com to book a consultation or contact Ursula Wesselingh on 07590 403 997.

Simon Horn Nursery Furniture   **020 7731 1279**
555 King's Road, Fulham, SW6 2EB
www.simonhorn.com
The Simon Horn nursery collection is based in the 18th Century Louis Philippe style made from Cherrywood or painted finishes and carries a brass plate engraved with the child's name and birth date or short dedication.

The Little White Company   **020 8166 0199**
4 Symons Street, Chelsea, SW3 2TJ
www.thewhiteco.com
Positioned to the rear of this flagship White Company Lifestyle store, the Little White Company offers a classic range of white nursery furniture, plaid blankets and linen. Open Mon-Sat 10am-7pm, Sun 10am-5pm.

The Nursery Window   **020 7581 3358**
83 Walton Street, Chelsea, SW3 2HP
www.nurserywindow.co.uk

Yummy Kids   **020 8201 8870**
1-2 Russel Parade, Golders Green Rd, NW11 9NN
www.yummykids.co.uk
Yummy Kids offers cots from East Coast, Izziwotnot and Kub from £200+. Open Mon-Thurs 10am-6pm, Fri 10am-2pm, Sun 10.30am-3pm.

cribs, cots and first beds

Babylist   **020 7371 5145**
The Broomhouse, 50 Sulivan Road, SW6 3DX
www.babylist.com
Babylist offers one of the largest ranges of cotbeds, including many high quality brands sourced from around the world. They come in all sorts of designs, as well as hand-painted or in solid beech, oak or cherry. And you have the luxury of looking at them all from the comfort of their showroom.

shopping

linens

Olli Ella 020 7713 8668
www.olliella.com
Olli Ella, makers of stylish accessories for the modern nursery, has a delightful collection of organic baby bedding (each piece is lovingly made in England) that design-savvy parents adore. The range includes bedding, wall art, baby sleep bags, receiving blankets - and even the sweetest toddler bean bags.

mattresses

The Little Green Sheep 0800 028 1433
www.thelittlegreensheep.co.uk
Looking for a baby mattress? Keep it simple, we do. The Little Green Sheep sell the only certified Organic baby mattress in the UK. Each mattress is chemical-free, extra breathable and naturally anti-dust mite for the best start in life.

Mattresses made by hand in Devon

Naturalmat 020 7985 0474
99 Talbot Road, Notting Hill, W11 2AT
www.naturalmat.co.uk
The one stop shop for all things natural for your nursery. The best natural fibre mattresses and organic bed linen on the market. Standard sizes and made to measure. Contemporary nursery furniture, wonderful lambswool blankets, organic clothing and lots more.

maternity shops

E15

Polarn O Pyret Stratford 020 8519 1461
13 The Arcade, E15 2EE
www.polarnopyret.co.uk
Mums rave about this functional and playful brand that offers mums-to-be high quality Swedish style at sensible prices. Open Mon-Fri 10am-8pm, Sat 9am-7pm, Sun 12-6pm.

N1

Pretty Pregnant Islington 020 7486 2531
271 Upper Street, N1 2UQ
www.prettypregnant.co.uk
Pretty Pregnant offers a one-stop solution for stylish, fashionable yet affordable maternity wear. They stock a vast range of maternity labels, European collections and a wide

selection of jeans. Styles range from casual basics to work, formal wear and lingerie as well as top nursing wear Boob, ideal for Mums who breastfeed: all to feel beautiful and comfortable throughout your pregnancy. Expect to find a relaxed environment with friendly staff, a playmat for the kids and a sofa for dads. Open Mon-Sat 10am-6pm.

N8

JoJo Maman Bebe Crouch End 020 8347 8139
47 The Broadway, N8 8DT
www.jojomamanbebe.co.uk
JoJo Maman Bebe is a one-stop shop for pregnancy and beyond, offering fashionable maternity wear for every occasion, quirky children's clothing and adorable babywear. The company also provides an extensive range of practical products, toys and gifts for your baby, nursery and family home. Open Mon-Sat 9.30am-5.30pm, Sun 10am-4pm.

NW2

Mamas & Papas Brent Cross 0845 268 2000
Brent Cross Shopping Park, Tilling Road, NW2 1LJ
www.mamasandpapas.com
Excellent one-stop shop with everything you'll ever need for mother and child - fashionable maternity and babywear, nursery furniture, feeding equipment, high chairs, car seats, colourful prams and pushchairs, bathtime accessories, toys and gifts. Open Mon-Fri 10am-8pm, Sat 10am-7pm, Sun 11am-5pm.

NW3

Seraphine Maternity 0844 287 0001
28 Kensington Church Street, W8 4EP
79B Hampstead High Street, NW3 1RE
www.seraphine.com
Seraphine is Europe's leading maternity wear retailer, offering chic and stylish clothes that are functional as well as fashionable. The celebrity and fashion editors destination of choice for their maternity wardrobe needs, Seraphine's range of Award Winning jeans, tops, dresses and nursing clothes are the perfect option for dressing your pregnant curves in style. Seraphine also now offers a luxe line of special event and bridal dresses.

NW4

Polarn O Pyret Brent Cross 020 8203 9781
1st Floor, Brent Cross Shopping Centre, NW4 3FP
www.polarnopyret.co.uk
Mums rave about this functional and playful brand that offers mums-to-be high quality Swedish style at sensible prices. Open Mon-Fri 10am-8pm, Sat 9am-7pm, Sun 12-6pm.

NW11

JoJo Maman Bebe Finchley 020 8731 8961
3 Ashbourne Parade, 1259 Finchley Rd, NW11 0AD

SE22

JoJo Maman Bebe Dulwich   020 8693 2123
6 Lordship Lane, SE22 8HN

Pretty Pregnant East Dulwich   020 8693 9010
61 North Cross Road, SE22 9ET

SE3

JoJo Maman Bebe Blackheath   020 8852 2058
21 Montpelier Vale, SE3 0TJ

SW1

9 London at Harrods   020 7730 1234
87-135 Brompton Road, SW1X 7XL
www.harrods.com
Harrods nursery department is situated on the 4th floor where
you will find a capsule collection from 9 London.

SW3

9 London by Emily Evans   020 7730 1318
190 Pavillion Road, SW3 2BF
www.9london.co.uk
Located off London's Sloane Square 9 London offer beautiful
maternity collections from around the world, mixed with
one-off vintage pieces and their own quirky collection.

Blossom Mother and Child   020 7589 7500
164 Walton Street, SW3 2JL
www.blossommotherandchild.com
Blossom offers mothers a one-stop shop for maternity
clothing and lingerie, designer baby and childrenswear, plus
adorable gifts for mother and baby. Brands include Levi's
Kids, Clements Ribeiro for Blossom, M. Missoni, See by
Chloe, Alice Temperley, Anya Hindmarch, La Perla Baby and
Toffee Moon, as well as Blossom's maternity collections.
Great designer maternity jeans and the only shop in Europe
to stock 7 For All Mankind and True Religion customised for
pregnancy. Gwyneth Paltrow and Brooke Shields are fans.
Open Mon-Sat 10am-6pm, Sun 10am-5pm.

JoJo Maman Bebe Chelsea Green   020 7589 9593
12 Cale Street, SW3 3QU

Petit Bateau Kings Road   020 7838 0818
106-108 Kings Road, SW3 4TZ
www.petit-bateau.fr
Stylish, classic French clothing for premature babies up to
10yrs. Also maternity wear, gifts and soft toys. Open Mon-Sat
10am-6.30pm, Wed-Thur 10am-7pm, Sun 12noon-6pm.

Pretty Pregnant Chelsea   020 7349 7450
186 King's Road, 266 Fulham Road, SW3 5XP

SW11

JoJo Maman Bebe Battersea   020 7228 0322
68 & 72 Northcote Road, SW11 6QL

shopping

Pretty Pregnant Clapham   **020 7924 4850**
102 Northcote Road, SW11 6QW

SW15

JoJo Maman Bebe Putney   **020 8780 5165**
30 Putney Exchange, SW15 1TW

SW18

Mamas & Papas Colliers Wood   **0845 268 2000**
Christchurch Road, SW18 2NX

W1

Blossom Mother and Child   **020 7486 6089**
69 Marylebone High Street , W1U 5JJ

John Lewis Oxford Street   **020 7629 7711**
Oxford Street, Mayfair, W1A 1EX

Mamas & Papas Oxford Circus   **0845 268 2000**
256-258 Regent Street, W1B 3AF
www.mamasandpapas.com
Mamas & Papas' flagship store and cafe, a spacious and stylish environment with great services, including personal shopping, fashion advisors, and their award-winning Baby Bump fitting service to help you visualize your changing shape. Everything you'll ever need for mother and child - fashionable maternity and babywear, nursery furniture and equipment, high chairs, car seats, colourful prams and pushchairs, bathtime accessories, toys and gifts. Open Mon-Fri 9am-5.30pm, Sat 9am-5pm, Sun 10am-5pm.

Polarn O Pyret House of Fraser   **020 7529 4700**
318 Oxford Street, W1C 1HF

W2

JoJo Maman Bebe Notting Hill   **020 7727 3578**
101 Westbourne Grove, Notting Hill, W2 4UW

W4

JoJo Maman Bebe Chiswick   **020 8994 0379**
80 Turnham Green Terrace, W4 1QN

The Maternity Co   **020 8995 4455**
42 Chiswick Lane, W4 2JQ
www.thematernityco.com
This long-established maternity boutique in Chiswick offers stylish maternity clothes from a range of international designers including Mamalicious, 9 Fashion, Valja, Attesa, Belly Button and Noppies; with maternity underwear from Hot Milk and Amoralia. Open Mon-Sat 10am-5.30pm (Thurs til 7pm).

W5

Baby e Ealing   **020 8840 8197**
20 The Green, W5 5DA
www.babye.co.uk
Boutique offering designer clothes for mum and baby aged

0-2, as well as shoes, toys by Steiff and Kaloo, pushchairs (Bugaboo) and highchairs, maternity and breastfeeding tops, christening and baby shower gifts. Brands include Baby Dior, Ralph Lauren and No Added Sugar. Open 10am-5.30pm Mon-Sat, 12noon-4pm Sun.

W8

Seraphine Maternity   **0844 287 0001**
28 Kensington Church Street, W8 4EP
79B Hampstead High Street, NW3 1RE
www.seraphine.com
Seraphine is Europe's leading maternity wear retailer, offering chic and stylish clothes that are functional as well as fashionable. The celebrity and fashion editors destination of choice for their maternity wardrobe needs, Seraphine's range of Award Winning jeans, tops, dresses and nursing clothes are the perfect option for dressing your pregnant curves in style. Seraphine also now offers a luxe line of special event and bridal dresses.

W12

Mamas & Papas Westfield   **0845 268 2000**
Westfield London Shopping Centre, W12 7GF
www.mamasandpapas.com
Fashionable maternity and babywear, nursery furniture, feeding equipment, high chairs, car seats, colourful prams and pushchairs, bathtime accessories, toys and gifts. Personal shopping, fashion advisors, and award-winning Baby Bump fitting service to help you visualise your changing shape. Open Mon-Fri 10am-9pm, Sat 9am-9pm, Sun 11am-5pm.

maternity bras

Mammae   **020 3583 0408**
www.mammae.co.uk
Mammae - A beautiful award winning underwired and lightly padded nursing bra. Conceals both nursing pads and nipples and can be worn under low cut clothing. Designed ultimately to preserve modesty, Mammae enables mums to publicly but discreetly nurse their babies. Visit our website to watch the demonstration video and view the full range.

maternity wear: online

A Beautiful Mummy   **01524 771 544**
www.abeautifulmummy.co.uk
Maternity Fashion for Yummy Mummies. A Beautiful Mummy offers a collection of fantastic breastfeeding clothes and maternity wear basics, plus mix and match clothing for any occasion. This year they launched their 'Simply Couture Maternity Collection' including dresses from Sweet Belly Couture, worldwide breastfeeding clothing and maternity celebrity favourites.

shopping

Amoralia
020 7940 8250
www.amoralia.com
Amoralia is a British luxury brand offering the most stylish, most comfortable, best quality maternity lingerie on the market. They also offer glamorous maternity swimwear and nightwear designed for comfortable and elegant nursing. Amoralia's aim is to make pregnant and nursing women feel, and look beautiful. A truly special treat!

Brides n Bumps
01252 377 725
www.bridesnbumps.com
Made to measure wedding dresses, bridesmaid dresses and evening gowns.

Bumpalicious Maternity
0845 0038301
www.bumpaliciousmaternity.co.uk
Bumpalicious Maternity specialises in beautiful maternity dresses for the woman who does not want to compromise on her style during her pregnancy. As well as their own signature occasion dresses, they sell gorgeous maternity evening and bridesmaid dresses in a wide range of colours from brands such as Ripe and Sweetbelly Couture.

Everyday Maternity
01244 681 061
www.everydaymaternity.com
A collection of international maternity brands are sold from this online only store including nursing tops from Boob, nursing bras from Emma-Jane and Carriwell and dresses from Fragile and Bellybutton.

Fun Mum
0141 882 6333
www.funmum.com
Based in Glasgow, Fun Mum have an comprehensive collection of maternity clothes for the modern mum-to-be. Great fabrics, sensible colours, comfy fit and a style guide for seasonal looks.

Harry Duley
01747 855023
www.harryduley.co.uk
Comfortable, stretchy and sexy maternity collection for a relaxed pregnancy, including maxi dresses, tops, tunics and trousers.

Isabella Oliver
0844 844 0448
www.isabellaoliver.com
The Isabella Oliver maternity collection features iconic silhouettes loved by the A-list crowd. Made from luxurious stretch fabrics and high quality cottons, the clothes are designed to hug your figure and accentuate your shapely bump.

Lulu Arver Maternity
01404 815 516
www.luluarver.com
Stylist approved, key maternity separates designed for smart girls in pursuit of gorgeous maternity clothes.

Melba London
020 8347 8811
www.melbamaternity.co.uk
Soft and luxurious maternity nightwear for stylish mums to be. Using gorgeous fabrics and clever design detail, Melba's essential maternity active and leisure wear collection will take you from month 1 to 9 in both comfort and style. Perfect for lounging elegantly at home or for a prenatal yoga class.

Picchu Maternity
0845 004 8606
www.picchumaternity.com
Gorgeous maternity dresses, evening tops, tunics and trousers in luxurious-looking jersey fabrics. Nightwear, swimwear and other everyday essentials also available.

Seraphine
www.seraphine.com
Seraphine is Europe's leading maternity wear retailer, offering chic and stylish clothes that are functional as well as fashionable. The celebrity and fashion editors destination of choice for their maternity wardrobe needs, Seraphine's range of Award Winning jeans, tops, dresses and nursing clothes are the perfect option for dressing your pregnant curves in style. Seraphine also now offers a luxe line of special event and bridal dresses.

Tiffany Rose Maternity
0870 420 8144
www.tiffanyrosematernity.com
Glamorous maternity dresses for A-list celebs, TV presenters and red-carpet fashionistas. Think Holly Willougby and Emma Bunton.

baby accessories

These suppliers have designed unique and stylish products that offer something practical with a great sense of style.

Babylist
020 7371 5145
The Broomhouse, 50 Sulivan Road, SW6 3DX
www.babylist.com
You might be wondering how much baby "stuff" is really all that necessary. If so, then you need to book an appointment with Babylist, the longest running nursery advisory service in London. They will take you through their list of essentials, as well as the nice-to-haves in the comfort of their showroom. This is not just an exclusive, A-list celebrities-only service (although they have had quite a few), but a thoroughly sensible way of tailoring your needs with the amazing range of products on offer.

Buggysnuggle
01869 340 694
www.buggysnuggle.com
Designed to keep kids warm and cosy, the Buggysnuggle fits all makes of pushchairs and is available in over 40 funky designs. Suitable from birth to over 3 years. Order online www.buggysnuggle.com.

Custard & Crumble
020 7183 3799
www.custardandcrumble.co.uk
Create a stylish and inspiring nursery with the help of Custard & Crumble. This online boutique presents a beautiful handpicked selection of baby nursery furniture, accessories and gifts, many of which you wont find on the high street. They guarantee free UK mainland delivery and offer a gift list service.

Oscar and Patch
0845 838 0680
www.oscarandpatch.co.uk
Oscar and Patch is a wonderful emporium of timeless

traditional luxuries for babies and children, offering the finest clothing, alongside the most magical toys and exquisite hand crafted nursery furniture. Referred by many as the Harrods of the online children's world, it's a unique and exciting concept bringing back the best of British craftsmanship.

Rosy Cheek Cosy   **01225 443 975**
www.rosycheekcosy.com
Exclusive designs by Tess Lambert, using 100% cotton prints and an eco collection in Organic Cotton and super soft Bamboo. Rosy Cheek Cosy specialise in stylish baby gifts, bedding and accessories. Quite simply everything we do focuses as much as possible on natural, high quality and planet-friendly. Designed and made with love in Bath, England.

birth announcements

Happyhands   **020 7274 1131**
www.happyhands.co.uk
Your baby's hand and foot prints on cards. Happyhands provide their customers with an ingenious ink-free kit which allows you to take your baby's hand or footprints without ink.

Built to Olympic proportions, this London Tote baby changing bag from **Babymel** comes equipped with a matching padded changing mat, insulated bottle holder, seven internal pockets and built in shoulder straps - a true British champion. **£45**

www.babymel.co.uk

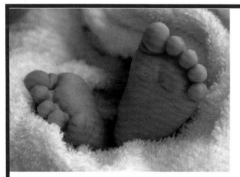

Your baby's hands and feet are truly amazing

Let **HappyHands** preserve the memory of them on cards, tiles and mugs

We provide you with an easy to use inkless kit to take your prints

Quote **LBD15** for a 10% discount

www.happyhands.co.uk
tel: 0845 466 0171 email: info@happyhands.co.uk

Franchise opportunities available, please call for more information

castings: hands & feet

Most mothers regret that they never got round to taking their baby's hand or foot prints or struggled with a tube of paint. These companies offer a range of styles (casts, prints and imprints) to suit all budgets.

First Impressions   020 8346 8666
www.firstimpressions.org.uk
First Impressions, the original baby casters are celebrating our 26th anniversary this year, with new gorgeous pieces to treasure. Have a peep at our micro collection... exquisite jewellery made from your baby's casts. Cufflinks, keyrings and charms. We have had to sign several confidentiality agreements this year so alas cannot tell you who is wearing our gorgeous jewellery! This of course, alongside our uniquely personal sculpture, creating exquisite casts of your baby's hands and feet and more, in silver, bronze, crystal, resins and plaster.

Happyhands   0845 466 0171
www.happyhands.co.uk
Hand and foot prints preserved on ceramic tiles and mugs.

Image Casting   07515 678 280
www.imagecasting.co.uk
We at First Impressions, the original baby casters, are celebrating our 26th anniversary this year, with new gorgeous

pieces to treasure. Have a peep at our micro collection... exquisite jewellery made from your baby's casts. Cufflinks, keyrings and charms. This of course, alongside our uniquely personal sculpture, creating exquisite casts of your baby's hands and feet and more, in silver, bronze, crystal, resins and plaster.

Wrightson & Platt   020 7639 9085
www.wrightsonandplatt.com
Precious memories cast from your own little work of art! Breathtaking sculpture and jewellery created by the finest artists and craftsmen. Commissions include baby feet, children holding hands and complex family pieces. All inclusive service offers FREE casting visit, gift packaging, delivery and archiving. Go on, make the moment last forever!

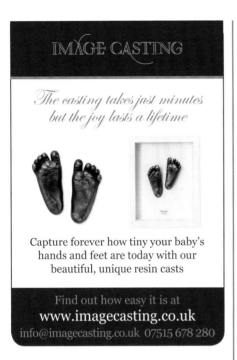

clothing shops

online

Balloons Designer Childrenswear   **01159 455 829**
www.balloonsweb.co.uk
Balloons provides high quality designer children's clothing and baby clothes through e-commerce on our website and our store in Nottingham. With over 15 years experience in the children's designer clothing business, Balloons is proud to offer a range of leading brands including: Catimini, Kenzo, IKKS, Oilily, Bonnie Baby, No Added Sugar, Scotch Shrunk, Scotch R'Belle, DKNY and Timberland. Balloons' designer children's clothes are available for all ages from newborn to 16 years for boys and girls. Balloons aims to complement their high quality designer children's clothes with excellent service.

boutiques - E2

Bob & Blossom   020 7739 4737
140 Columbia Road, Shoreditch, E2 7RG
www.bobandblossom.co.uk
Bob & Blossom design cool sleepsuits and matching hats, t-shirts, baby blankets in stripes or with heart or star motifs in sizes from0-6yrs. Also toys and gifts with the emphasis on quality and nostalgia. Only open Sun 9am-3pm to coincide with the Columbia Road flower market.

E3

Jakss   020 8981 2233
469 Roman Road, Bow, E3 5LX
www.jakss.co.uk
This is a well established friendly children's boutique for 0-16yrs. Wide range of brands including Fendi, Ralph Lauren, Oilily, Juicy Couture and Jottum. Also stock Birkenstock sandals. Open Mon-Sat 10am-5.30pm.

E8

Buggies and Bikes   020 7241 5382
23 Broadway Market, Hackney, E8 4PH
www.buggiesandbikes.net
As well as buggies, bikes and toys, this shop stocks an innovative range of separates, occasion wear and accessories created for babies and toddlers up to 36 months. They also provide a room for children's activities such as Sing and Sign, pregnancy yoga and baby massage. Open Mon-Sat 10am-6.30pm, Sun 11am-5pm.

N1

Brora   020 7354 4246
186 Upper Street, Islington, N1 1RQ
www.brora.co.uk
Scottish cashmere cardigans, trousers and hats as well as pram blankets and personalised cot blankets. Mon-Sat 10am-6pm, Sun 12-5pm.

shopping

Felix & Lilys   020 7424 5423
3 Camden Passage, Islington, N1 8EA
www.felixandlilys.com
Funky, colourful clothes for babies and children, from orange babygrows to puffball skirts and rockabilly shirts. Labels include Oh Baby, Their Nibs and Mini Rodini. Also traditional wooden toys from doll's houses and car parks to musical instruments. Online shop for clothes only. Open Mon-Fri 10am-6pm, Sat 10am-7pm, Sun 11am-5pm.

Igloo Kids Islington   020 7354 7300
300 Upper Street, Islington, N1 2TU
www.iglookids.co.uk
Modern shop with extensive product ranges for 0-8yrs. Loads of designer brands, including No Added Sugar, Bob & Blossom, Frilly Lily and Petit Bateau. Also stock shoes, outdoor and swimming gear, toys, gifts and toiletries. Open Mon-Wed 10am-6.30pm, Thur 9.30am-7pm, Fri-Sat 9.30am-6.30pm and Sun 11am-5.30pm.

N10

Frocks Away   020 8444 9309
81-83 Fortis Green Road, Muswell Hill, N10 3HP
www.frocksaway.co.uk
Fantastic one-stop shop where you can buy everything from children's clothes and shoes for 0-12yrs to designer wear for yourself. Brands include Catimini, Petit Bateau, Molo and Scotch & Soda. Shoe fittings for such labels as Camper, Geox, Crocs and Start-rite. Open Mon-Sat, 9.30am-5.30pm, Sun 11am-5pm

Obaby   020 8444 8742
126 Fortis Green Road, Muswell Hill, N10 3DU
Set up by Alyson Spiro (think Emmerdale) this shop specialises in fairtrade, organic baby clothing from 0-4yrs. Also stocks wooden toys, knitted animals, organic skin and hair care products. Open 9.30am-5.30pm Mon-Sun.

N16

Frere Jacques   020 7249 5655
121 Stoke Newington Church Street, N16 0UH
Children and baby clothing, shoes and accessories for 0-7yrs. Brands include Minymo, Ecco, Petit Bateau, Justine et Lea and Alphabet. They have a shoe fitting service and a kids hair salon which is open on Saturdays. Open Tue-Fri 10-5pm, Sat 11am-6pm.

Kiddie Chic   020 8880 1500
19 Amhurst Parade, Stamford Hill, N16 5AA
Kiddie Chic is a welcoming shop with lovely range of children's clothes for 0-16yrs. Brands include DKNY, Baby Graziella, Jean Bourget, IKKS and Mona Lisa. Toy basket and play area keeps little ones amused. Open Mon-Thur 10am-5.30pm, Fri 10am-12pm, Sat closed, Sun 10am-2pm.

Olive loves Alfie   020 7241 4212
84 Stoke Newington Church Street, N16 0AP
www.olivelovesalfie.co.uk
Olive loves Alfie don't buy into mass-produced or hyped products. Here you will find funky, contemporary, colourful designs from around the world, including Marimekko, Ej Sikke Lej, No Added Sugar and Ziestha, bright T shirts from Katvig

---

Need to Know: Daily deals and flash sales

There is much to recommend the new daily deal and flash sale websites, offering known and coveted brands as well as introducing you to new products and services and saving you 50% in the process. Sign up via email or iphone app.

LittleBird.co.uk Offering discounted tickets for events such as shows at the Southbank, activities and treats for mum and dad, this site focuses on premium brands and experiences that its two founder mums feel are genuine goodies.

UrbanExplorers.co.uk For parents around town, this site keeps its finger on the pulse with a weekly what's on newsletter as well as daily offerings for urban dwellers with tots in tow.

Halfpintchic.com An early runner of flash sale sites selling designer baby clothes, children's party dresses, shoes and acces-

sories. Brands have included Simonetta, Tartine et Chocolat and Baby Graziella.

Casabu.com Launched this spring, Casabu offers flash sales of European designer clothes, toys (we've just spotted Lego), maternity changing bags and other leading brands. Technically this site looks the most leading edge.

Zulily.com Another one to watch with a wide selection of high quality brands including Toby Tiger, Rufflebutts and French label Right Bank Babies. Also includes deals for mums such as Lancaster sunglasses and Cool Mint fashion.

and rainwear from Kozi Kids. Shop online or at the store, Mon-Fri 9.30am-5.30pm, Sat 10am-6pm, Sun 12-5pm.

Three Potato Four 020 7704 2228
44-45 Newington Green, N16 9QH
www.threepotatofour.co.uk
This unique children's boutique was set up in 2008 by Genna Savastio and is a popular hub for local parents. Integrating children's fashion, traditional and stylish toys (think retro Fisher Price and Le Toy Van) and vintage interior finds, Genna has selected an eclectic range of local designers and traditional brands. Children's wear favourites include the French brand Dis Une Couleur, Fub, Kik-Kid, Smafolk and Milibe, as well as soft baby shoes from Bobux, Tip Toey Joey and Nowali moccasins. Also tucked towards the back is an exquisite hairdressing salon with ornate mirrors and orange and yellow padded high chairs set against vintage wallpaper and comfy leather chairs. Open Mon-Fri 10am-5pm, Sat 9.30am-5pm and Sun 10am-5pm.

N6

Notsobig 020 8340 4455
31a Highgate High Street, Highgate, N6 5JT
Wonderfully friendly shop with a fantastic range of children's clothes. Brands include Mini-a-ture, American Outfitters, I Love Gorgeous and Hucklebones. For 0-12yrs.Open 10am-6pm Mon-Sat, 11am-5pm Sun.

N8

Aravore Babies 020 8347 5752
31 Park Road, Crouch End, N8 8TE
www.aravore-babies.com
Luxury organic brand Aravore Babies' concept store in Crouch End stocks Aravore's own range for little ones (0-6yrs) including gorgeous vintage knits, matching accessories and exquisite baby shawls and blankets as well as a hand-picked selection of like-minded organic clothing, toys and toiletries brands. Open Mon-Sat 10am-5.30pm.

JoJo Maman Bebe Crouch End 020 8347 8139
47 The Broadway, Crouch End, N8 8DT
www.jojomamanbebe.co.uk
JoJo Maman Bebe is a one-stop shop for pregnancy and beyond, offering fashionable maternity wear for every occasion, quirky children's clothing and adorable babywear. The company also provides an extensive range of practical products, toys and gifts for your baby, nursery and family home. Free P&P on all UK mainland orders. Open Mon-Sat 9.30am-5.30pm, Sun 10am-4pm.

Mini Kin 020 8341 6898
22 Broadway Parade, Crouch End, N8 9DE
www.minikin.co.uk
Designer wear for 0-8yrs, including No Added Sugar, Noah Noah, Bonnie Baby and I Love Gorgeous. Also changing bags, gifts and toiletries by Green People, Burt Bees and Earth Friendly Baby. Their own children's specialist haird-ressing salon. Open 9.30am-5.30pm Mon-Sat, 10.30am-4.30pm Sun.

NW1

Elias & Grace 020 7449 0574
158 Regents Park Road, Primrose Hill, NW1 8XN
www.eliasandgrace.com
A great store for mother and child, frequented by A listers Kate Moss, Sadie Frost, Luella Bartley, Sam Taylor Wood and Jools Oliver. In store or online, a modern and versatile mix of super cool fashion and shoes for 0-10 yrs, including their own label, Nurtured by Nature, Chloe, Miller and Quincy. Also hand-knitted soft toys, mobiles and gifts. Open Mon-Sat 10am-6pm, Sun 12-5pm.

NW10

Kidsen 020 8969 7565
111 Chamberlayne Road, Kensal Rise, NW10 3NS
www.kidsen.co.uk
Great Scandinavian kids' store with everything you need for 0-7yrs, from top-brand baby clothing, shoes and accessories to nursery furniture, toys and unique gifts. Items are handpicked by Swedish born Corina Papadopoulou. Open Mon-Fri 10am-5.30pm, Sat 10am-5pm.

Their Nibs Kensal Rise 020 8964 8444
79 Chamberlayne Road, Kensal Rise, NW10 3ND
www.theirnibs.com
Exclusive and distinctive in-house designed prints are used for their retro clothing collection for children aged 0-10yrs. These include the Cowboy, Cowboys and Indians, Gardening Girl, Pirate, Retro Cars and the Vintage Fairy print. Open Mon-Fri 9.30am-5.30pm, Sat 10am-6pm, Sun 12-5pm. Children's hairdressing also available Weds 3-5.30pm, Thurs 4-6pm and Sat 10am-1pm (booking recommended). Online shopping available.

NW2

Mamas & Papas Brent Cross 0845 268 2000
Brent Cross Shopping Park, Tilling Road, NW2 1LJ
www.mamasandpapas.com
Excellent one-stop shop with everything you'll ever need for mother and child - fashionable maternity and babywear, nursery furniture, feeding equipment, high chairs, car seats, colourful prams and pushchairs, bathtime accessories, toys and gifts. Open Mon-Fri 10am-8pm, Sat 10am-7pm, Sun 11am-5pm.

NW7

Tartan Turtle 020 8959 9938
52 The Broadway, Mill Hill, NW7 3LH
www.tartanturtle.co.uk
Well stocked shop with variety of brands that change with the seasons, but usually including Nolita, Rare, Two Religions, Pepe, Kate Mack and Baby Graziella. Open Mon-Sat 9.30am-5.30pm, Sun 10am-2pm.

shopping

NW8

Igloo Kids St John's Wood 020 7483 2332
80 St John's Wood High Street, NW8 7SH
www.iglookids.co.uk
Modern shop with extensive product ranges for 0-8yrs.
Loads of designer brands, including No Added Sugar, Bob &
Blossom, Frilly Lily, Antik Batik, Ver de Terre and Petit Bateau.
Also stock shoes, active and swimming gear, toys, gifts and
toiletries. Open Mon-Sat 9.30am-6pm, Sun 11am-5.30pm.

Tiddlywinks 020 7722 3033
23 St John's Wood High Street, St John's Wood,
NW8 7NH
www.tiddlywinks.co.uk
Well stocked designer shop for 0-8yrs. Brands include Baby
Dior, Ralph Lauren and Tiddlywinks' own cute baby frocks,
frou-frou party wear, Armani Baby cargoes and jeans, and
other mini delights. Collections updated seasonally. Gorgeous
own brand, Baby Graziella and Tip Toey Joey shoes. Gift
boxes. Open Mon-Sat 9.30am-6pm, Sun 11am-5pm.

SE3

Ottie and the Bea 020 8465 5318
12 Old Dover Road, Blackheath, SE3 7BT
www.ottieandthebea.co.uk
Launched in 2010 this fab children's shop in South East
London offers local parents a great selection of creative and
imaginative games (eg Little Experience and Cloth Kits
creative crafts); great toys such as Djeco and Flensted
mobiles; exclusive books (think of hard-back, collector's
items you see at the Tate); and clothes including the much-
loved brands Poppy, Dandy Star and Animal Tales. They also
host loads of creative events, such as storytelling and puppet
making. Open Mon-Fri 9am-5pm and Sat 9.30am-5.30pm.

SE10

United Ideas 020 8858 4006
11 Greenwich Market, Greenwich, SE10 9HZ
www.unitedideas.co.uk
Beautiful embroidered knitwear, designed in England and
made in Peru. Also cute dresses. Open Mon-Fri 10.30am-
5pm, Sat-Sun 10am-5.30pm. Limited range also in the
Jubilee Market Hall, Covent Garden Market, at weekends.

SE13

Love Me Again 020 8244 0172
37 Staplehurst Road, Hither Green, SE13 5ND
www.homeandkids.co.uk
Brilliant children's boutique offering hand-picked children's
new and nearly new clothing and toys. Favoured brands are
D&G, Kenzo, Ralph Lauren, Burberry, Gap, Molly & Jack,
Zara and Mini Boden, and stylish footwear labels Gumbies,
Smelly Wellies and home furnishing. Mon-Sat 9.30am-5pm.

SE16

Olivia Rose 020 7740 1111
194 Southwark Park Road, Bermondsey, SE16 3RP

www.olivia-rose.co.uk
Set up by local mother of 3, Sarah Mash, this excellent
designer children's store has many exclusive brands from
Spain such as Mayoral and Torres, as well as Darcy Brown,
Oililly and Katie Mack. The shop also sells its own brand of
shoes (ballerinas, Mary Janes and Moccasins for boys).
Clothing accessories, hair bows and other gifts such as
changing bags, luxury pram liners etc. Open Mon-Sat 10am-
5pm.

SE21

Biff Kids Dulwich 020 8299 0911
41-43 Dulwich Village, Dulwich, SE21 7BN
www.biffkids.com
An excellent children's boutique stocking a mixture of
affordable brands such as Joules and Petit Bateau, plus
some great items from Catimini, I Love Gorgeous and
Timberland. In the second half of the store they fit children's
shoes (Start-rite, Geox, Lelli Kelly, Crocs). Wellies too. Also
great for accessories and school must-haves: plimsolls,
swimwear and school uniforms. Open Mon-Fri 9.30am-
5.30pm, Sat 10am-6pm, Sun 11.30am-4.30pm

SE22

JoJo Maman Bebe Dulwich 020 8693 2123
6 Lordship Lane, East Dulwich, SE22 8HN
www.jojomamanbebe.co.uk
JoJo Maman Bébé is a one-stop shop for pregnancy and
beyond, offering fashionable maternity wear for every occasion, quirky children's clothing and adorable babywear. The
company also provides an extensive range of practical
products, toys and gifts for your baby, nursery and family
home. Free P&P on all UK mainland orders. Open Mon-Sat
9.30am-5.30pm, Sun11-5.

Sparkle and Spin 020 8299 6606
14 Melbourne Grove, East Dulwich, SE22 8QZ
www.sparkleandspin.co.uk
Popular East Dulwich children's boutique with a range of
unique clothing labels such as Katvig, Milibe, Molo, Freoli,
Hollys, Louie Louis and Soft Gallery; shoes from Angulus and
Bergstein wellington boots. The store also has a stylish range
of contemporary toys and gifts. Open Mon-Sat 10am-3pm
(opening to 5pm on some days).

SW3

Bonpoint South Kensington 020 3263 5057
256 Brompton Road, South Kensington, SW3 2AS
www.bonpoint.com
Exquisite classic French designer wear for 0-18yrs (girls) 0-
4yrs (boys). Open 10am-6pm Mon-Sat, Sun 11-5pm.

SW10

Pure Baby 020 7751 5544
208 Fulham Road, SW10 9PJ
www.purebaby.co.uk
Luxury baby and toddler boutique with clothing for 0-3yrs,

conveniently situated opposite the Chelsea & Westminster hospital. We stock a wide range of baby clothing, also in cashmere, toys, gifts and a full range of nursery furniture. Open Mon-Sat 10am-6.30pm, Thu 10am-7pm, Sun 11am-5pm.

SW11

JoJo Maman Bebe Battersea 020 7228 0322
68 & 72 Northcote Road, Clapham, SW11 6QL
www.jojomamanbebe.co.uk
In Northcote Road you have the chance to visit their specialist maternity store with a much increased collection and a wide variety of nursing bras and tops. Two doors down at 72 Northcote Road is their baby and children's store which carries almost the whole catalogue collection of clothing, nursery products and toys with the exception of furniture and bulky items. Open Mon-Fri 9.30am-5.30pm, Sun 11am-5pm.

Lizzies 020 7738 2973
71 Webbs Road, Battersea, SW11 6PX
Lifestyle shop that stocks traditional clothing for 0-6yrs including Kissy Kissy and a new Spanish label, Bykiss. Also toys (Jellycat, Maileg and Christening and personalised chairs). Open 10am-6pm, Mon-Sat.

Quackers 020 7978 4235
155d Northcote Road, Battersea, SW11 6QB
Friendly shop with good range of clothes for 0-8yrs including the delightful brand Weekend a la Mer, as well as Katvig, Molo and Mayoral. Also soft baby shoes and ballet clothes. Open 9.30am-5.30pm Mon-Fr, 10am-5.30pm Sat.

Trotters Clapham 020 7585 0572
86 Northcote Road, Clapham, SW11 6QN
www.trotters.co.uk
Classy traditional baby and children's clothes for 0-10 yrs, as well as shoes, books, toys and haircuts. Open Mon-Sat 9am-6pm, Sun 10am-6pm.

SW12

Twist 020 3558 6229
11 Balham High Road, Balham, SW12 9AP
www.twistkids.com
Following a relocation to this new shop in October 2010, this excellent Balham baby and children's independent nursery and clothing shop sells a range of clothing (Organics for Kids, Bob & Blossom, Lilly and Side, Bibbles), urban puschairs including Joolz, Stokke, Phil & Teds and Baby Jogger; toys and games as well as cots (Stokke and Bednest).

SW13

Membery's 020 8876 2910
1 Church Road, Barnes, SW13 9HE
www.memberylondon.com
Where 0-10s flock for dressy frocks, from christening gowns to Sally Membery's wonderful made-to-measure or off-the-peg bridesmaid dresses. Liberty print dresses too, and designer wear by Petit Bateau and Paul Smith. Open 10am-5pm, Mon-Sat.

SW15

JoJo Maman Bebe Putney 020 8780 5165
30 Putney Exchange, Putney High Street, Putney, SW15 1TW
www.jojomamanbebe.co.uk
JoJo Maman Bébé is a one-stop shop for pregnancy and beyond, offering fashionable maternity wear for every occasion, quirky children's clothing and adorable babywear. The company also provides an extensive range of practical products, toys and gifts for your baby, nursery and family home. Free P&P on all UK mainland orders. Open Mon-Sat 9am-6pm, Sun 11am-5pm

SW18

Mamas & Papas Colliers Wood 0845 268 2000
Tandem Shopping Centre, Christchurch Road, Colliers Wood, SW18 2NX
www.mamasandpapas.com
Excellent one-stop shop with everything you'll ever need for mother and child - fashionable maternity and babywear, nursery furniture, feeding equipment, high chairs, car seats, colourful prams and pushchairs, bathtime accessories, toys and gifts. Open Mon-Fri 10am-8pm, Sat 10am-6pm, Sun 11am-5pm.

shopping

SW1V

Little Bevan   020 7821 9499
53 Moreton Street, Pimlico, SW1V 2NY
www.littlebevan.co.uk
Made to measure partywear for smart occasions, weddings and christenings. If you don't want to visit the studio in Pimlico, Sarah Colfer offers a home visit service (for a fee). She also stocks a selection from D'Arcy Brown, Olive and Moss, Anna Fie, Mini-a-ture, and Lille Barn. Also a good selection of newborn gifts, accessories and party shoes. Open Mon-Sat 10am-5pm, Thurs 10am-6pm

SW1W

Peter Jones   020 7730 3434
Sloane Square, Chelsea, SW1W 8EL
www.johnlewis.com
Department store heaven for Chelsea mums, for everything you need prior to and after the birth, including expert advice from well-trained nursery advisors. A good range of car seats, puschairs and prams, nursery furniture and linens as well as highchairs and other necessary equipment (all never knowingly undersold, with full guarantees). Clothes, shoes and essential kit for mum, baby and older children. Their popular nursery advisory service (similar to their wedding list service) allows friends and family to buy things from your list. A great stash of toys from rocking horses and dolls' houses to Ben 10 and all the popular TV character toys and games, as well as stocking fillers, cars and trains, Fisher-Price, educational toys, board games, puzzles - truly something for everyone.

Semmalina Starbags   020 7730 9333
225 Ebury Street, Pimlico, SW1W 8UT
www.starbags.info
Set up by showbiz sisters Emma Forbes and Sarah Standing, Semmalina Starbags offersa quirky mix of fun contemporary and vintage clothing for 0-8yrs, as well as enchanting toys, sweets and Starbag party bags. Open Mon-Sat 9.30am-5.30pm.

SW1

Baby Dior   020 7823 2039
6 Harriet Street, Belgravia, SW1X 9JW
www.dior.com
The ultimate in French chic. Designer clothes and accessories for 0-12-plus yrs. Open 10am-6.30pm Mon-Sat, 10am-7pm Wed. Website is for adult rather than children's wear.

Bonpoint Chelsea   020 7235 1441
15 Sloane Street, Chelsea, SW1X 9NB
www.bonpoint.com
Exquisite classic French designer wear for 0-18yrs (girls), 0-12yrs (boys). Open 10am-6pm Mon-Sat, Sun 12-5pm.

Caramel Baby and Child   020 7730 2564
259 Pavilion Road, Chelsea, SW1X 0BP
www.caramel-shop.co.uk
Gorgeous clothes and shoes in unique fabrics and designs,

for 0-12yrs. This is the largest and sleekest of Caramel's 3 London stores. Open 10am-6pm Mon-Sat, 12noon-5pm Sun. Excellent online shop also.

Harrods   020 7730 1234
87-135 Brompton Road, Knightsbridge, SW1X 7XL
www.harrods.com
Harrods nursery department is situated on the 4th floor where you will find the top of the range in nursery furniture, furnishings, fashion, toys, maternity wear, collectables and a kids' hair dressing salon. Open Mon-Sat 10am-8pm, Sun 11.30am-6pm.

Kidspace   020 7235 3730
3 Sloane Street, Knightsbridge, SW1X 9QX
www.kidspace.it
An Italian clothing boutique selling such popular Italian ranges as Miss Bluemarine, Iceberg and Parrot. The collections are from newborn to 14yrs, casual and formalwear as well as some footwear. They also have a VIP personal shopping lounge, where new collections are presented to customers. Open Mon-Sat 10am-6pm, Sun 12noon-6pm.

La Stupenderia   020 7245 6656
16 Motcomb Street, Belgravia, SW1X 8LB
www.lastupenderia.com
Beautiful Italian clothing boutique in Belgravia with sizes from newborn clothing to 16yrs, popular with celebrities such as Angelina Jolie. Open Mon-Sat 10am-7pm, Sun 12-5pm. There is also a small selection to be found in Harrods (Knightsbridge).

Marie-Chantal Chelsea   020 7730 8662
133a Sloane Street, Chelsea, SW1X 9AX
www.mariechantal.com
Classic, timeless collections capturing the innocence of childhood. From newborn to 12 yrs, Marie-Chantal uses only the finest fabrics to create the most adorable selection of casual and formal wear with accessories to match. Open Mon-Thur 10am-6pm, Fri-Sat 10am-6.30,Sun 12-5

Rachel Riley   020 7259 5969
14 Pont Street, Knightsbridge, SW1X 9EN
www.rachelriley.co.uk
Exquisite hand-made children's clothing using beautiful fabrics. Traditional Sunday best outfits with fine smocking and embroidery; fun florals, retro ginghams and polka dots. Traditional leather shoes too. Open 10am-6pm, Mon-Sat.

SW3

Amaia Kids   020 7590 0999
14 Cale Street, Chelsea, SW3 3QU
www.amaiakids.co.uk
Amaia offer beautiful Spanish clothes for 0-10yrs as well as shoes and hair accessories. They also have a large range of styles and colours for weddings and first Communion. Open 10-6pm Mon-Sat, 12-5

Blossom Mother and Child   020 7589 7500
164 Walton Street, Belgravia, SW3 2JL
www.blossommotherandchild.com

Blossom offers mothers a one-stop shop for maternity clothing and lingerie, designer baby and childrenswear, plus adorable gifts for mother and baby. Brands include Levi's Kids, Clements Ribeiro for Blossom, M. Missoni, See by Chloe, Alice Temperley, Anya Hindmarch, La Perla Baby and Toffee Moon, as well as Blossom's maternity collections. Great designer maternity jeans and the only shop in Europe to stock 7 For All Mankind and True Religion customised for pregnancy. Gwyneth Paltrow and Brooke Shields are fans. Opens Mon-Sat 10am-6pm, Sun 10am-5pm

Bonpoint South Kensington   020 3263 5057
256 Brompton Road, South Kensington, SW3 2AS
www.bonpoint.com
Exquisite classic French designer wear for 0-18yrs (girls) 0-14yrs (boys). Open 10am-6pm Mon-Sat.

Brora   020 7352 3697
344 King's Road, Chelsea, SW3 5UR
www.brora.co.uk
Scottish cashmere cardigans, trousers and hats as well as pram blankets and personalised cot blankets. Open Mon-Sat 10am-6pm, Sun 12am-5pm. Branch also at 66-68 Ledbury Road, Notting Hill, W11 2AJ (020 7229 1515).

Caramel Baby and Child   020 7589 7001
291 Brompton Road, South Kensington, SW3 2DY
www.caramel-shop.co.uk
Sleek store offering gorgeous clothes and shoes in unique fabrics and designs for 0-12yrs. Open 10am-6pm Mon-Sat, 11am-5pm Sun. Larger store in SW1.

Catimini   020 7824 8897
33c Kings Road, Chelsea, SW3 4LX
www.catimini.com
Gorgeous children's clothing from 0-14yrs from this quintessential French label. Open Mon-Sat 10am-6.30pm (7pm on Wed), Sun 12-6pm.

Igloo Kids Chelsea   020 7352 4572
227 Kings Road, Chelsea, SW3 5EJ
www.iglookids.co.uk
Modern shop with extensive product ranges for 0-8yrs. Loads of designer brands, including No Added Sugar and Petit Bateau. Also stock shoes, active and swimming gear, toys and gifts. Open Mon-Sat 9.30am-6.30pm, Wed-Thur 9.30am-7pm, Fri-Sat 9.30am-6.30pm and Sun 11am-5.30pm.

Marie Chantal   020 7730 8662
148 Walton Street, Knightsbridge, SW3 2JJ
www.mariechantal.co.uk
Classic, timeless collections capturing the innocence of childhood. From newborn to 12 yrs, Marie-Chantal uses only the finest fabrics to create the most adorable selection of casual and formal wear with accessories to match. Open Mon-Sat 10am-6pm.

Trotters Kings Road   020 7259 9620
34 Kings Road, Chelsea, SW3 4UD
www.trotters.co.uk
Classy traditional baby and children's clothes for 0-10 yrs, as well as shoes, books, toys and haircuts. Open Mon-Sat 9am-7pm, Sun 10am-6pm.

SW6

Chocolate Wardrobe   020 7731 0262
201 New Kings Road, Parsons Green, SW6 4ST
www.chocolatewardrobe.co.uk
Chocolate Wardrobe offers a selection of eclectic, contemporary children's clothing, toys and accessories for discerning parents and children. You will find quality, popular brands like Mona Lisa, Tartine et Chocolat, Angel's Face, DKNY, Hugo Boss, Calvin Klein, Juicy Couture, Mini a Ture, Olive and Moss, Mexx, Mini a ture and more. Open Mon-Sat 10am-5pm.

Pollyanna   020 7731 0673
811 Fulham Road, Fulham, SW6 5HG
This is a long-established and family run children's shoe and clothing shop with an expert shoe fitting service. Popular brands are are Start-rite, Mod8, Timberland, Crocs, Birkenstock, Geox, Darcy Brown, I Love Gorgeus, Emu, Camper, Vans and Petit Bateau. Open Mon-Sat 9.30am-5.30pm.

W10

Dotty Dot   020 7460 3405
67a St Helens Gardens, Ladbroke Grove, W10 6LL
www.dotty-dot.com
High quality, beautifully designed toys, books, clothes and vintage homewares. Open Mon-Sat 10am-5pm.

Sasti   020 8960 1125
Unit 6, 281 Portobello Road, Notting Hill, W10 5TY
www.sasti.co.uk
Run by Julie Brown and Rosie Carpenter, Sasti sells their own designs under the Ten Fingers Ten Toes and R. Life labels, for children 0-11yrs. Playful, funky, functional designs. Play area for children. Open Mon-Sat 10am-6pm, Sun 12noon-5pm. Online shopping soon available.

W11

Bonpoint Notting Hill   020 7792 2515
197 Westbourne Grove, Notting Hill, W11 2SE
www.bonpoint.com
Exquisite classic French designer wear. This store specialises in 0-12yrs (girls) and 0-8yrs (boys). Open 10am-6pm, Mon-Sat.

Caramel Baby and Child   020 7727 0906
77 Lebury Road, Notting Hill, W11 2AG
www.caramel-shop.co.uk
Sleek store offering gorgeous clothes and shoes in unique fabrics and designs for 0-12yrs. Open 10am-6pm Mon-Sat, 12noon-5pm Sun. Larger store in SW1. Excellent online shop too.

Hop like a Bunny   020 7221 6116
12 Portland Road, Notting Hill, W11 4LA
www.hoplikeabunny.co.uk
Hop Like a Bunny is a charming children's boutique opened

shopping

in April 2010 by London mother of 3, Maria Torregrosa. The store offers the full range of Elefantino clothing and shoes, as well as other collections from leading designer branch such as: Christina Rhode, Mini A Ture, Lily & the Funky Boys. Open Mon-Sat 10am-6pm.

I Love Gorgeous   020 7229 5855
52 Ledbury Road, Notting Hill, W11 2AJ
www.ilovegorgeous.co.uk
Set up in 2007 by two friends Sophie and Lucy, ilovegorgeous design beautiful clothes for girls aged 0-12yrs. Their love of fabrics and Indian prints are a constant source of inspiration. Open Mon-Sat 10am-6pm, Sun 12-6pm.

Marie-Chantal Notting Hill   020 7243 0220
61a Ledbury Road, Notting Hill, W11 2AA
www.mariechantal.com
Classic, timeless collections capturing the beauty and innocence of childhood. From newborn to age 12 years Marie-Chantal uses only the finest fabrics and has the most adorable selection of both casual and formal wear with beautiful and fun accessories to match. Open Mon-Sat 10am-6pm, Wed 10am-7pm.

Nanos   020 7243 0299
183 Westbourne Grove, Notting Hill, W11 2SB
www.nanos.es
A classic collection of Spanish childrenswear from 0-16yrs. This brand uses liberty prints for dresses and rompers, soft cotton shirts teamed with fine wool coats, cashmere woollens and leather shoes. They also have a "Karpi" range which caters for a casual look and inludes jeans, cotton shirts and chinos. Each collection is beautifully laid out in this small boutique, but allowing plenty of access for prams and pushchairs. Open Mon-Sat 10am-5pm.

Petit Aime   020 7221 3123
34 Ledbury Road, Notting Hill, W11 2AB
www.aimelondon.com
Popular baby and children's boutique selling a range of clothing from classic European brands such as Bonton, Mann, Gold and Dandy. They also sell a rane of other nursery and homeware items. Gifts, toys, books, cards and wrapping paper also make this a great gift shop destination or if you need to find favours for party bags. Open Mon-Sat 10am-6.30pm.

The Cross   020 7727 6760
141 Portland Road, Holland Park, W11 4LR
www.thecrossshop.co.uk
Delightful treasure trove of designer goodies for adults and children 0-8yrs, with quirky modern gear from Dandy, classic cashmere by English Weather, toys and gifts. Open 10am-6pm, Mon-Sat. You'll need to visit rather than shop online.

W12

Bebe Bisou   020 8740 9434
Westfield Shopping Centre, W12 7GB
Luxury boutique catering for all your child's needs from newborn to 6yrs. Ranges include Baby Dior, Ralph Lauren, D&G Junior, Gucci and Jean-Paul Gaultier. Timeless nursery

furniture from Europe, bedding, accessories, prams by Aprica for Fendi and Roberto Cavalli, collections of soft toys from Kaloo and unique bikes and cars. Opens Mon-Wed 10am-9pm, Thur & Fri 10am-10pm, Sat 9am-9pmr, Sun 12-6pm.

W1

Mamas & Papas   0845 268 2000
256-258 Regent Street, Oxford Circus, W1B 3AF
www.mamasandpapas.com
Mamas & Papas' flagship store and cafe, a spacious and stylish environment with great services, including personal shopping, fashion advisors, and their award-winning Baby Bump fitting service to help you visualize your changing shape. Everything you'll ever need for mother and child - fashionable maternity and babywear, nursery furniture and equipment, high chairs, car seats, colourful prams and pushchairs, bathtime accessories, toys and gifts. Open Mon-Fri 10am-8pm, Sat 9am-8pm, Sun 12am-6pm with late night opening on Thursday until 9pm.

So Tiny London   020 7636 2501
64 Great Titchfield Street, W1W 7QH
www.sotinylondon.com
Situated minutes from Oxford Circus, So Tiny London is a baby and children's boutique with a range of unique slogan babygros and t-shirts with British themes incuding the Beatles and Pink Floyd, film memorabilia such as Star Wars and Superman as well as many bespoke designs. In addition they sell popular baby toys (eg Sophie the Giraffe and Manhattan soft toys), soft shoes and other exclusive gifts. Open daily from Mon-Fri 10am-7pm, Sat 10-6pm, Sun 11-5pm. Also available online.

Please Mum   020 7486 1100
24 Orchard Street, W1H 6HJ
www.pleasemum.co.uk
Well established designer shop with A-list clientele including numerous royal families. As well as their own brand they stock the likes of Roberto Cavalli, Armani, D&G and Monnalisa. Boys catered for at this branch, girls at 140 Wigmore Street W1U 3SQ. Also at 85 Knightsbridge SW1X 7RB. Open Mon-Sun 10am-6pm.

Catimini   020 7629 8099
52 South Molton Street, Mayfair, W1K 5SE
www.catimini.com
Gorgeous children's clothing from this quintessential French label from 0-14yrs. Open Mon-Sat 10am-6.30pm (7pm on Thurs), Sun 12-6pm.

Tartine et Chocolat   020 7629 7233
66 South Molton Street, W1K 5ST
www.tartine-et-chocolat.fr
Very traditional French clothing for 0-10yrs, as well as accessories and toys. Open 10-6pm Mon-Sat.

Burberry   020 3402 1500
21-23 New Bond Street, W1S 2RE
www.burberry.com
Kit the littl'uns out like the Beckham boys. Mini trenchcoats and capes and cutting-edge twists on classics, from the

Burberry check bikini to checked wellies. 0-12 yrs. Open 10am-7pm, Mon-Sat, 12-6pm Sun.

Ralph Lauren Kids Store   020 7535 4600
143 New Bond Street, W1S 2TP
www.ralphlauren.co.uk
Mini sportswear, button-down collared shirts, jackets, frocks, footwear and lifestyle goods for budding Preppies, plus newborn clothing and accessories including baby blankets and pram shoes. Caters for 0-20yrs (boys) and 0-16 yrs (girls). Open 10am-6pm Mon-Sat, 10am-7pm Thur, 12noon-6pm Sun.

Blossom Mother and Child   020 7486 6089
69 Marylebone High Street , Marylebone, W1U 5JJ
www.blossommotherandchild.com
Blossom offers mothers a one-stop shop for maternity clothing and lingerie, designer baby and childrenswear, plus adorable gifts for mother and baby. Brands include Levi's Kids, Clements Ribeiro for Blossom, M. Missoni, See by Chloe, Alice Temperley, Anya Hindmarch, La Perla Baby and Toffee Moon, as well as Blossom's maternity collections. Gwyneth Paltrow and Brooke Shields are fans. Open Mon-Sat, Sun 12-5pm

Bonpoint Marylebone   020 7487 2512
52-54 Marylebone High Street, W1U 5HR
www.bonpoint.com
Exquisite classic French designer wear for boys and girls, 0-12yrs at this branch. Open 10am-6pm, Mon-Sat, Sun 11am-5pm.

Brora   020 7224 5040
81 Marylebone High Street, W1U 4QJ
www.brora.co.uk
Scottish cashmere cardigans, trousers and hats as well as pram blankets and personalised cot blankets. Open Mon-Sat 10am-6pm, Sun 12-5pm.

Rachel Riley   020 7935 8345
82 Marylebone High Street, W1U 4QW
www.rachelriley.co.uk
Exquisite hand-made children's clothing using beautiful fabrics. Traditional Sunday best outfits with fine smocking and embroidery; fun florals, retro ginghams and polka dots. Trad leather shoes, too. Open 10am-6.30pm Mon-Sat, 10.30am-5.30pm Sun.

W2
....

JoJo Maman Bebe   020 7727 3578
101 Westbourne Grove, Notting Hill, W2 4UW
www.jojomamanbebe.co.uk
JoJo Maman Bebe is a one-stop shop for pregnancy and beyond, offering fashionable maternity wear for every occasion, quirky children's clothing and adorable babywear. The company also provides an extensive range of practical products, toys and gifts for your baby, nursery and family home. Free P&P on all UK mainland orders. Open Mon-Sat 10am-6pm, Sun 11am-5pm.

W4
....

JoJo Maman Bebe   020 8994 0379
80 Turnham Green Terrace, Chiswick, W4 1QN
www.jojomamanbebe.co.uk
JoJo Maman Bébé is a one-stop shop for pregnancy and beyond, offering fashionable maternity wear for every occasion, quirky children's clothing and adorable babywear. The company also provides an extensive range of practical products, toys and gifts for your baby, nursery and family home. Free P&P on all UK mainland orders. Open Mon-Sat 10-6pm, Sun 11am-5pm.

Tots in the Terrace Chiswick   020 8995 0520
39 Turnham Green Terrace, Chiswick, W4 1RG
www.totschiswick.com
Small friendly shop offering European children's clothing for 0-14yrs. Brands include Catimini, Kenzo, Mini a ture, Timberland and Gant. Open Mon-Sat 10am-6pm, Sun 12-5pm.

Trotters Turnham Green   020 8742 1195
84 Turnham Green, Chiswick, W4 1QN
www.trotters.co.uk
Classy traditional baby and children's clothes for 0-10 yrs, as well as shoes, books, toys and haircuts. Open Mon-Sat 9am-6pm, Sun 10am-6pm.

W5
....

Baby e   020 8840 8197
20 The Green Ealing, W5 5DA
www.babye.co.uk
Boutique offering designer clothes for mum and baby aged 0-2, as well as shoes, toys by Steiff and Kaloo, pushchairs and highchairs, breastfeeding ware, christening and baby shower gifts. Brands include Baby Dior, Ralph Lauren, Burberry and Chloe. Open 10am-5.30pm Mon-Sat, 12noon-4pm Sun. Excellent online shop.

W8
....

Trotters Kensington   020 7937 9373
127 Kensington High Street, Kensington, W8 5SF
www.trotters.co.uk
Classy traditional clothes for newborns up to 10 yrs, as well as shoes, books, toys and haircuts. Open Mon-Sat 9am-7pm, Sun 10am-6pm.

W9
....

Jou Jou & Lucy   020 7289 0866
32 Clifton Road, Maida Vale, W9 1ST
www.joujouandlucy.co.uk
European designer clothes for 0-6yrs (boys) and 0-10yrs (girls). Brands stocked include Catimini, Ralph Lauren, Kenzo, Tartine et Chocolat and Baby Graziella. Open 10am-6pm Mon-Sat, 11am-5pm Sun.

Masiel Bebe   020 3490 7216
18 Bristol Gardens, Maida Vale, London, W9 2JQ
www.masielbebe.co.uk
A new baby and children's wear shop in Maida Vale, Masiel

Bebe, brings a unique collection of Spanish brands to London. You'll find classic styles from Pili Carrera, Tutto Piccolo and Foque to contemporary fashion from Agatha Ruiz de la Prada and Cosan Baby. In addition to clothing (0-10yrs), there are children's accessories, gifts (blankets and linen), soft shoes and first boots as well as decorative items for the nursery. Open Mon-Sat 9.15am-7pm.

gifts

Babylist   **020 7371 5145**
The Broomhouse, 50 Sulivan Road, SW6 3DX
www.babylist.com
Wonderful hand-embroidered range of clothing from Dimples, or Babylist's own range of smocked nighties. Babylist also offers a wish list service to clients who come in for full consultations, where clients can choose their own list of gifts which are made available to friends and family to purchase.

Rosy Cheek Cosy   **01225 443 975**
www.rosycheekcosy.com
Exclusive designs by Tess Lambert, using 100% cotton prints and an eco collection in Organic Cotton and super soft Bamboo. Rosy Cheek Cosy specialise in stylish baby gifts, bedding and accessories. Quite simply everything we do focuses as much as possible on natural, high quality and planet-friendly. Designed and made with love in Bath, England.

TreatBaby.com   **08456170891**
www.treatbaby.com
TreatBaby.com is the best place to find beautiful gift ideas for babies and mums. Whether it's your precious new arrival you'd like to celebrate, or for a mum you know that deserves some serious treating, choose from their exquisite range of personalised and heart-warming gift ideas. Use the exclusive code BABYD2505 and get 10% off.

personalised

Anne Taylor Designs   **020 8748 9279**
www.anne-taylor.co.uk
Visit our online shop to find lots of adorable gifts for children. Our hand-painted and personalised furniture and accessories make perfect Birthday and Christening presents. Products range from photograph frames, plaques and pegboards, to keepsake boxes, toy chests and chairs.

Happyhands   **0845 466 0171**
www.happyhands.co.uk
Your baby's hand and foot prints on mugs, tiles and cards.

name tapes

My Name Label   **0870 8507 897**
www.mynamelabel.co.uk
Sick of your child loosing things at school or nursery? My Name Label has the simple solution to help find their belongings. We offer a wide range of Vinyl and Iron on labels in bright attractive colours that you can personalise using pictures and a choice of lettering styles.

Easy2Name   **01635 298 326**
www.easy2name.com
You name it - we label it!

shoe shops

online

Starchild Shoes   **01509 817 601**
www.starchildshoes.co.uk
Our shoes are all handmade in England from the finest Italian leather, and recommended by mums and paediatricians. Soft leather allows feet to breath move and grow naturally. The suede sole gives grip on tiled, wood and laminated floors and the elasticated ankle means these shoes "really do stay on" little feet. We have over 200 designs with huge choice of colours. FREE delivery for UK customers. We ship world wide. 48 Hr despatch. Celebrity customer include Maddona, Prince, Ozzy, The Beckhams, Gwen Stefani, Amanda Holden, and many more.

shops - E3

Jakss   **020 8981 2233**
469 Roman Road, Bow, E3 5LX
www.jakss.co.uk
Well established friendly children's boutique for 0-16yrs. Wide range of brands including D&G, Ralph Lauren, Oilily, Diesel and Jottum. Also stock Birkenstock sandals. Open 10am-5.30pm Tues-Sat.

N1

Igloo Kids   **020 7354 7300**
300 Upper Street, Islington, N1 2TU
www.iglookids.co.uk
Modern shop with extensive shoe ranges for 0-8yrs. Open Mon-Wed 10am-6.30pm, Thur 9.30am-7pm, Fri-Sat 9.30am-6.30pm and Sun 11am-5.30pm.

One Small Step One Giant Leap   **020 7354 4126**
46 Cross Street, Islington, N1 2BA
www.onesmallsteponegiantleap.com
Wonderful range of designer shoes including Ralph Lauren and Pom d'Api. Stock a wide range of slippers and wellington boots. Open 10am-6pm Mon-Sat, 11am-5pm Sun.

N8

The Red Shoes 020 8341 9555
30 Topsfield Parade, Crouch End, N8 8QB
www.theredshoes.co.uk
An award winning local children's shoe shop with expert fitting services. Great range of brands including the classic Start-rites, Angulus, Bisgaard and Tip Toey Joey. Open Mon-Sat 10am-5.30pm, Sun 12-4.30pm.

N10

Frocks Away 020 8444 9309
81-83 Fortis Green Road, Muswell Hill, N10 3HP
www.frocksaway.co.uk
Fantastic one-stop shop where you can buy everything from children's clothes and shoes for 0-12yrs to designer wear for yourself. Brands include Catimini, Petit Bateau, Molo and Scotch & Soda. Shoe fittings for such labels as Camper, Geox, Crocs and Start-rite. Open Mon-Sun, 9.30am-5.30pm.

N16

Frere Jacques 020 7249 5655
121 Stoke Newington Church Street, Stoke Newington, N16 0UH
Children's shoes and accessories for 0-7yrs. Open Tue-Fri 10-5pm, Sat 11am-6pm.

Kidstep Shoes 020 8800 7055
122 Holmleigh Road, N16 5PY
Popular north London shoe shop with a broad range of sizes and styles including a new Portuguese brand Atlantic Mocassin. Open Mon-Sat 9.30am-6pm.

Shoe & Fashion Boutique 020 8806 5581
28 Stamford Hill, Stamford, N16 6XZ
Good local children's shoe shop with expert fitting services and stocking brands such as Start-rite, Petasil, and other continental brands. Open Mon-Fri 11am-6pm, Sun 11am-3pm (closed Sat).

shopping

Elias & Grace 020 7449 0574
158 Regents Park Road, Primrose Hill, NW1 8XN
www.eliasandgrace.com
A great store for mother and child, frequented by A-listers
Kate Moss, Sadie Frost, Luella Bartley, Sam Taylor Wood and
Jools Oliver. In store or online, a modern and versatile mix of
super cool fashion and shoes for 0-10 yrs, including their own
label, Nurtured by Nature, Chloe, Miller and Quincy. Also
hand-knitted soft toys, mobiles and gifts. Open 10am-6pm
Mon-Sat, 12-6pm Sun.

NW3

One Step Beyond 020 7435 3377
96 Belsize Lane, Hampstead, NW3 5BE
One Step beyond is tucked in beside the family-friendly
Oliver's Cafe in Hampstead's Belsize Lane. The shop stocks
a number of popular brands as well as Bobux baby shoes,
Step-2wo, Pediped and Buckle My Shoe. Open Mon-Fri
10am-5.30pm, Sat 10.30am-5pm.

NW8

Igloo Kids 020 7483 2332
80 St John's Wood High Street, NW8 7SH
www.iglookids.co.uk
Modern shop with extensive shoe ranges for 0-8yrs. Open
Mon-Wed 10am-6.30pm, Thur 9.30am-7pm, Fri-Sat 9.30am-
6.30pm and Sun 11am-5.30pm.

NW11

Brians Children's Shoes 020 8455 7001
2 Hallswelle Parade, Finchley Road, NW11 0DL
Stocking a good range of children's brands including
Naturino, Geox, Primigi, Ricosta, Ecco and Lelli Kelly. Open
Mon-Sat 9.15am-5.30pm, Sun 10.30am-1.30pm.

SE3

Pares Footwear 020 8297 0785
24 Tranquil Vale, Blackheath, SE3 0AX
www.paresfootwear.co.uk
This is a specialist children's shoe fitting shop with a good
quantity of excellent brands including Start-rite, Clarks,
Ricosta, Ecco. Open Mon-Fri 9.30am-6pm, Sat 9am-6pm,
Sun 10am-5pm.

SE13

Love Me Again 020 8244 0172
37 Staplehurst Road, Hither Green, SE13 5ND
www.love-me-again.co.uk
Brilliant children's boutique offering hand-picked children's
new and nearly new clothing and toys (you can bring in your
little-worn items, as long as they're from a top-drawer label).
Favoured brands are D&G, Kenzo, Ralph Lauren, Burberry,
Gap, Molly & Jack, Zara and Mini Boden, and stylish footwear
labels Gumbies and Smelly Wellies. Open Tues-Sat 10am-5pm.

SE16

Olivia Rose 020 7740 1111
194 Southwark Park Road, Bermondsey, SE16 3RP
www.olivia-rose.co.uk
Set up by local mother of 3, Sarah Mash, this excellent
designer children's store has many exclusive brands from
Spain. The shop also sells its own brand of shoes (ballerinas,
Mary Janes and Moccasins). Open Mon-Sat 10am-5pm.

SE19

Merlin Shoes 020 8771 5194
44 Westow Street, Crystal Palace, SE19 3AH
This is a popular local shoe shop in Crystal Palace with a
good range of practical school shoe ranges from Start-rite
and Geox as well as football boots, slippers and other party
shoe brands like Primigi. Also a small selection of adult shoes
in the entrance area. Open Mon-Sat 10am-5pm.

SE21

Biff 020 8299 0911
41-43 Dulwich Village, Dulwich, SE21 7BN
www.biffkids.com
An excellent children's boutique stocking a mixture of
affordable brands such as Joules and Petit Bateau. In the
second half of the store they fit children's shoes (Start-rite,
Geox, Lelli Kelly, Crocs). Wellies too. Also great for accessories and school must-haves: plimsolls, swimwear. Open
Mon-Fri 9.30am-5.30pm, Sat 10am-6pm.

SE22

Sparkle and Spin 020 8299 6606
14 Melbourne Grove, East Dulwich, SE22 8QZ
www.sparkleandspin.co.uk
Popular East Dulwich children's boutique with a range of
unique clothing labels and shoes from Angulus and Bergstein
wellington boots. Open Mon-Sat 10am-3pm. (Occasionaly 5pm).

SW1

Papouelli 020 7730 6690
43 Elizabeth Street, Pimlico, SW1W 9PP
www.papouelli.com
Popular local children's shoe shop in Pimlico with unique
range of elegant of school shoes, casuals and sandals. Open
10am-6pm Mon-Fri, 9.30am-5pm Sat. **New branch: 98,
Marylebone Lane. London W1U 2QA.Tel 020 7486 5530.**

One Small Step One Giant Leap 020 7225 6896
Harrods, Knightsbridge, SW1X 7XL
www.ossogl.co.uk
Wonderful range of designer shoes including Ralph Lauren
and Pom d'Api. Stock a wide range of slippers and wellington
boots. Open Mon-Sat 10am-8pm, Sun 11.30am-6pm.

SW3

Igloo Kids 020 7352 4572
227 Kings Road, Chelsea, SW3 5EJ

www.iglookids.co.uk
Modern shop with extensive product ranges for 0-8yrs. Loads of designer brands, including No Added Sugar, Bob & Blossom, Frilly Lily and Petit Bateau. Also stock shoes, active and swimming gear, toys, gifts and toiletries. Open Mon-Sat 9.30am-6.30pm, Wed-Thur 9.30am-7pm, Fri-Sat 9.30am-6.30pm and Sun 11am-5.30pm.

Trotters   020 7259 9620
34 Kings Road, Chelsea, SW3 4UD
www.trotters.co.uk
Classy traditional baby and children's clothes for 0-10 yrs, as well as shoes, books, toys and haircuts. Open Mon-Sat 9am-7pm, Sun 10am-6pm.

SW6

Pollyanna   020 7731 0673
811 Fulham Road, Fulham, SW6 5HG
This is a long-established and family run children's shoe and clothing shop with an expert shoe fitting service. Popular brands are are Start-rite, Mod8 and Petit Bateau clothing. Open Mon-Sat 9.30am-5.30pm.

SW11

One Small Step One Giant Leap   020 7223 9314
49 Northcote Road, SW11 1NJ
www.onesmallsteponegiantleap.com
Good range of designer shoes including Ralph Lauren and Pom d'Api as well as slippers and wellingtons. Open Mon-Fri 10am-6pm, Sat 9am-6pm, Sun 11am-5pm.

Trotters   020 7585 0572
86 Northcote Road, Clapham, SW11 6QN
www.trotters.co.uk
Classy traditional baby and children's clothes for 0-10 yrs, as well as shoes, books, toys and haircuts. Open Mon-Sat 9am-6pm, Sun 10am-6pm.

SW14

One Small Step One Giant Leap   020 8487 1288
409 Upper Richmond Road West, SW14 7NX
www.onesmallsteponegiantleap.com
Good range of designer shoes including Ralph Lauren and Pom d'Api. Stock a wide range of slippers and wellingtons. Open 10am-6pm Mon-Fri, 9am-6pm Sat, 11am-5pm Sun.

SW15

One Small Step One Giant Leap   020 8789 2046
The Exchange, Putney High St, SW15 1TW
www.onesmallsteponegiantleap.com
Wonderful range of designer shoes including Ralph Lauren and Pom d'Api. Stock a wide range of slippers and wellington boots. Open 10am-6pm Mon-Sat, 11am-5pm Sun.

Pied Piper   020 8788 1635
234 Upper Richmond Road, Putney, SW15 6TG
www.piedpiperputney.co.uk
Well established shop selling ballet, dancewear and a wide

range of children's shoes including Start-rite, Ricosta and Primigi. Open 9.30am-6pm Mon-Sat (closes 5.30pm Sat).

W1

One Small Step One Giant Leap
3 Blenheim Crescent, W11 2EE   020 7243 0535
www.onesmallsteponegiantleap.com
Good range of designer shoes including Ralph Lauren and Pom d'Api. Stock a wide range of slippers and wellington boots. 10am-6pm Mon-Fri, 9am-6pm Sat, 11am-5pm Sun.

Papouelli   020 7486 5530
98 Marylebone Lane, W1U 2QA
www.papouelli.com
Papillon manufacture their own range of children's shoes including ballerinas, moccasins, canvas mules and the most elegant of school shoes. Open Mon-Sat 10am-6pm.

W4

Trotters   020 8742 1195
84 Turnham Green, Chiswick, W4 1QN
www.trotters.co.uk
Classy traditional baby and children's clothes for 0-10 yrs, as well as shoes, books, toys and haircuts. Open Mon-Sat 9am-6pm, Sun 10am-6pm.

W5

One Small Step One Giant Leap   020 8840 8605
4 The Green, Ealing, W5 5DA
www.onesmallsteponegiantleap.com
Good range of designer shoes including Ralph Lauren and Pom d'Api. Stock a wide range of slippers and wellington boots. 10am-6pm Mon-Fri, 9am-6pm Sat, 11am-5pm Sun.

toy shops

online

Build-a-Bear Workshops   0800 542 0635
www.buildabear.co.uk
This franchise business has grown rapidly with seven branches across London, and is enormously popular with children. Children choose a bear (or dog and penguin), select a heart and then the bear is stuffed by a giant machine. Passport style certificates are produced and clothes and accessories can be purchased. Beware however, as clothes are fiendishly expensive, and often pricier than baby clothing available in the high street (clothing also available online). Branches are: Bromley, Croydon, Kingston, Covent Garden, Hamleys, Westfields Stratford and White City.

Custard & Crumble   020 7183 3799
www.custardandcrumble.co.uk
Create a stylish and inspiring nursery with the help of Custard & Crumble. This online boutique presents a beautiful handpicked selection of baby nursery furniture, accessories and gifts, many of which you won¡t find on the high street.

shopping

They guarantee free UK mainland delivery and offer a gift list service.

Toyella **0800 542 6857**
www.toyella.com
Award winning Toyella offer toys and gifts that have that something different. Style and good design is the common theme within all our original products. The toys are aimed at children up to 12 years old. Shipping is worldwide with free delivery on UK orders.

shops - E10

Ditchfields 020 8539 2821
792 High Road, Leyton, E10 6AE
www.ditchfields.co.uk
Long-established family-run toy and bike shop, stocking Power Rangers, trikes and scooters, rocking horses, radio-controlled cars, planes and boats. They also stock the major brands such as Brio, Revell model kits, Wow, Zapf dolls, Scalextric, V-Tech, Barbie, Playmobil, Lego, Meccano, Mattel, Fisher-Price and good range of garden toys. Open Mon-Sat 9.15am-5.30pm (Thurs 5pm).

E15

Westfield Stratford City
Montfitchet Road, Stratford, E15 2JU
www.uk.westfield.com
Not only nestling the Olympic site, but a shopping centre of Olympic proportions, Westfield Stratford is the shoppers' paradise in East London. Toy stores abound with a Build-a-Bear workshop, Disney store, ELC, Lego and the Entertainer toy shops. All open Mon-Fri 10am-pm, Sat 9am-9pm, Sun 12-6pm.

N5

Sylvanian Families 020 7226 1329
68 Mountgrove Road, Highbury, N5 2LT
www.sylvanianfamilies.com
For the last 17 years this small shop has been selling Sylvanian Families and is the official home of the Sylvanian Families Collector's Club. Open Mon-Fri .9.30am-5.30pm, Sat 9am-6pm, Sun 10am-4pm.

N8

Soup Dragon 020 8348 0224
27 Topsfield Parade, Tottenham Lane, Crouch End, N8 8PT
www.soup-dragon.co.uk
This lovely shop specialises in fun things for small people to suit every pocket. Unusual wooden toys, puzzles and games; beautiful kids clothing and fancy dress. From perfect party-bag pressies to baby rompers, wooden dolls' houses to fairy dresses. Open Mon-Sat 9.30am-6pm, Sun 11am-5pm.

N10

Fagin's Toys 020 8444 0282
84 Fortis Green Road, Muswell Hill, N10 3HN

Toys for 0-5yrs including pop-up toys, Vtech, Playnest and Jenny Kitten soft toys. Open Mon-Sat 9am-5.30pm, Sun 10am-3pm.

Never Never Land 020 8883 3997
3 Midhurst Parade, Fortis Green, N10 3EJ
www.never-never-land.co.uk
Very small toy shop crammed with dolls' houses and accessories, tea sets, wooden puzzles, knights and castles, etc. Open 10am-5pm Tues, Wed, Fri and Sat.

N11

Smyths Friern Barnet 020 8361 7345
Friern Barnet Retail Park, Pegasus Way, N11 3PW
www.smythstoys.com
Smyths Toy Shop is a large warehouse style store selling a good range of nursery products (Brixtax, Cosatto, Graco), toys (Lego, mini figures from TV/Films), bikes and scooters and games. Open Mon-Fri 10am-6pm, Sat 9am-6pm, Sun 11am-6pm.

N18

Early Learning Centre 020 8807 5518
Ravenside Retail Park, Angel Road, N18 3HA
www.elc.co.uk
The well-known specialist retailer of toys for pre-school children. Open Mon-Fri 9am-8pm, Sat 10am-6pm, Sun 10.30am-4.30pm.

NW2

Toys R Us Brent Cross 020 8209 0019
Tilling Road, Brent Cross, NW2 1LW
www.toysrus.co.uk
Warehouse style toy shopping. Whatever you need you'll find it here, from rattles to bicycles. Wide aisles and easy parking. The catalogue and website offer even more variety and better discounts than in store. Open Mon-Sat 9am-10pm, Sun 11am-17pm.

NW3

Huggle 020 7483 2826
8-10 Winchester Road, NW3 3NT
www.huggle.co.uk
Huggle had done the hard work so you don't have to! A unique nursery, toy and gift store offering a wide range of the best in stylish and modern baby products. From furniture and buggies to feeding, bathing, toys and gifts.

Kristin Baybars 020 7267 0934
7 Mansfield Road, Kentish Town, NW3 2JD
This "everything-pink" toy shop is packed to the rafters with craft toys, dolls' houses and miniatures and hence no buggy room is available. Nevertheless, a great place to browse with the kids. Open Tue-Sat 11am-6pm.

NW4

Early Learning Centre 020 8202 6948
Unit D1, Brent Cross Shopping Centre, NW4 3FE

Double award winning online toy and gift retailer

Selling unique world toys and shipping worldwide. Free UK delivery.

Junior DESIGN AWARDS 2011
BEST ONLINE TOY RETAILER
WINNER

Junior DESIGN AWARDS 2012
WINNER
BEST ONLINE TOY & GIFT RETAILER
www.juniormagazine.co.uk

www.elc.co.uk
The well-known specialist retailer of toys for pre-school children. Open Mon-Fri 10am-8pm, Sat 9am-7pm, Sun 12-6pm.

SE3

2nd Impressions　　　　　　　020 8852 6192
10 Montpelier Vale, Blackheath, SE3 0TA
Three floors of classic and unique toys such as Cheeky Rascals and Orchard puzzles. Good for outdoor activity toys, children's books, jewellery and bags. Open Mon-Sat 9.30am-5.30pm, Sun 10.30am-4.30pm.

SE9

Early Learning Centre　　　　　020 8294 1057
7 St Mary's Place, High Street, SE9 1BL
www.elc.co.uk
The well-known specialist retailer of toys for pre-school children. Open Mon-Sat 9am-5.30pm, Sun 10am-3.30pm.

SE10

Chock a Block Toys　　　　　　020 8616 3308
5 Nelson Road, Greenwich, SE10 9JB
www.chock-a-blocktoys.co.uk
Based in the heart of Greenwich, Chock-a-Block Toys offers a range of toys for children aged 0-10yrs. Young babies will love their selection of sensory toys, rattles and teethers;

toddlers can choose from jigsaws and puzzles to balls, soft toys, puppets and balance bikes. Brands include John Crane (wooden toys), Manhanttan soft toys, Galt and Orchard Toys as well as fairtrade and multicultural brands such as Lanke Kade. Open Mon-Fri 11am-6pm, Sat-Sun 10am-6pm.

SE13

Early Learning Centre　　　　　020 8318 0610
1 Lewisham Retail Park, Lewisham, SE13 7RZ
The well-known specialist retailer of toys for pre-school children. Open Mon-Sat 9.30am-6pm, Sun 11am-5pm.

SE15

Toys R Us Peckham　　　　　　020 7732 7322
760 Old Kent Road, Peckham, SE15 1NJ
www.toysrus.co.uk
Warehouse-style toy shopping. Whatever you need you'll find it here, from rattles to bicycles. Wide aisles and easy parking. The catalogue and website offer even more variety and better discounts than in store. Open Mon-Fri 9am-8pm, Sat 9am-7pm, Sun 11am-5pm.

SE22

Hope and Greenwood　　　　　020 8613 1777
20 North Cross Road, East Dulwich, SE22 9EU
www.hopeandgreenwood.co.uk
Miss Hope and Mr Greenwood run an old-fashioned sweet

shopping

shop, selling retro, traditional and nostalgic sweets, from fudge and toffee to gums and jellies, as well as new confections like Fizz! Bang! Wallops! The shop is usually packed with lots of children gazing longingly at the glass sweetie jars packed with a selection of strawberry shoelaces, smarties, fizzy cola bottles and more. Open Mon-Sat 10am-6pm, Sun 11am-5pm. Fun nostalgic website where you can stock up online.

Just Williams Toys   020 8299 3444
106 Grove Vale, East Dulwich, SE22 8DR
www.justwilliamstoys.com
This large toy shop has a great selection of popular brands (Lego, Power Rangers) as well as knights and animals, dressing up outfits, dolls, art materials and pocket-money items. Open Mon-Sat 9.30am-6pm.

Soup Dragon   020 8693 5575
106 Lordship Lane, East Dulwich, SE22 8HF
www.soup-dragon.co.uk
This lovely shop specialises in fun things for small people to suit every pocket. Unusual wooden toys, puzzles and games; beautiful kids clothing and fancy dress. From perfect party-bag pressies to baby rompers, wooden dolls' houses to fairy dresses. Open Mon-Sat 9.30am-6pm.

SE24

Just Williams Toys Herne Hill   020 7733 9995
18 Half Moon Lane, Herne Hill, SE24 9HU
www.justwilliamstoys.com
This independent toy shop opened in Herne Hill over 5 years ago and was an instant hit with local families. Its cram-packed shelves offer everything from puzzles, games, Lego and Playmobil to arts and crafts, dressing up gear and a wide range of pocket-money toys and collectables (gogos, Match Attax, etc). Open Mon-Sat 9.30am-6pm.

SW1

Peter Jones   020 7730 3434
Sloane Square, Chelsea, SW1W 8EL
www.johnlewis.com
A great stash of toys from rocking horses and dolls' houses to Ben 10 and all the popular TV character toys and games, as well as stocking fillers, cars and trains, Fisher-Price, educational toys, board games, puzzles - truly something for everyone. Mon, Tues, Thur, Fri, Sat 9.30am-7pm, Weds 9.30am-8pm, Sun 11am-5pm.

Harrods   020 7730 1234
87-135 Brompton Road, Knightsbridge, SW1X 7XL
www.harrods.com
Harrods toy department is moving this year to the third floor following a complete refit. It will stock a huge selection of top brands (and TV merchandise) as well as preschool favourites and family games. Electronic toys are usually supported with in-house demonstrations. Open Mon-Sat 10am-8pm, Sun 11.30am-6pm.

SW3

Chelsea Toys   020 7352 1718
53 Godfrey Street, Chelsea, SW3 3SX
www.chelseatoys.co.uk
This shop is bursting with colourful wooden toys, designer dolls, stuffed bears, children's bedding, designer clothing and delightful speciality toys crafted by the best European designers. Classic gifts that will last for years and won’t go out of style. Mon-Thurs 10am-5.30pm, Fri-Sat 10am-6pm, Sun 12-4pm.

SW6

Little Heroes   020 7348 7907
638 Fulham Road, Fulham, SW6 5RT
www.littleheroes.co.uk
A great local toy shop in Fulham with unique and unusual brands as well as traditional favourites such as Playmobil, Brio and US toy brand Melissa and Doug. The range includes dressing up and construction toys, craft activities, ride-on toys and traditional games and puzzles. Open Mon-Fri 9.30am-5.30pm, Sat 10am-6pm, Sun 11am-4pm.

Patrick's Toys & Games   020 7385 9864
107-111 Lillie Road, Fulham, SW6 7SX
www.patricktoys.co.uk
Traditional toy shop established 1948 stocking everything from quality wooden puzzles to Hornby trains.Open Mon-Sat 9.30am-5.30pm.

SW8

Puppet Planet   020 7627 0111
787 Wandsworth Road, Clapham, SW8 3JQ
www.puppetplanet.co.uk
A treasure trove of puppets and marionettes from around the world including drop-in puppet-making sessions and storytelling. They also host puppet parties or can bring puppets to your party at home or another venue. There's something for everyone from toys suitable for babies to collector's items including unique brands such as Folkmanis, Fiesta Crafts, Trullala and Egmont. Open Tues-Sat 9am-4pm.

SW11

Letterbox   0844 573 4561
99 Northcote Road, Clapham, London, SW11 6PL
www.letterbox.co.uk
This was the first Letterbox shop to open on the back of their very successful toy catalogue and acquisition of the Hawkin's bazaar chain (although the only other branch is in Norwich). This store sells many of the catalogue items, but principally toys for the 0-5yr age group. This includes construction and craft kits, dressing up clothes, ride-on toys and traditional games and puzzles. Open Mon-Sat 9am-6pm, Sun 11am-5pm.

QT Toys   020 7223 8637
90 Northcote Road, London, SW11 6QN
www.qttoys.com
Great little shop stocking all the most popular crazes as well

as the traditional favourites. Also stocks books, story tapes and other educational products for all age groups. Open Mon-Sat 9.30am-5.30pm, Sun 9.30am-5pm.

SW12

Just Williams Toys 020 3538 6798
8b Balham Hill, Clapham South, SW12 9EA
www.justwilliamstoys.com
This family-run, independent toy shop opened in Clapham South last year and has been an instant hit with local families. Its cram-packed shelves offer everything from puzzles, games, Lego and Playmobil to arts and crafts, dressing up gear and a wide range of pocket-money toys and collectables (gogo, Match Attax, etc). Open Mon-Sat 9.30am-6pm, Sun 10.30am-4.30pm.

SW14

Play Inside Out 020 8876 5229
377 Upper Richmond Road West, East Sheen, SW14 7NX
www.playinsideout.com
Traditional children's toy shop with a mixture of natural wooden toys and top brands including Lego, Sylvanian families, Villac, Pintoy etc. Open 9am-5.30pm Mon-Fri. 9.30am-6pm Sat. 11am-4pm Sun. Branches also at 63 Broad Street, Teddington, TW11 8QZ Tel 020 8614 5628; 54 High Street, Walton on Thames, KT12 1BY Tel 01932 246 124.

SW15

Early Learning Centre 020 8780 1074
8 Putney Exchange Centre, Putney, SW15 1TW
www.elc.co.uk
The well-known specialist retailer of toys for pre-school children. Open Mon-Sat 10am-6pm, Sun 11am-5pm.

SW18

The Entertainer 0844 800 5136
Southside Shopping Centre, Wandsworth, SW18 4FT
www.thetoyshop.com
A well-known shop which provides a huge range of toys for all ages starting from pre-school toys, and stocking all the latest and leading brands. Events are organized on Saturdays and during holidays. Open Mon-Sat 9am-5.30pm. Closed Sun.

SW19

Early Learning Centre 020 8944 0355
111 Centre Court Shopping Centre, Wimbledon, SW19 8YE
www.elc.co.uk
The well-known specialist retailer of toys for pre-school children. Open Mon-Fri 9.30am-7pm, Sat 9am-6pm.

The Entertainer 0844 800 5133
29 The Broadway, unit 7, Wimbledon, SW19 1PS
www.thetoyshop.com
A well-known toy chain providing toys for all ages starting

Toys Ryan's Road Trip £16.99
www.wowtoys.com

from pre-school toys to the latest crazes. Events are organized during weekends and holidays. Open Mon-Sat 9.30pm-6pm. Closed Sun.

W1

John Lewis Oxford Street 020 7629 7711
Oxford Street, W1A 1EX
www.johnlewis.com
A great stash of toys from rocking horses and dolls' houses to Ben 10 and all the popular TV character toys and games, as well as stocking fillers, cars and trains, Fisher-Price, educational toys, board games, puzzles - truly something for everyone. Open Mon-Sat 9.30am-8pm, Sun 12-6pm.

The Disney Store 020 7491 9136
350-352 Oxford Street, W1C 1JH
www.disneystore.co.uk
Apart from Disney toys the Disney Stores also include newborn clothing, boys' and girls' clothing and accessories, videos, DVDs, books, stationery and costumes. Stores also at 22-26 The Broadway Shopping Centre, Hammersmith, W6 (020 8748 8886) and 91 The Piazza, Covent Garden, WC2 (020 7836 5037). Open Mon-Fri 8am-9pm. Sat-Sun 10am-6pm.

Hamleys 0870 333 2455
188-196 Regent Street, W1R 6BT
www.hamleys.com
London's most famous toy shop, founded in 1760 and on this site since 1881, a huge emporium on 7 floors where you will find everything from arts and crafts, dolls, action toys, outdoor games and building toys to pre-school goods, soft toys and trains, planes and automobiles. Loads of demonstrations and excited young customers make this a buzzy place for an extended visit. Open Mon-Fri 10am-8pm, Sat 9pm-8pm,Sun 12-6pm. Also branches in Covent Garden and Heathrow Airport.

W4

Snap Dragon 020 8995 6618
56 Turnham Green Terrace, Chiswick, W4 1QP
Excellent toy shop with the right balance of traditional, hand-crafted toys and popular branded ones. Open Mon-Sat 9.30am-5.30pm, Sun 11am-4pm.

shopping

studiodeidre.com

Lego games, Harry Potter-themed sets, the Creator and City lines as well as Lego Duplo sets for pre-school children. The store also hosts themed lego-building events for families so check the what's on pages

photography

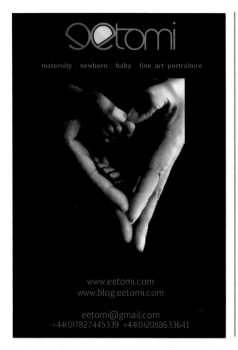

Vanessa Berberian Photography
portraits of your family in their natural environment

vanessaberberian.com
Tel: 07984026633

Beautiful photographs that capture the fun of childhood

HELEN BARTLETT PHOTOGRAPHY

info@helenbartlett.co.uk • 0845 603 1373 • www.helenbartlett.co.uk

Green shopping

It's amazing how many parents-to-be start thinking about organic eating and buying 100% natural products, often for the first time in their lives. And once their baby is born, it's hard not to consider what might be the best for that tender little body. For many, along with the responsibility to their child comes the responsibility to the planet their child will be living in.

Toiletries

Infants' skin is thinner and more absorbent than that of adults. Happily, the demand for skin-kind, chemical free baby skincare products has seen the mainstream embrace green toiletries and now brands like purepotions, Burt's Bees and other organic skincare labels are widely stocked in supermarkets and high street pharmacies.

Clothing

It's not just about chemical-free processes to protect the planet and organic cottons against your little one's skin, there is a far bigger issue with green clothing – ethical production. Do you really want your child wearing cheap and easy clothes at the expense of another child or woman somewhere in the world who is working in poverty?

Look for ecologically-friendly sourced textiles (organic cotton, silk, bamboo, wool, hemp and linen) and authenticated claims that their production processes reduce harm to the environment, as well as clothes produced in fair-labour conditions.

Toys

The wave of plastic toys that enter most families' homes is enough to send even a half-hearted eco warrior into a panic. Go for longer-lasting wooden toys from certifiably sustainable sources, fair trade soft toys that have been produced in labour-friendly conditions, and beautiful designer kids' gifts made from recyclable materials.

Lifestyle

From cot mattresses to furniture for the family lounge, it's easier than ever to buy green at reasonable prices and find styles that look as chic as they are eco-friendly. Go for wooden nursery and home furniture from sustainable sources, rugs dyed with natural colourings and other furnishings in organic cottons or hemp.

Bedding

cosylambs.co.uk British wool has found a new niche with this natural and organic bedding company. Their cot duvets made from 100% wool, are encased in cotton to help children get a good night's sleep, avoide asthma, and banish dust mites. Or see their new 100% Bluefaced Leicester wool baby shawls.

www.naturalmat.com Experts in hand-made organic mattresses made from coir, organic lambswool, mohair and latex. They also have lovely brushed organic cotton sheets and mattress protectors.

thelittlegreensheep.co.uk An award-wining brand using natural materials for everything from cot mattresses (including the clever Twist design) to sleeping bags and massage mats.

Clothing

welovefrugi.com Practical organic clothes for babies and children up to 8 years, plus nursing dresses and breastfeeding tops for new mothers.

aravore.com An award-wining brand using organic and natural fabrics.

naturally4baby.com Organic babywear from New Zealand including babygros, sleeping bags and cute little Possum pixie boots.

organicsforkids.com Spots, stripes, frogs, elephants, this organic range of babygros is simple, stylish and all made in the UK using organic cotton.

redurchin.co.uk If the sight of yet more baby pastels makes you queasy then turn to Red Urchin's richly coloured organic babygros in dark greens, blues and reds with edgy little animal designs.

minimoroc.com Flash about in these brightly coloured kaftan tops designed by new mum, Nadia Tribak. Made from organic cottons in her home town in Turkey.

Health & Beauty

foreverliving.com Aloe Vera has long been known to heel a number of skin conditions including the sorest baby's bottom. Try their Aloe Vera drinks and teas for an internal health boost.

naturallycoolkids.com Natural sun and after sun creams for babies and children which are made free from dairy, nut and soya. Plus a hair and body wash with soothing lavendar and mandarin essential oils. Smells delicious.

purepotions.biz Babies have extremely sensitive skins so look out for this new brand which has developed a "skin salvation" ointment for nappy rash, as well as bath and massage oils.

Nursery

amoralia.com Treat yourself to comfortable and flattering underwear and nursing bras made from the softest organic cotton.

rosycheekcosy.com Using organic cottons and bamboo fabrics, Tess Lambert designs and makes gorgeous baby towels, muslins and blankets from her studio in Bath. Unique gift ideas you wont find on the highstreet.

totsbots.co.uk Founders Marcus and Fiona Smyth were determined to develop a cloth nappy which was as easy to use as a disposable, save you hundreds of pounds, and give you a clear conscience. Their range includes the Bamboozle, the Flexitot and the Easyfit.

vupbaby.co.uk This impressive business has grown rapidly by only offering products that are completely non-toxic (ie free from BPA, PVC and Phthalates). You'll find stylish and practical nursery equipment, toys and gifts.

Toys & Gifts

greenowltoys.co.uk Encouraging children's natural creativity, is the focus of this leading online toy company. All toys are sourced from sustainable sources and are built to last several generations.

sewheartfelt.co.uk You'll fall in love with these handmade felt slippers designed by Sonia Spencer. Foxes, mice, piglets and donkeys with cute little tails.

bynature.co.uk From gorgeous green treats for mummy and daddy (including recycled martini glasses and fairly traded spices) to green baby-wear, toys and toiletries, bynature has it all covered.

go green

baby hampers & gifts

Lulu et Compagnie 020 7378 6320
www.luluetcompagnie.co.uk
Beautiful range of organic baby hampers, perfect gift for new baby or ideal present for baby shower. All hampers are arranged in a natural eco-friendly gift box. Gorgeous organic hand knitted baby wear and nursery decorations too.

natural baby products

Cool in Cloth 01271 324 450
www.coolincloth.co.ukc
Eco-Chic childrens clothes & shoes boutique up to the age of 8 years. Lots of New Bright Cool clothes & Barefoot Technology shoes. Moms cool clothes and maternity. Baby Directory reader offer - Quote FREEPOST in promotional code box at check out.

"FROM PLAY
TO KNOWLEDGE**"**

Green Owl Toys 020 8851 9904
www.greenowltoys.co.uk
An unique toy shop offering toys only made in Europe. They guarantee top quality and interesting toys and games for children from birth to 10 years old. All toys, games and art supplies are eco-friendly and have an educational element to them. They are fun and safe for every child.

NATURALLY COOL KIDS

Naturally Cool Kids Skincare 01274 861 542
www.naturallycoolkids.com
Winter and Summer natural skincare products that are fun for children and free from nasties giving parents peace of mind that their children are safe when using them. All of our products are soy, nut and dairy free and are suitable for children with sensitive and eczema prone skin.

Naturally4Baby 01303 814 048
www.naturally4baby.com
At Naturally4Baby we have searched to find the perfect products that are of such quality and uniqueness, that only your little one deserves. Beautiful organic designer baby clothes, super soft leather baby shoes, aromatherapy products for babies and young children.

Lulu et Compagnie
LONDON

Organic Baby Wear & Gifts

Baby First Bath Hamper

All our **hampers** are beautifully arranged in a gorgeous **eco - friendly** natural gift box.

www.LuluEtCompagnie.co.uk
020 7378 6320

naturalmat®
Mattresses made by hand in Devon

Naturalmat 020 7985 0474
99 Talbot Road, Notting Hill, W11 2AT
www.naturalmat.co.uk
The one stop shop for all things natural for your nursery. The best natural fibre mattresses and organic bed linen on the market. Standard sizes and made to measure. Contemporary nursery furniture, wonderful lambswool blankets, organic clothing and lots more.

Rosy Cheek Cosy 01225 443 975
www.rosycheekcosy.com
Exclusive designs by Tess Lambert, using 100% cotton prints and an eco collection in Organic Cotton and super soft Bamboo. Rosy Cheek Cosy specialise in stylish baby gifts, bedding and accessories. Quite simply everything we do focuses as much as possible on natural, high quality and planet-friendly. Designed and made with love in Bath, England.

Cosy Lambs *from* NATUREWARM

Cot Blanket

Bedtime bliss for babies with cot blankets and baby shawls made from 100% Bluefaced Leicester wool, and cot duvets made from British wool encased in 100% cotton

Baby Shawl

www.naturewarm.co.uk
www.cosylambs.co.uk
sales@naturewarm.co.uk
Tel: 01572 767258

Naturally4Baby

Organic clothing and natural products exclusively chosen for your precious little one

www.naturally4baby.com

Cosy Lambs   **01572 767 258**
from Naturewarm Ltd
www.cosylambs.co.uk
The Cosy Lambs range now comprises cot blankets and shawls made from soft Bluefaced Leicester wool, and cot duvets filled with British wool. Restful sleep for babies and toddlers and their parents.

natural health & beauty products

Forever Living Products   **07867 524 343**
www.shop-aloe.myflpbiz.com
Aloe Vera is a powerful natural health tonic. Containing over 75 different vitamins, minerals and amino acids, aloe balances the immune system, assists in healthy digestion, produces healthy, glowing skin, maintains healthy joints and helps the body balance itself. Contact Caroline Glassell for more information.

organic maternity wear

Amoralia   **020 7940 8250**
www.amoralia.com
Amoralia is a British luxury maternity lingerie brand. Their stylish and supportive second skin organic range is made from certified organic cotton. Amoralia's aim is to make pregnant and nursing women feel, and look beautiful. A truly special treat!

The Food Stork

The Food Stork is a personal food delivery service delivering freshly cooked, nutritious food specifically created for new mothers direct to their door.

Each order is made from scratch.

Store in your fridge or freezer and eat at your leisure.

www.thefoodstork.com
01386 858701

The London Baby Directory Awards 2012

After 16 years of scouring the streets of London and the internet for the best services, reviewing products and sourcing ideas that any new family could need in London, the Baby Directory celebrates the best products that will make any new family's life better in the weeks and months ahead. Many other parenting awards invite companies to pay to nominate their own products but here we have selected the winners based purely on our experience of these items as used by real parents.

From established brands and tried and tested baby equipment to new names in fields such as pushchairs and skincare, our Urban Parent awards not only take into account high performance and thoughtful design, but innovation and imagination in this vast field. All this, plus the unique perspective of being the only parent product awards which are specifically looking for those winners that perform well in city homes and within an urban lifestyle. After all, the funkiest pram might never fit into an apartment lift, a city car boot or get you safely round your favourite boutique!

We were delighted to work with **BabyList** on these awards. Matching our years of experience as London-based parents and parenting journalists, the team at **BabyList** are specialists in advising parents to be and new families on the whole range of baby goods they might need, according to each different family's needs and style. Sourcing these goods for over 16 years, **BabyList** have their eye on tried and tested quality, what urban families really need, and what new ideas are evolving within the market all the time.

After hours of shortlists and re-drafted shortlists - and the most pedantic discussions around feeding, baby bedtimes and car journeys - we hope you find our urban baby awards inspiring and genuinely useful.

Babylist and the London Baby Directory

Preparing you for parenthood
Now close to celebrating their 18th birthday, Babylist is the original nursery planning service. Babylist guides parents-to-be through every aspect of the nesting process to help you create the perfect nursery for your new family.

At Babylist - bespoke rules
Becoming a parent is one of life's greatest joys. You move from individual to family unit, but this isn't to say that you lose your individuality.

Babylist's totally tailored approach enables you to make the right choices for you and your new family.

If you are looking for a buggy, whether you drive a hatchback, are a keen runner or have stairs up to your home will all play a part in choosing what is right for you and your soon-to-be family.

It's about family
Babylist is a family-run business based in West London; Anita - Babylist's nursery guru - has become famous amongst friends and clients for her warmth of character, fabulous independent advice and experienced eye. If it's out there Anita will have seen it, tried it and will enable you to make an informed choice about it.

An unrivalled range that's right for you
In an internet-age of ready information, the choice of products, fashions and styles can be bewildering. Babylist cuts through the noise and listens to your individual needs. Babylist's world-class, hand-picked product range, including the best brands as well as their own exclusive discoveries, has been honed, tried and tested, which means clients can be wholly confident in their choices.

The Babylist experience
The Babylist process begins with a two hour consultation at their beautiful nursery with Anita or another trusted nursery guru. Consultations are one on one, private and relaxed. Babylist then works with clients to create a list of everything you and your baby need. Everything at Babylist is ordered individually for the client, which enables them to focus entirely on the client's needs. Discreet and dedicated, Babylist then delivers everything to your door before helping to create your perfect nursery.

Contact Babylist
For the most personalised advice from experienced professionals who have been there before and for the most stylish and practical product range, call Babylist on **0207 371 5145** or email **joey@babylist.com** and book your complimentary consultation in their West London nursery.

Winner
From birth pushchair

iCANDY PEACH

Most pushchair and pram combinations at the higher end of the market now tick all the boxes in terms of being easy to fold, store and adjust for different uses. They usually even have some cute extras. But for your baby's first walk about town, what parent wouldn't want a little bit of wow factor? We feel the iCandy Peach, with it's confident maneuverability, comfortable carrycot and seat options, and range of stylish finishes is a real winner.

The Uppababy Vista (last year's Baby Directory winner) continues to impress, and we expect the forthcoming Quinny Moodd (in cool Apple-esque white) to turn heads, but for now, the iCandy Peach, with its lightweight aluminium chassis, luxuriously large shopping basket and flexible front and rear facing modes, truly distinguishes itself as an urban baby chariot that can take on the countryside too. (Plus the special London edition out-Bugaboos Bugaboo for contemporary cool!) **www.icandyworld.com**

Winner
Double pushchair

BUGABOO DOUBLE

The double buggy is one of the most hotly debated categories when it comes to a best buy. After all, who is it for? Twins or two siblings of different ages? Is one child at nursery and needs collecting by car? Are you going out with just one today so you only need a single pushchair? And ultimately, is this a model you can physically squeeze through your front door? So many questions – and that's the last thing a parent with two small children needs to be worrying about. So, we've plumped for the bugaboo donkey.

The Mountain Buggy Duet is a strong performer too, with its flexible combinations of pushchair, pram and infant carrier fittings, but the Bugaboo donkey is stylish, durable and in its range of two-seat combinations, seems to be considering where life is going to take you and your child – from birth to later toddlerhood, all in three little clicks. Added to this, the space to store and carry bags can be altered – a simple yet much appreciated innovation! **www.bugaboo.com**

Pushchairs

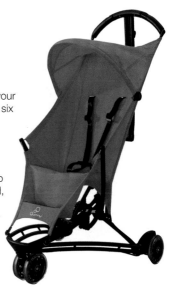

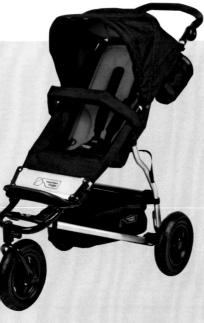

Winner
Buggies and lightweight strollers
QUINNY YEZZ

A lightweight buggy is not going to perform at the same level as your big-buy from-birth pram or pushchair, but once your baby is over six months, something smaller and nippy will become your best buy. And when it comes to small and nippy, the Yezz surges ahead of the pack.

Compact when open and freestanding when it's closed, you can also carry it over your shoulder on days when your child prefers to toddle. It's not the ideal solution if you're looking for a flip-flop fold, but it does have a one-action release and it weighs a mere 5kg thanks to its molded, composite glass fibre frame. Plus its unique skate wheels mean you can weave in and out of the tightest spaces on the street and in stores. Essential for the parent and child about town…
www.quinny.com

Winner
Three-wheeler
MOUNTAIN BUGGY SWIFT

Imagine all the features you want from a three-wheeler – confident handling, a stable ride for your child, sleek design – but with the slim frame you would expect in a regular from-birth four-wheeler. It's all here in the swift.

We still love the Mountain Buggy Terrain – especially for weekends in the country – but with the arrival of the swift, the discerning urbanite no longer has to compromise on performance just because most London roads were built centuries before the pushchair had been invented. Considering it weighs less than 10kg, the swift is an impressive option that offers comfort for newborns and enough support to convey a child as old as 6!
mountainbuggy.com

Winner
From birth car seat
MAXI-COSI OPAL

In recent years the argument for having young toddlers as well as babies travel backwards in cars has been made a great deal stronger, so car seats that manage both directions with reassuring durability are a wise buy. Maxi-Cosi can always be relied upon to innovate in this field, and along with the Pebble (which has proved popular since its introduction), the Opal is an excellent choice.

Suitable from birth to about three and a half years, the Opal offers good value and is easy to adapt as your child grows; you use the seat belt to secure the seat in the same way whether the Opal is rearward or forward facing. You can use it for longer even when it faces rearward too, thanks to the multi-direction adjustability to give more leg and body room whilst maintaining the best head support as your child grows.
www.maxi-cosi.com

Winner
From 9 months
BESAFE IZI COMBI ISOFIX

It's possible to have your child sitting rearward facing until the age of 4 with this sporty looking car seat, with easy to fit Isofix securings. But, if the time comes when your child wants to ride forward facing, the seat is designed so it's especially easy to thread with a safe, advance belt routing system..

With great side impact protection and four different sitting or sleeping positions, and added cushioning for use with smaller infants, even the most wriggly child should find a comfy way to ride happily.
www.besafe.com

Car seats

Winner
From 4 years
MAXI-COSI RODIFIX

As your child gets older, the arguments of, 'Do I really still need a car seat?' will become more frequent. The RodiFix, with its sporty design and excellent support for your child (even when he or she has fallen asleep on long, 'booor-ing' drives) should put paid to those disputes.

Other details which encouraged our judges to deem it 'practically perfect' include the patented AirProtect side impact protection in the headrest, as well as side impact protection for the lower back and hips. The RodiFix also has easily adjustable recline action which allows you to fit it suited to whatever angle your car seats are set at. All this, plus easy to thread seat belt routing and easy glide action when you want to make a quick getaway.
www.maxi-cosi.com

Winner
Carrier
BABYBJÖRN MIRACLE

Slings are popular, but with the design of baby carriers becoming ever softer, lighter and reflecting how we instinctively keep our babies close to us, the carrier still tends to offer the more convincing option for parent and baby support and comfort. Pioneers of the baby carrier, BabyBjörn have scored high again with their latest model, the Miracle.

Launched about a year ago, the Miracle has quickly proved to be a success. A premium model, it's suitable for use with babies from birth to about 15 months and offers great back support for the parent, with easy to follow markings which allow you always to gauge at what height on your body your growing baby should be positioned. As your child gets heavier, you can simply adjust the carrier, in order to spread the load across your own body. Plus you can choose from different finishes – soft cotton, organic cotton or airy mesh. An intelligent design that still feels wonderfully natural.
www.babybjorn.co.uk

Winner Monitor
BT MONITOR AND PACIFIER

All basic monitors will serve you well if you just want to know when your baby is awake or crying. But these days, video cameras, room thermometers and lullaby programmes are treasured extras. The BT Monitor and Pacifier goes further. With a pretty light show projection, a wider range of tinkly bedtime tunes to play and even an MP3 plug for you to select your own musical or storytime choices, it's the next best thing to you standing by the cot yourself all evening.
www.shop.bt.com

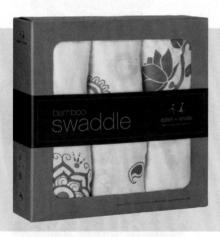

Winner Bed linen and sleeping bags
ADEN + ANAIS

Raegan Moya-Jones created her baby bedding inspired by the simple muslin cloth wraps her mother and grandmother has used decades before. Updating these with pretty, modern designs, she has created a beautiful range of swaddles, sheets and sleeping bags that are warm but never stiflingly hot, even in summer.
www.adenandanais.co.uk

Winner
BABY DAN

New arrivals appear all the time in the travel cot market, yet the Baby Dan blue and mesh model has been an enduring favourite for years. Easy to open and fold down, with wheels to make it easy to move around and padded bumper rails, it's not the whizziest cot on the market, but it's a reliable performer every time.
www.babydan.com

In the nursery

Winner Mattress
LITTLE GREEN SHEEP TWIST

You might not be serving up a mattress as salad, but Little Green Sheep argue a strong case for going organic when it comes to bedtime. The natural properties in organic fabrics perform better as long-lasting, breathable mattress materials compared with cheaper synthetic options, which means your baby is sleeping on something that's more eco-friendly and free from dyes, pesticides and chemicals.

Little Green Sheep uses coconut coir and natural fleece wool as the starting point for all its mattresses, but for the Twist, which we particularly like, there is also a layer of natural latex. This acts as a good support when your baby becomes a more lively toddler. Suitable from newborn to 5 years, it's a great investment. www.thelittlegreensheep.co.uk

Winner Gadget
TOMMEE TIPPEE DIGITAL EAR THERMOMETER

Baby temperatures can play havoc with your nerves! More often than not, a briefly raised temperature is just a symptom of a teething phase or the body fighting off a minor bug. But of course, you want to know when it might signal something more serious. At times like this, an ear thermometer can take an accurate reading quickly, with little inconvenience to the out-of-sorts 'patient'.

The Tommee Tippee model is especially good because the tip which goes into the ear is very small so it fits even a newborn ear, but can be used for children and adults too. It also has a fever alert for high readings. www.tommeetippee.co.uk

Winner Nursing chair
OLLI ELLA

Why should your baby's bedroom look any less stylish than the rest of your home? Investing now in a few key pieces that will stay in your home for years will give you far more pleasure than flimsy make-do items, and during those long nursing sessions in the middle of the night, you deserve to be sitting pretty.

Olli Ella's beautiful, British-made gliding chairs allow you to smoothly move back and for as if you were rocking your baby off to sleep as you feed. Despite its soft suede feel, the upholstery is actually stain resistant and wipeable and the foam filling is chemical free. While there are a few luxury nursing chairs on the market, the shape and finish of Olli Ella chairs puts them in a different class. We especially love the crisp, rich blue model for retro appeal. www.olliella.com

Winner
Disposable nappies
HUGGIES

These days you should easily be able to find a well-designed nappy that doesn't chafe on your baby's legs and doesn't leak even when it hasn't been changed overnight. However, in this competitive market, there are still cute new innovations to be made, and we like Huggies for their clever little wetness indicator stripe that shows you clearly when a change is needed. More importantly, and why they really go to the top of the class, we love the newborn range which includes an umbilical cord cutaway so that the nappy doesn't rub on your new baby's tenderest parts. **www.huggiesclub.co.uk**

Winner
Wipes
DERMAH2O WATER WIPES

Last year's winner hasn't been bettered, so here it is again! In the early months, many parents only use water and cotton wool to clean their baby's delicate bottom, but when you're out and about, wipes are so much easier. But do you really want to use something with (even quite gentle) chemicals in? With water wipes you have the best of both worlds.

We also like the idea of Cheeky Wipes – which are reusable baby wipes – but they involve a whole cleansing kit process and the simplicity of Water Wipes really does take some beating. **www.dermah2o.com**

Winner
Toiletries PUREPOTIONS

The Brighton-based skincare company Purepotions have seen amazing results with their 100% natural range of products. Suitable for a range of skin problems, their lotions and creams are ideal for babies, children and even adults.

Their Skin Salve, Lavender Nappy Slave and Camomile Bathy Oil are particular favourites for simplicity and effectiveness.
www.purepotions.biz

Everyday essentials

Winner Changing bag
IL TUTTO BRIGITTE

We like baby changing bags that look like properly posh handbags. It's not that we don't want to shout about being new mums, but something of quality that we can enjoy long after the nappies have come off is surely a bonus. There are many on the market which look like something Audrey Hepburn would have taken away with her on a weekend break, but we especially love Il Tutto for sheer quality at a great price (around £149), and their Brigitte is truly gorgeous.

The fashionable shape and style of the Brigitte competes with any regular handbag you'd see all year, with added panels and pockets inside to accommodate all your bottle, wipe and nappy needs. Plus the finish and the pretty lining can't help but raise a smile even when you're in a restaurant loo changing the third unscheduled stinky nappy of the day… www.iltutto.co.uk

Winner
Playmat
SKIP HOP TREETOP ACTIVITY MAT

One wise investment during the earliest months is a great activity mat. For those days when your baby wants to explore with eyes and fingers, and even for quiet times, a pretty activity mat provides a cosy resting place with stimulating toys and visual features within easy reach.

We love Skip Hop's softly colourful designs because they look great in the nursery and in the lounge, so their Treetop Activity Mat has to be a winner. With five hanging toys, a mirror, built-in sounds and differing textures in the fabric design, it'll keep your baby fascinated for hours.
www.skiphop.com

Winner
Baby chair

NUNA LEAF

If you have the space for this luxuriously sleek baby lounger, we highly recommend it. Instead of bouncing as your baby wriggles, it gently swivels on a smooth-running pivot system, lulling your baby off for naps and making the chair a cosy place to try first weaning experiences.
www.nuna.eu

Winner
Highchair

BABY DAN DANCHAIR

There are some wild and funky designs around in the feeding chair world, but we still admire the simplicity of a wooden chair that 'grows' with your child, eventually becoming a regular stool that blends in with other kitchen furniture rather than being consigned to the broom cupboard.

In the Stokke style, the Baby Dan Danchair has several adjustable levels so the seat and footrest can be changed easily as your child grows. Plus it's designed with extra long feet so it remains stable, whoever is having lunch on it...
www.babydan.com

Feeding

Winner
Babyfood preparation at home
BEABA BABYCOOK

Easy to use, utterly gorgeous to look at and designed with intelligent parent instincts in mind, the Babycook range is all you need to make your child's meals. Helping you prepare food so it preserves its vitamins, and including clever pots that allow you to cook fast without too much time-consuming supervision, the Babycook range is easily the best in its field.

From simple first weaning dishes that need to be steamed and mashed, to food for older babies and toddlers, you will have everything you need for prep, serving and storing. In fact, you'll probably still be using their steamer-cooker-blender for yourselves when the kids have left for college…
www.beaba.com

Winner
Food on the go
BABY ZILLI

With the best will in the world, sometimes you need to buy readymade baby foods, and when you're out and about, pouch packaging is by far the easiest way of serving just as much food as your baby wants without spoiling the leftovers for later.

In this area, while we like the ranges offered by Ella's Kitchen and Plum Baby, we love Baby Zilli from the kitchen of celeb chef Aldo Zilli. The range features tasty organic dishes, starting with simple veg and fruit choices for babies from 4 months, then moving on to salmon, potato and pea, chicken and parsnip, and even a cock-a-leekie recipe. Available in a wide range of high street stores, they are great value too.
www.zillibaby.co.uk

Winner
Baby toy

SOPHIE LA GIRAFE

An icon of the baby nursery in France since it was first introduced in 1961, Sophie has become a popular baby toy here too. Handmade from natural rubber, she looks cute, feels interesting and can be a wonderful comforter when your baby wants to chew away the teething blues.

The range also includes three alien-looking fungi toys called Chan, Pie and Gnon. (As in 'champignon'!)
www.sophielagirafe.co.uk

Winner
Toys 3-5 years

MINI-MICRO SCOOTER

Once your child is toddling, speed is king! The Mini-Micro Scooter, with its two wheels at the front and one at the back, is one of the lightest yet most stable ride-on toys and it's easy to carry with you for any unscheduled park visits.

The Mini-Micro is suitable for 3 to 5 year olds, but you can buy a seat adaptor which turns it into a ride-on toy for over-1s and then gradually raise the handlebars as your child grows. Now why didn't we think of that?
www.micro-scooters.co.uk

Toys

Winner
Best online retailer
TOYELLA

There are a multitude of toy retailers on the internet these days, but few source imaginative, beautiful playthings quite so well as fledgling company Toyella. Who wants a boring old pretend tea set when you can buy a fabric sushi meal or dress in a play costume that's classy enough to be seen on a film set?

Find everything you want here, but just that little bit more cool and cleverer than you'll see elsewhere ... from games and puzzles and toys for all ages, to bedroom accessories and weird and wonderful building kits that will amaze and amuse even a hard-to-please big brother or sister.
www.toyella.com

Winner
Toddler toys
WOW TOYS

Imaginative role play and pretending are all part of a preschool child's way of learning about the world around them. And that's just what this London based toy designer, Wow Toys, has perfected with its range of brightly colour, tactile vehicles. Each toy is a combination of elements, which can fit together or can be played with separately creating a wide range of imaginative scenarios. Parents love this brand for the the simple fact that they are not battery powered, but have friction motors which allow preschoolers to control speed and direction. And this year they are bang on trend with a cupcake bakery for girls and Ryan's road trip camping for boys.
www.wowtoys.com

Winner
Maternity seasonal collections
PRETTY PREGNANT

There are easy staples in any maternity collection, but just because you're pregnant, you really don't have to settle for something practical when you're turning up for a party where everyone else is on-trend.

Pretty Pregnant is a vibrant and imaginative maternitywear company that has added a touch of youthful style to collections for pregnant women since it launched in 2004. With four London boutiques (Chelsea, Clapham, Dulwich and Islington) and an online store, they cover the essentials as well as adding seasonal twists that work with your changing shape.

Winner
Maternity evening/occasion (and brida...
SERAPHINE

Seraphine's maternitywear is glamorous in shape, style and even fabric, indulging in silk and lace for those times when you want to feel particularly gorgeous.

Their catalogue includes playful short silk evening dresses with just enough of a sleeve to hide those flashes of flesh (on nights when your pregnancy temperature is on the high side), floaty maxi dresses to make you glide even if you feel like you're waddling underneath, and even stunning wedding dresses for women who want to celebrate the most treasured guest on their special day. In fact, there's an entire maternity wedding boutique for brides and bridesmaids. Classy stuff.
www.seraphine.com

Maternity

MELBA

Instead of adapting a pair of your other half's pyjamas, why not treat yourself to maternity nightwear? After all, when you get to hospital, it's your jim-jams you'll be in half the time.

London-based company Melba make nightwear the star attraction in their small but perfectly formed maternitywear range. Robes, nightdresses and PJs are designed to stay comfortable at night but still look glamorous at breakfast time. In colours like navy and lilac, with buttlermilk trim, you can mix and match camisoles and robes, so you can also lounge around the house feeling good enough to never get dressed!
www.melbamaternity.co.uk

Winner
Nursing bra
MAMMAE

When you are breastfeeding, you might continue to use your maternity bra and cover yourself up with tactfully placed tops, but investing in a couple of good nursing bras will go a big way to making breastfeeding feel like a more natural part of your new exciting life and not just a chore.

Beyond their pretty designs, these bras feature clever details that reflect what new mums really need. An outer layer to the bra covers up nipples or any breast pads you might be wearing, and also helps to create a fuller bra shape concealing any outline of a pull-down flap. Bravissimo's range of nursing bras range from DD to K cups too, offering great support and stylish design, but overall, it's the padded extras that make Mammae a winner. mammae.co.uk

Babylist's Best of the Best

At Babylist, finding products that perfectly fit the needs, style and lifestyle of their clients is everything. What do they look for when handpicking products for their world-class range? Practicality, style, personalisation and timelessness. We've selected six of Babylist's best-loved products - some enduring client favourites; others hot off the press; all fabulous, all available at Babylist.

ANYA HINDMARCH CHANGING BAG
Practical elegance with the baby-ready 'it' bag

Bridging style and substance - an elegant bag from the British mistress of style.

Babylist's Anita says; *'Every mother needs a changing bag, but that bag doesn't have to look out of place in her wardrobe. Babylist believes that understanding your life and style is key to understanding how best to make you baby-ready.'*

BEAUTIFUL 'BEIGE BEES' BED LINEN
Timeless style in softest cotton

Beautifully soft, hand-embroidered bed linen in a classic style, perfect for tucking in tiny ones for a quiet night's sleep.
Anita says; *'You will want your baby's bed to be as comfy, cosy and welcoming as possible. This elegant bed linen is just the thing to tempt tired little ones gently to sleep, while bringing some timeless style to the nursery.'*

THE BABYLIST BOUNCY CHAIR
Simply the best

Recommended by top private ante-natal classes in London, the Babylist bouncy chair is loved by parents and babies alike.

Anita says; *'The Babylist bouncy chair is critically acclaimed and very popular with our parents and babies alike. The integrated wooden board allows baby to lie totally flat from day one and the cover is removable and washable - by far the most easy on the eye for parents too!'*

BABY CLOTHES HAND-KNITTED IN ENGLAND
Bespoke baby luxury

Softest Loro Piana cashmere, merino or cotton for the most delicate skin, these baby clothes are entirely personalised - made with your baby in mind.

Anita says; *'Choose cashmere, merino or cotton depending on the season in your own unique style, colour and size - these pieces become treasured heirlooms. Babylist clients return annually for these unique and long-lasting garments.'*

KORBELL NAPPY BIN
Perfectly practical parenting essential

Cleverly-designed and odour-free, the sleekly-styled Korbell nappy bin means you can dispose of used nappies quickly, easily and hygienically.

Anita says; *'Crucially this nappy bin is pedal-operated, so you can use it while keeping a safe hand on your baby. The internally-stored biodegradable nappy bags keep your nursery clutter-free and a sealed internal unit stores more than any other bin on the market. We know it's the best because our clients rave about it.'*

BABYLIST PHOTOGRAPHERS
Beautiful photographs in timeless style

Babylist photographers are experts in taking beautiful baby portraits. Traditional or contemporary, they will create elegant portraits to suit your style.

Anita says; *'Beautifully-shot photography is a lasting memento and fitting tribute to joys of the early days. Our tried and trusted expert photographers capture those special moments in stunning pictures that you will treasure.'*

shopping

changing bags

Y ou're going to use this bag everyday for two years (or more depending on when you potty train), so grab something stylish and practical from our selection of favourites.

. . . .

1. Il Tutto- Brigitte tote bag- £149.00
This sleek and sophisticated tote bag has all the essentials that a new mum needs. A removable waterproof lining, a changing mat, and all the small pockets and compartments that help you store whatever you need. *www.iltutto.co.uk*

2. OiOi- Retro circular floral messenger £80
This bag is 100% cotton, with an easy to clean nylon lining. With its fun and funky exterior, the bag contains all the extras you'd expect including a case for wipes, an insulated bottle holder and a large microfibre changing mat.
www.oioibaby.co.uk

3. Storksak- Helena Leather Rose £275
Even after your child has grown up, you will still be able to use this leather changing bag. While remaining chic and stylish as the day you bought it, it features a detachable zipped bag, detachable strap, and a large elasticised pocket.
www.storksak.co.uk

4. Pink Lining- Poppins bag blue butterflies £65
With a whimsical butterfly and bird pattern this bag has been made a little bigger than your average changing bag. There are pockets for all your bits and bobs and a strap long enough to fit over a pram. *www.pinklining.co.uk*

5. Baby Mel- London studio Tote £45
Babymel's London inspired tote is a refreshing change design wise and it has all the customary features that we love from Babymel, including a padded changing mat, seven internal pockets and an insulated bottleholder.
www.babymel.com

education

As soon as your child is born you'll be thinking about their education. And it's never too early to register for pre-school care as the most popular nurseries and childminders get booked up frighteningly early.

What are your pre-school childcare options?

Day Nurseries (£8 per hour, all year round): from 6 weeks - normally privately run and offering care from 8am-6pm or by the half-day in specially adapted and Ofsted inspected premises. Ideal for working parents who have to be at their desk by 9am.

Childminders (£8 per hour, all year round): from 6 weeks childminders take children into their own home like a small family sized group.

Private Nursery schools (Fee paying, termtime): from 2½-5yrs usually attached to independent pre-prep schools.

Pre-schools/playgroups (contributions accepted, termtime): from 2½yrs - mainly run by parent or volunteer committees that are not-for-profit and employ their own staff. Based in church halls or community centres.

Primary School nurseries (Free, termtime): from 3-4yrs. Most of these are attached to local primary schools, although a place at nursery does not guarantee a place at the primary school. You must put your name down as soon as possible as there may well be a waiting list and you'll find parents with older siblings have got there first.

Primary Schools (Free, termtime): from 4 rising 5 to 11yrs. You will need to apply for your child's primary school place when they are 3 rising 4 years - or at least a year before they start (which is usually the term before they turn 5yrs). For nearly all nurseries and schools in the private sector, early registration is highly recommended particularly in Kensington, Hampstead and Richmond, so ring, visit with babe in arms and register ahead of time, even if you later decide not to pursue that option.

For a list of state-run nurseries ie state primary schools with nursery classes contact your local Council.

Ofsted inspect nurseries regularly and rank them accordingly: Outstanding, Good, Satisfactory and inadequate. The reports are available online for parents to read at (ofsted.gov.uk). This will give you an indication of how they're performing.

Many private schools are not inspected by Ofsted, but by the **ISI** (Independent Schools Inspectorate). They don't rank schools in the same way as Ofsted, but give a good overall impression about educational objectives and achievements, ethos and social care. Reports are online at (isi.net).

FIND MY CHILD A SCHOOL

Marina Dawson-Damer
School Placement Consultant

I offer a unique, bespoke service assisting parents within the UK Independent School system, guiding them through the process of finding the right school for their child within Central London.

SCHOOL PLACEMENT CONSULTANT

Find my child a school

www.findmychildaschool.co.uk
Telephone 020 73513811   Mobile 0777 4444479

---

educational consultant

Find My Child a School   **020 7351 3811**
-Marina Dawson-Damer   **07774 444 479**
www.findmychildaschool.co.uk
Marina Dawson-Damer offers parents in London a unique, bespoke Service, assisting them in finding the right school for their child within the Independent School system. With over 20 years teaching experience from Nursery to Preparatory School she has extensive knowledge of the London Day School system.

extra tuition

Victoria Page   **07050 246 810**
Private Tutor   **020 7381 9911**
Victoria Page is a Private Tutor in Maths, English, Verbal and Non-Verbal Reasonsing. She teaches the Nursery Syllabus, Reading, Writing to preschool children as well as offering Remedial help where necessary. Exam preparation for common entrance, prep-school entry at 7+, 8+ and 11+ Scholarship. Great at building confidence and skills for any entry including Nursery. 2½-11yrs+. Holiday's or termtime, UK and overseas clients. Fully qualified teacher, Exceptional references. Established 1982.Telephone for advice or to discuss requirements.

Greycoat Childcare   **020 7233 9950**
& Education
www.greycoatchildcare.co.uk
For all your additional educational needs - our professional service helps you find the ideal Private Tutor for your child to ensure he/she reaches their full potential. All subjects and levels catered for. Call our dedicated Consultant today.

speach, language and hearing

Speech, Language and   **020 7383 3834**
Hearing Centre
1-5 Christopher Place, Chalton Street, NW1 1JF
www.speech-lang.org.uk
Specialist centre for babies/toddlers with hearing or speech impairment.

educational training

Montessori Centre   **020 7493 8300**
International
18 Balderton Street, W1K 6TG
www.montessori.org.uk
Not just a job... a way of life. Become a Montessori Teacher with MCI. Europe's largest Montessori training college, in central London. Full-time, part-time & distance learning courses available. Attend our monthly open evenings to find out more. Email: career@montessori.uk.com

nurseries

East postcodes - E1

Dreammaker Day Nursery   020 7480 7166
65 Cartwright Street, Tower Bridge, E1 8NB

Green Gables Montessori School   020 7488 2374
St Georges in the East Church, 16 Cannon Street
Road, E1 0BH

Matilda Community Day Nursery   020 7480 6396
St Katherine's Way, Wapping, E1W 1LQ

Spitalfields Children's Centre   020 7375 0775
21 Lamb Street, Spitalfields, E1 6EA

The Nursery at St Pauls   020 7265 0098
St Paul's Church, Dock Street, Wapping, E1 8JN

E2

Bethnal Green Montessori School   020 7739 4343
68 Warner Place, E2 7DA

S Gatehouse School   020 8980 2978
Sewardstone Road, Victoria Park, Bethnal Green,
E2 9JG

Happy Nest Nursery   020 7739 3193
Fellows Court Family Centre, Weymouth Terrace,
Hackney, E2 8LR

Noah's Ark   020 7739 2317
within Mildmay Hospital, Hackney Road, E2 7NA

Noah's Ark Community   **020 7739 2317**
Nursery
Little Oak's Children's Centre, Pelter Street, E2 7PE
www.leyf.org.uk
6mths-5yrs. 8am-6pm. 51wks. Hoping to return to work,
looking to boost your child's development - or just prepare
them for big school? Award-winning charity LEYF actively
supports lower-income families by helping to reduce the cost
to parents of high quality childcare. Ask our highly qualified &
friendly Nursery staff in Westminster and Camden about
leading childcare you can afford.

Rachel Keeling Nursery School   020 8980 5856
Bullards Place, Morpeth Street, E2 0PS

E3

Bow Childcare at Tudor Lodge   020 8983 7973
95 Bromley High Street, Bow, E3 3EN

Bow Nursery Centre   020 8981 0483
1 Bruce Road, Bow, E3 3HN

Overland Children's Centre   020 8981 1619
60 Pardell Road, E3 2RU

education

Pillar Box Gardens Nursery 020 8983 7431
49 Fairfield Road, Bow, E3 2QA

Pillar Box Montessori Nursery 020 8980 0700
City House, 107 Bow Road, Bow, E3 2AN

E4

Ainslie Wood Nursery 020 8523 9910
140 Ainslie Wood Road, Chingford, E4 9DD

Amhurst Nursery 020 8527 1614
13 The Avenue, E4 9LB

Billet's Corner Nursery 020 8523 3823
11 Walthamstow Avenue, Chingford, E4 8ST

Buttercups 020 8527 2902
22 Marborough Road, Chingford, E4 9AL

Childs Play Day Nursery 020 8529 6058
283 Hall Lane, Chingford, E4 8NU

Childs Play Day Nursery 020 8523 7208
1 Hatch Lane, Chingford, E4 6LP

Chingford Day Nursery 020 8529 6101
Sewardstone Road, Chingford, E4 7SD

Friday Hill Nursery 020 8529 6101
58 Friday Hill, Chingford, E4 6EZ

Need to Know: Development

From birth your baby is developing skills rapidly, but there are a few key milestones which begin to show at around the ages below. Do bear in mind these vary from child to child so don't worry if your child hasn't hit a new achievement on a set date!

- **First smile:** around two to three months
- **First attempts to hold or grip:** four to six months
- **Pushing up:** from four to six months
- **Sitting up:** from seven to nine months
- **Crawling:** from seven to 11 months
- **Or shuffling on bottom:** from eight to 11 months
- **Standing and cruising:** from 10 to 13 months
- **Toddling:** from 12 to 16 months

For more information on development visit our Health Clinic online at **www.babydirectory.com/health_clinic**

Highams Park Day Nursery 020 8531 0713
16a Handsworth Avenue, E4 9PJ

Leapfrog Day Nursery 020 8524 7063
2 Larkswood Leisure Park, 175 New Road, Chingford, E4 9EY

Merryfield Montessori 020 8524 7697
Nursery
76 Station Road, Chingford, E4 7BA

S Normanhurst School 020 8529 4307
68-74 Station Road, Chingford, E4 7BA

Tiny Tots 020 8523 5046
101 Higham Station Avenue, E4 9AY

Waterlily Day Nursery 020 8524 6745
3 Friday Hill West, Chingford Hatch, E4 6JS

E5

Rooftop Nursery 020 8986 2006
6 Ottaway Street, Clapton, E5 8PX /07930 380 443

St Michael's Nursery 020 8985 2886
59 Thistlewaite Road, Clapton, E5 0QG

Sunflower Children's Nursery 020 8985 6686
36 Colne Road, E5 0HR

Teddy Bear School House Nursery 020 8985 6486
51 Mayola Road, E5 0RE

E6

Alphabet House Nursery 020 8552 0078
Canberra Road, East Ham, E6 2RW

Alphabet House Nursery 020 7476 0222
Stroud Pavillion, Savage Gardens, Becton, E6 5NB

Enchanted Castle Nursery 020 8552 6777
557-565 Barking Road, East Ham, E6 2LW

Little Butterflies 020 8475 0898
Pilgrims Way Church, Pilgrims Way, East Ham, E6 1HW

Seahorse Children's Day Nursery 020 7473 3522
116 Evelyn Dennington Road, E6 5YU

St Stephens Children's Centre 020 8471 1366
St Stephens Road, E6 1AX

E7

Chestnut Nursery School 020 8503 0394
177 Earlham Grove, Forest Gate, E7 9AP

S Grangewood Independent 020 8472 3552
School
Chester Road, Forest Gate, E7 8QT

Stepping Stones Day Nursery   020 8470 6999
St Bonaventure's School, Boleyn Road, E7 9QD

E8

Independent Place Nursery   020 7275 7755
26-27 Independent Place, 76 Shacklewell Lane, E8 2HD

Kingsland Day Nursery   020 7241 2411
3 Birkbeck Mews, Dalston, E8 2LE

Market Day Nursery   020 7241 0978
Wilde Close, Hackney, E8 4JS

New Generation Nursery   020 7249 9826
179 Haggerston Road, Haggerston, E8 4JA

Teddy Bear Nursery   020 7249 4433
The Trinity Centre, Beechwood Road, E8 3DY

E9

Bloombers Day Nursery   07946 864 118
Homerton High Street, Homerton, E9 6DF

Homerton Roundabout Nursery   020 8510 8951
14 Kenworthy Road, E9 5TD

Little Saint Nursery School   020 8533 6600
Homerton High Road, E9 5QB

Places for Children Nursery   020 8986 0051
106-108 Morning Lane, E9 6LG

Wentworth Nursery School   020 8985 3491
Cassland Road, E9 5BY

Wetherell Nursery   020 8533 1072
17 Iveagh Close, E9 7BW

E10

Bright Kids Day Nursery   020 8558 0666
1 The Square, High Road, E10 5NR

Chesterfield Day Nursery   020 8539 5541
38 Chesterfield Road, E10 6EW

Little Ones Nursery   020 8558 8573
56 Leyton Park road, E10 5RL

Nappy Gang Nursery   020 8539 9005
71 Vicarage Road, E10 5EF

Nappy Gang Nursery   020 8539 8359
100 Oliver Road, Leyton, E10 5JY

Smilers Day Nursery   020 8558 1810
29 Vicarage Road, Leyton, E10 5EF

Sybourn Centre   020 8558 9597
Perth Road, Leyton, E10 7PB

Twinkels Day Nursery   020 8925 8674
44 Colchester Road, Leyton, E10

E11

Acacia Nursery School   020 8558 4444
Cecil Road, E11 3HE

Excel Day Nursery   020 8556 1732
62 Hainault Road, E11 1EQ

Foot Steps Day Nursery   020 8530 5471
2 Preston Road, E11 1NN

Giggles Childcare   020 8556 3791
392 Grove Green Road, E11 4AP

Humpty Dumpty Nursery   020 8539 3810
24/26 Fairlop Road, E11 1BN

Just Learning Nursery   020 8988 0818
Whipps Cross Road, E11 1NR

Little Green Man Day Nursery   020 8539 7228
15 Lemna Road, E11 1HX

Sunbeams Day Nursery   020 8530 2784
10 Bushwood, E11 3AY

Sunshine Day Nursery   020 8556 6889
167 Wallwood Road, E11 1AQ

Treehouse Nursery School   020 8532 2535
35 Woodbine Place, Wanstead, E11 2RH

E12

Chestnut Nursery School   020 8478 2246
Lawrence Avenue, E12 5QP

Smartstarts Day Nursery   020 8478 2700
Little Ilford Centre, Church Road, E12 6HA

Wisdom Kids Nursery   020 8478 2805
524 High Street, E12 6QN

E13

Alphabet House Nursery School   020 8548 9466
23 Harold Road, Upton Park, E13 0SQ

Coccinelle   020 8552 3340
663 Barking Road, E13 9EX

Foster Road Nursery   020 8472 8700
Foster Road, Plaistow, E13 8bT

Smarty Pants Day Nursery   020 8471 2620
1 Plashet Road, E13 0PZ

E14

Bushytails Private Day Nursery   020 7537 7776
Wood Wharf Business Park, Docklands, E14 9LZ

Lanterns Nursery & Pre-School   020 7363 0951
F4-F7 Lanterns Court, 22 Millharbour, E14 9TU

education

Limehouse Arches Day Nursery 020 7515 1480 21-23 Trinidad Street, Limehouse, E14 8AA	**Koala Bear Day Nursery** 020 8520 0762 1 Church Hill, E17 3AB
Little Herons Centre 020 7719 0719 50 Bank Street, Canary Wharf, E14 5NS	**Magic Roundabout Nursery** 020 8523 5551 161 Wadham Road, E17 4HU
Little Unicorn Day Nursery 020 7519 1010 20 Canada Square, Canary Wharf, E14 5NN	**Rascals Day Nurseries** 020 8520 2417 34 Verulam Avenue, E17 8ER
Little Unicorn Day Nursery 020 7519 6519 2 Westferry Circus, Canary Wharf, E14 4HD	**Tinkerbells Nursery** 020 8520 8338 185 Coppermill Lane, E17 7HU
Little Unicorn Day Nursery 020 7513 0505 13 Columbus Courtyard, Canary Wharf, E14 4DA	**Tom Thumb Nursery** 020 8520 1329 20 Shirley Close, 1-7 Beulah Road, E17 9LZ
Magic Roundabout Nursery 020 7364 6028 2 Lawn House Close, Marshwall, E14 9YQ	**Uplands House Nursery** 020 8531 6326 1 Uplands House, Business Centre, E17 5QT

E15

Alphabet House Nursery School   020 8519 2023
37 Windmill Lane, Stratford, E15 1PG

Bright Kids Kindergarten   020 8519 2100
9 Brydges Road, Stratford, E15 1NA

Olive Day Nursery   020 8522 0622
375-377 High Street, Stratford, E15 4QZ

Ronald Openshaw Nursery   020 8534 6196
Henniker Road, Stratford, E15 1JP

Stepping Stones Childcare   020 8534 8777
Brickfields Centre, Welfare Road, E15 4HT

E16

Children's Garden   020 8223 2663
4-6 University Way, E16 2RD

Kimberley Road Nursery   020 8472 8700
Kimberley Road, E16 4NT

Leapfrog Day Nursery   0207 474 7487
Royal Victoria Docks, E16 1XL

E17

Carville Day Nursery   020 8521 7612
43a West Avenue Road, E17 9SF

Chapel End Early Years Centre   020 8527 9192
Brookscroft Road, E17 4LH

Church Hill Nursery   020 8520 9196
Woodbury Road, E17 9SB

Climbers Nursery   020 8521 0783
215 Queens Road, E17 8PJ

Happy Child Day Nursery   020 8520 8880
The Old Town Hall, 14b Orford Road, E17 9NL

Just Learning Day Nursery   020 8527 9711
20 Sutton Road, Higham Hill, E17 5QA

Walthamstow Montessori School   020 8523 2968
Penrhyn Hall, Penrhyn Avenue, E17 5DA

Walthamstow Nursery   020 8523 5551
161 Wadham Road, E17 4HU

E18

Fareacres Nursery   020 8505 3248
1 Chelmsford Road, E18 2PW

Fullers Hall Community Nursery   020 8505 5779
64a Fullers Road, E18 2QA

Playdays Day Nursery   020 8530 8688
52-54 Chigwell Road, E18 1NN

Rainbow Kids Nursery   020 8504 1036
2 Malmesbury Road, E18 2NN

EC1

Smithfield House Childrens Nursery 020 7236 1000
14 West Smithfield, Barbican, EC1A 9HY

Kidsunlimited Nurseries   0845 365 2908
Mango Tree
62-66 Farringdon Road, EC1R 3GA

East West Community Nursery   020 7490 1790
Mitchell Street, Islington, EC1V 3QD

Hopes and Dreams Nursery   020 7833 9388
339-341 City Road, Islington, EC1V 1LJ

EC2

Leapfrog Day Nursery   020 7422 0088
49 Clifton Street, EC2A 4EX

Barbican Playgroup   020 7638 2718
Level 1& 2, Andrewes House, Barbican, EC2Y 8AX

City Child Nursery   020 7374 0939
1 Bridgewater Square, EC2Y 8AH

S City of London School for Girls   020 7847 5500

St Giles Terrace, Barbican, EC2Y 8BB

Newpark Childcare – Barbican   020 7638 5550
1 St. Giles Terrace, Barbican, EC2Y 8DU

EC3

Tower Hill Nursery   020 7320 1780
100 Minories, EC3N 1JY

Middlesex postcodes (north of the M4)
EN1

Alice Nursery   **020 8886 1135**
85 Wellington Rd, Bush Hill Park, Enfield, EN1 2PL
www.pghs.co.uk
The Alice Nursery is a brand new purpose built nursery for
3-4 year old girls and is the pre-school for Palmers Green
High School. Opening times are 8.45am -3.45pm during
term time. Admissions are by assessment and/or interview.
Please contact the school for further details or visit our
website.

Enfield Nursery   020 8367 0069
Carterhatch Lane, Enfield, EN1 4LF

Goldstar Montessori Nursery   020 8364 6876
466 Baker Street, Enfield, EN1 3QS

EN2

Cedar Park Nursery   020 8367 3800
50 Hadley Road, Enfield, EN2 8JY

EN3

Southbury Nursery   020 8805 1144
8 Glyn Road, Enfield, EN3 4JL

Tara Kindergarten   020 8804 7710
198 High Street, Ponders End, Enfield, EN3 4EZ

EN5

S Norfolk Lodge School   **020 8447 1565**
Dancers Hill Road, Barnet, Herts, EN5 4RP
www.NorfolkLodgeSchool.co.uk
Norfolk Lodge Montessori is based in a large, tranquil country
mansion in Dancers Hill Road, Barnet. The nursery enjoys a
beautiful play garden at the rear and is surrounded by
woodlands. Babies can join Little Gems baby room from
three months old and progress on to pre-nursery and nursery
classes in due course.

HA0

Bringing Up Baby   020 8385 1928
Vale Farm, Watford Road, Wembley, HA0 3HG

Colours Nursery   020 8902 2226
Mount Pleasant, Wembley, HA0 1SH

Little Jems Nursery   020 8904 2644
Sudbury Avenue, Wembley, HA0 3BG

HA1

Happy Days Nursery   020 8424 0102
Sea Cadet Hall, Woodlands Road, HA1 2RT

North Harrow Day Nursery   020 8427 0114
42-44 Gloucester Road, HA1 4PR

Quainton Hall School   020 8427 1304
Hindes Road, HA1 1RX

HA2

Newton Farm Nursery   020 8864 8081
Ravenswood Crescent, HA2 9JU

HA3

Asquith Nursery Kenton   020 8909 9850
9 The Ridgeway, Kenton, Harrow, HA3 OLJ

Learning Tree Nursery   020 8904 9413
309 Preston Road, Harrow, HA3 0QQ

Stanmore Daycare Centre   020 8416 3721
123 Uxbridge Road, Harrow, HA3 6DJ

Woodcock Nursery School   020 8907 2818
Woodcock Hill, St Johns Church, HA3 0JH

education

HA4

Lady Bankes Eye Nursery 01895 636 765
Dawlish Drive, Ruislip, HA4 9SF

Once Upon A Time Day Nursery 020 8866 7258
Field End Road, Eastcote, HA4 9PG

White House Nursery 01895 632 681
97 West End Road, Ruislip, HA4 6JN

Woodlands Nursery 01895 622 140
Woodford Hall, Poplars Close, Ruislip, HA4 7BU

HA5

4 Street Nursery 01895 623 288
Fore Street, Eastcote, Pinner, HA5 2HX

Hatch End Nursery 020 8421 5471
3 Hillview Road, Hatch End, Pinner, HA5 4PB

Rosewood Montessori 020 8866 7653
Cuckoo Hill Road, Pinner, HA5 1AS

St Vincents Day Nursery 020 8426 1490
St Vincents Hospital, Wiltshire Lane, Pinner, HA5 2N

HA6

Mount Vernon Day Nursery 01923 844 141
Rickmansworth Road, Northwood, HA6 2RN

Riverside Nursery 01923 848 041
Riverside Club, Ducks Hill Road, Northwood, HA6 2DR

HA7

Stanmore Park Children's Centre 020 8954 2015
William Drive, Stanmore, HA7 4FZ

HA8

Smiley Totz 020 8958 6164
Stonegrove Gardens Hall, Stonegrove Gardens,
Edgware, HA8 7TE

HA9

Happy Days Montessori School 020 8903 6221
St John Bosco, Empire Way, Wembley, HA9

Honeypot Nursery 020 8903 9367
Ujima House, 388 High Road, Wembley, HA9 6AR

Windermere Nursery 020 8904 3327
Windermere Avenue, Wembley, HA9 8QT

North postcodes - N1

Comet Nursery School 020 7729 0936
20 Halcomb Street, N1 5RF

Floral Place Nursery 020 7354 9945
2 Floral Place, Northampton Grove, N1 2PL

Kate Greenaway Nursery School 020 7837 4982
York Way Court, Copenhagen Street, N1 0UH

Little Angels Schoolhouse 020 7336 8833
3 Bletchley Street, N1 7QG

Mars Montessori Bilingual Nursery 020 7704 2805
4 Collins Yard, N1 2XQ

New River Green Childrens Centre 020 7527 4817
23 Ramsey Walk, N1 2SX

Rosemary Works EYC 020 7613 5500
2a Branch Place, Southgate Road, N1 5PH

St Andrew's Montessori 020 7700 2961
St Andrew's Church, Thornhill Square, N1 1BQ

The Children's House 020 7354 2113
77 Elmore Street, N1 3AQ
www.childrenshouseschool.co.uk
Nursery school and Upper school for children aged 2½-7yrs.
Sessional for the nursery and 9am-3.30pm for the Upper
School. Termtime only. Nursery 99 places, Upper School 60
places. Registration recommended as soon as possible.

S The Gower School 020 7278 2020
10 Cynthia Street, Islington, N1 9JF
www.thegowerschool.co.uk
4-11yrs. 8.45am-3.30pm. Termtime. Also wrap around care
from 8am-6pm and holiday activity clubs. This friendly state
of the art school offers an accredited Montessori approach
up to 11yrs. Qualified, experienced teachers with high ratios.
Outside there is a science and nature garden, pets corner as
well as an allotment garden. There is a suite of practice
rooms for individual music tuition, a dance s

The Grove Nursery 020 7226 4037
83-93 Shepperton Road, Islington, N1 3DF

N2

S Annemount Nursery 020 8455 2132
18 Holne Chase, N2 0QN

Fortis Green Nursery 020 8883 1266
70 Fortis Green, N2 9EP

Scribbles Nursery 020 8883 8546
2 Hertford Road, Barnet, N2 9BU

N3

Early Learning Years 020 8349 3492
19 The Grove, N3 1QN

Pardes House 020 8371 8292
Hendon Lane, N3 1SA

Pentland Nursery 020 8970 2441
224 Squires Lane, N3 2QL

The Rocking Horse Nursery 020 8346 3682
5 Victoria Avenue, N3 1BD

B.C.L Nursery   020 8211 7107
Woodberry Down, N4 2SH

Blythwod Community Nursery   020 7263 5070
Holly Hall, Blythwood Road, Islington, N4 4EU

Crouch Hill Day Nursery   020 7561 1533
33 Crouch Hill, Islington, N4 4AP

Finsbury Park Day Nursery   020 7263 3090
Dulas Street, Islington, N4 3AF

Holly Park Montessori School   0207 435 3646
Holly Park Church Hall, Crouch Hill, N4 4BY

St Angela's Day Nursery   020 8800 5228
34-36 Adolphus Road, N4 2AY

St Thomas Playgroup   020 7354 9347
St Thomas's Church, Monsell Rd, Islington, N4 2QY

Twinkle Stars   020 8802 0550
416 Seven Sisters Road, N4 2LX

Woodberry Down EYC   020 8800 1444
Springpark Drive, Green Lanes, N4 2NP

N5

Aberdeen Park Nursery   020 7226 2610
143 Highbury New Park, N5 2LJ

Little Angels Day Nursery   020 7354 5070
and Pre-School
217 Blackstock Road, N5 2LL

Martineau Community Nursery   020 7359 9911
1 Elwood Street, N5 1EB

New Park Nursery   020 7226 1109
67 Highbury New Park, Islington, N5 2EU

N6

Activity Nurseries   020 8348 9248
1 Church Road, Highgate, N6 4QH

Avenue Nursery School   020 8348 6815
2 Highgate Avenue, Highgate, N6 5RX

S Highgate Pre-Prep   020 8340 9196
7 Bishopswood Road, N6 4PH

Ladybird Montessori School   020 7586 0740
The Scout Hall, Sheldon Avenue, Highgate, N6 4ND

Nursery Montessori Highgate   020 8374 0289
23 Woodside Avenue, Highgate, N6 4SP

Rainbow Montessori School   020 7328 8986
Highgate Church, Pond Square, Highgate, N6 6BA

THE GOWER SCHOOL

A Montessori School for 4-11's in Barnsbury

where every child matters

Telephone: 020 7278 2020 www.thegowerschool.co.uk

N7

Kidsunlimited Nurseries   0845 365 2921
Tollington Way, N7 6QX

Mount Carmel EYC   020 7697 7370
18 Eden Grove, Holloway, N7 8EQ

Paradise Park Nursery   020 7697 7341
164 Mackenzie Road, N7 8SE

Rosedale Early Years Centre   020 7609 2344
24 Bride Street, N7 8RP

Spanish Sisters of Charity   020 7607 3974
95 Huddleston Road, Islington, N7 0AE

The Gower School   **020 7700 2445**
18 North Road, N7 9EY
www.thegowerschool.co.uk
3mths-5yrs. 8am-6.30pm. 48wks. This is a high quality,
accredited Montessori nursery offering a wide range of extra
activities such as Music, Baby Yoga, French, Mini Tennis,
Football and Tiny Talk signing classes. Trips and outings each
term. Qualified, experienced longstanding staff – a friendly,
family atmosphere with parents workshops and a range of
family activities make it the perfect place for your child to
make great progress. There is a large, sunny garden and an
allotment to introduce children to the production of organic
food. They offer freshly prepared vegetarian home cooking.
Awarded by Islington for Quality Assurance and the Green
Mark for commitment to the environment.

Willow Children's Centre   020 7527 1990
Holbrooke Court, N7 0BF

N8

Active Learning Nursery   020 3031 9094
Tivoli Road, Crouch End, N8 8RG

Adventure Land Day Nursery   020 8347 6951
18 Gisburn Road, N8 7BS

African Caribbean Day Nursery   020 8889 4222
30 Hornsey Park Road, Hornsey, N8 0JP

Bowlers Community Nursery	02072 812 832	**Teddies New Southgate**	020 8368 7915
81 Crouch Hill, N8 9EG		60 Beaconsfield Road, New Southgate, N11 3AE	

N12

Hollybush Nursery   020 8348 8537
5 Redston Road, N8 7HL

Active Learning Nursery   0800 081 1620
10-11 Moss Hall Crescent, N12 8NY

Keiki Day Care   020 8340 3841
7 Harold Road, Crouch End, N8 7DE

Finchley Reform Synagogue   020 8445 6807
Fallow Court Avenue, N12 0BE

Little Tree Montessori   020 8342 9231
143 Ferme Park Road, N8 9SG

S North London Intl School   020 8920 0634
88 Woodside Park Road, N12 8SH

North London Steiner   0208 341 3770
1-3 The Campsbourne, Hornsey High St, N8 7PN

N13

Orange Day Nursery   020 8340 3104
24 Willoughby Road, Hornsey, N8 0JE

Aplomb Day Nursery   020 3232 1030
32 Bourne Hill, N13 4LY

Planet Tiny   020 8348 8222
Priory Road, Hornsey, N8 7HR

Tottenhall Children's Centre   020 8829 1100
Tottenhall Road, Palmers Green, N13 6HX

St John's Busy Bunnies   020 8348 7744
Wightman Road, N8 0LY

N14

Starshine Nursery   020 8348 9909
34 Crescent Road, Crouch End, N8 8AX

Blue Planet Montessori Nursery   020 8441 6712
Bramley Road, Oakwood, N14 4HL

N9

Inspirations Montessori Nursery   020 8886 2400
Waterfall Road, Southgate, N14 7JZ

Edmonton Day Nursery   020 8807 9649
24 Cyprus Road, N9 9PG

Salcombe Day Nursery   020 8882 2136
33 The Green, Southgate, N14 6EN

New Horizons Nursery   020 8351 8280
Walbrook House, 1 Huntingdon Road, N9 8LS

S Salcombe Prep School   020 8441 5282
224-226 Chase Side, Southgate, N14 4PL

Rainbow Nursery Firs Farm   020 8807 9078
1-4 Kipling Terrace, Great Cambridge Rd, N9 9UJ

Southgate Day Nursery   020 8886 2824
25 Oakwood Avenue, Southgate, N14 6QH

Tara Kindergarten   020 8804 4484
310-314 Hartford Road, N9 7HB

Tara Kindergarten   020 8886 6163
2-16 Burleigh Parade, Burleigh Gardens, N14 5AD

N10

S Vita et Pax Preparatory School   020 8449 8336
6a Priory Close, Green Road, Southgate, N14 4AT

345 Pre-School   07966 541 889
77 Church Crescent, N10 3TS

N15

Greygates Nursery   020 8883 5640
182 Muswell Hill Road, N10 3NG

Rainbow Nursery   020 8826 0674
Derby Hall, West Green Road, N15 3PJ

Montessori House   020 8444 4399
5 Prince's Avenue, N10 3LS

Sugar Plum Nursery   020 8800 7560
255 West Green Road, N15 5JN

S Norfolk House Prep School   020 8883 4584
10 Muswell Avenue, N10 2EG

Woodlands Park Nursery   020 8802 0041
74-86 Woodlands Park Road, N15 3SD

Nursery Montessori   020 8883 7958
24 Tetherdown, N10 1NB

N16

Rosemount Nursery School   020 8883 5842
6 Grosvenor Road, N10 2DS

Academic Day Nursery   020 7254 9200
Weslyan School, 41-47 Leswin Road, N16 7NX

N11

Apple Blossoms   020 8806 3525
59a Osbaldeston Road, N16 7DL

Little Leo's Nursery   020 8211 3119
Oakleigh Road South, New Southgate, N11 1GN

Coconut Nursery   020 7923 0720

133 Stoke Newington Church Street, N16 0UH

Mini Home   020 7249 0725
14 Allen Road, N16 8SD

Sunrise Nursery   020 8806 6279
1 Cazenove Road, N16 6PA

The Factory Community Nursery   020 7241 1520
107 Matthias Road, N16 8NP

N17

Assure Day Nursery   020 8808 7373
33 Forster Road, N17 6QD

Blossoms Nursery   020 8808 0178
Imperial House, 64 Willoughby Lane, N17 0SP

N18

Angel Raynham Children's Centre   020 8807 4726
Raynham Avenue, Edmonton, N18 2JQ

Ashland Private Day Nursery   020 8345 5752
36 Weir Hall Road, N18 1EJ

Tinkerbells Nursery   020 8372 7682
2 Amersham Avenue, N18 1DT

N19

Archway Children's Centre   020 7272 3350
Vorley Road, N19 5HE

Konstam Nursery Centre   020 7272 3594
75 Chester Road, N19 5DH

Leaping Lizards Day Nursery   020 7619 3624
Whittington Park Centre, Yerbury Road, N19 4RS

Little Angels Day Nursery   020 7281 3514
70 Bredgar Road, Highgate, N19 5BF

Montpelier Nursery   020 7485 9813
115 Brecknock Road, N19 5AH

N20

Academy 4 Kids Day Nursery   020 8446 9988
209 Friern Barnet Lane, Whetstone, N20 0NG

Magic Daycare Nursery   020 8343 7766
Grangeview Road, Whetstone, N20 9EA

N21

Busy Bees Nursery   020 8360 6610
2 Florey Square, Highlands Village, N21 1UJ

S Keble Prep School   020 8360 3359
Wades Hill, Winchmore Hill, N21 1BG

S Palmers Green High School   020 8886 1135
104 Hoppers Road, N21 3LJ
www.pghs.co.uk
Palmers Green High School is an independent day school for
approximately 300 girls aged 3-16. Alice Nursery (3-4 years),
Lower School (4-10 years), Senior School (11-16 years).
Admissions are by assessment and/or interview. Please
contact the school for further details or visit our website.

Teddys Day Nursery   020 8364 3842
18 Green Dragon Lane, N21 2LD

Woodberry Day Nursery   020 8882 6917
63 Church Hill, Winchmore Hill, N21 1LE

N22

Bowes Park Nursery   020 8888 1142
63-65 Whittington Road, N22 8YR

TAB Children's Centre   020 8888 2797
Palmeston Road, Bounds Green, N22 8RA

NW1

S Abingdon House School   0845 230 0426
Broadley Terrace, Regent's Park, NW1 6LG

Auden Place Community Nursery   020 7586 0098
1 Auden Place, Manley Street, NW1 8LT
info@audenplace.co.uk   www.audenplace.co.uk
Auden Place Community Nursery is a 40 place nursery for
children 6 months to 5 years. As a community nursery,
Auden are committed to offering high quality childcare at
affordable prices, which includes all meals, outings and extra
curricular activities.

Regents Park Nursery   020 7935 7274
15 Gloucester Gate, Regent's Park, NW1 4HG

Camden Chinese Nursery   020 7485 4156
United Reformed Church, Buck Street, NW1 8NJ

Dolphin Montessori School   020 7267 3994

education

Church Hall, Leighton Crescent, NW1 2QY

S Francis Holland School   0207 723 0176
Clarence Gate, Ivor Place, NW1 6XR

Hampden Nursery Centre   020 7387 1822
80 Polygon Road, NW1 1HQ

Kidsunlimited Nurseries   0845 365 2923
1 Regents Place, Longford Street, NW1 3FN

Ready Steady Go Camden   020 7267 4241
123 St Pancras Way, Camden, NW1 0SY

Ready Steady Go Fitzroy Road   020 7722 2488
Fitzroy Road, Primrose Hill, NW1 8TN

Regents Park Nursery Centre   020 7387 2382
Augustus Street, NW1 3TJ

St Mark's Square   **020 7586 8383**
Nursery School   **020 7585 9012**
`OUTSTANDING OFSTED`
St Mark's Church, St Mark's Square, NW1 7TN
www.stmarkssquarenurseryschool.org.uk
2-6yrs. Full day nursery school established for 28 years offering an exciting, broad curriculum, which is holistic and consciousness based, including yoga, violin and ballet, and trips to London's art galleries. It has an Outstanding Ofsted report, and a headmistress that has been nominated for a 'Nursery Management Today Lifetime Achievement Award' and excellent links to top schools including: Trevor Roberts, Arnold House, South Hampstead, St Christophers and The Hall.

S The Cavendish School   020 7485 1958
31 Inverness Street, NW1 7HB

The Speech Language   **020 7383 3834**
and Hearing Centre
1-5 Christopher Place, Chalton Street, NW1 1JF
www.speech-lang.org.uk
The Speech, Language and Hearing Centre is for babies and children under 5 who have hearing impairment or delay in speech, language and communication or more complex needs. The Centre combines teaching and therapy from an interdisciplinary professional team.

Woodentots Montessori School   020 7485 0053
6 Rochester Road, NW1 9JH

NW2

Abbey Nursery School   020 8208 2202
Cricklewood Baptist Church, Sneyd Rd, NW2 6AP

Crickets Montessori   07811 102 085
Chatsworth Road, NW2 4BL

Ellen Louise Nursery   020 8208 2202
Gladstone Centre, Anson Road, NW2 6BH

Fordwych Nursery   020 8208 2591
107 Fordwych Road, NW2 3TL

Kidz First Nursery   020 8438 8285
Brent Terrace, Brent Cross, NW2 1LT

Living Spring Montessori   020 8830 7331
Church Hall, St Michaels Road, NW2 6XG

Mulberry House   020 8452 7340
7 Minster Road, NW2 3SD

Neasden Montessori   020 8208 1631
St Catherine's Church, Dudden Hill Lane, NW2 7RX

Pinocchio Nursery   07957 966139
St Cuthbert's Church, Fordwych Road, NW2 3TN

NW3

S Devonshire House School   **020 7435 1916**
69 Fitzjohn's Avenue, Hampstead, NW3 6PD
www.devonshirehouseschool.co.uk
Co-ed 2½-13yrs. Also see Oak Tree Nursery.

Eton Nursery Montessori School   020 7722 1532
45 Buckland Crescent, NW3 5DJ

Hampstead Activity Nursery   020 7435 0054
Christ Church, Hampstead Square, NW3 1AB

North Bridge House   020 7435 9641
33 Fitzjohns Avenue, Hampstead, NW3 5JY

Oak Tree Nursery   **020 7435 1916**
2 Arkwright Road, NW3 6AE
www.devonshirehouseschool.co.uk
2½-11yrs Girls, 13yrs Boys. Part of Devonshire House School.

Octagon Nursery School   020 7586 3206
Saint Saviour's Church Hall, Eton Road, NW3 4SU

Olivers Montessori   020 7435 5898
52 Belsize Square, NW3 4HN

Peter Piper Nursery School   020 7431 7402
Kidderpore Avenue, Hampstead, NW3 7SU

Puss in Boots Nursery School   020 7281 5485
Agincourt Road, NW3 2NT

Ready Steady Go Primrose Hill   020 7586 6289
12a King Henry's Road, Primrose Hill, NW3 3RP

S South Hampstead High School   020 7794 7198
5 Netherhall Gardens, NW3 5RN

Swiss Cottage Pre-School   020 7916 7090
19 Winchester Road, NW3 3NR

Three Acres Pre-School   020 7722 3812
29-31 Parkhill Road, NW3 2YH

Village School   020 7485 4673
2 Parkhill Road, NW3 2YN

Willoughby Hall Dyslexia Centre   020 7794 3538
1 Willoughby Road, NW3 1RP

NW4

Asquith Nursery Hendon   020 8203 9020
46 Allington Road, Hendon, NW4 3DE

Hasmonean Day Nursery   020 8202 7704
8-10 Shirehall Lane, Hendon, NW4 2PD

S Hendon Preparatory School   020 8203 7727
20 Tenterden Grove, NW4 1TD

Hill Park Day Nursery   020 8201 5816
5 Sunningfields Road, Hendon, NW4 4QR

Nancy Reuben Kindergarten   020 8202 5646
48-50 Finchley Lane, Hendon, NW4 1DJ

Talpiyot Nursery   020 8202 9611
Ner Yisrael Synagogue, The Crest, NW4 2HY

The Kindergarten Nursery Schools 020 8202 5687
Christ Church, Heriot Road, Hendon, NW4 2EG

NW5

Bluebells Nursery   020 7284 3952
Lady Margaret Road, NW5 2NE

Bringing Up Baby   020 7284 3600
37 Ryland Road, NW5 3EH

Caversham Children's Centre   020 7974 3377
Vadnie Bish House, 33-43 Caversham Rd, NW5 2DR

Chaston Nursery   020 7482 0701
Chaston Place, off Grafton Terrace, NW5 4JH

Gospel Oak Nursery Centre   020 7267 4517
5 Lismore Circus, NW5 4RA

Highgate Children's Centre   020 7485 5252
53-79 Highgate Road, Kentish Town, NW5 1TL

Rooftops Nursery   020 7267 7949
Athlone Street, Kentish Town, NW5 4LN

The Dolphin Montessori School   020 7267 3994
Leighton Crescent, NW5 2QY

York Rise Nursery   020 7485 7962
York Rise, NW5 1SB

DEVONSHIRE HOUSE PREPARATORY SCHOOL
THE OAK TREE NURSERY

The Oak Tree Nursery is for children from the age of two and a half. Devonshire House is a co-educational school for children from two and a half to thirteen years of age. Parents interested in further information, or in applying for a place for a child, should contact the Admissions' Secretary.

enquiries@devonshirehouseprepschool.co.uk
www.devonshirehouseschool.co.uk
Devonshire House School, 69 Fitzjohn's Avenue, Hampstead, London NW3 6PD.
Tel: 020 7435 1916. Fax: 020 7431 4787.

NW6

Acol Nursery Centre   020 7624 2937
16 Acol Road, NW6 3AG

Active Learning Nursery   020 3031 9097
88 Compayne Gardens, NW6 3RU

Beehive Montessori   020 8969 2235
147 Chevening Road, NW6 6DZ

Bright Futures Nursery   07817 677 144
Winterleys House, Albert Road, Kilburn, NW6 5DR

S Broadhurst School   020 7328 4280
19 Greencroft Gardens, NW6 3LP

Chaston Nursery School   020 7372 2120
30-31 Palmerston Road, NW6 2JL

Happy Child Day Nursery   020 7328 8791
2 Victoria Road, NW6 6QG

Hopscotch Nursery   020 8969 9792
215A Chevening Road, NW6 6DT

Jelli Tots Nursery   020 8451 5477
Christchurch Avenue, West Hampstead, NW6 7BJ

Kilburn Grange Children's Centre 020 7974 5089
1 Palmerston Road, NW6 2JL

education

Lymington Road Montessori   07772 112299
1 Dresden Close, Hampstead, NW6 1XP

Maria Montessori School   020 7435 3646
134a Abbey Road, West Hampstead, NW6 4SN

Rainbow Montessori   020 7328 8986
13 Woodchurch Road, NW6 3PL

Rainbow Montessori Nursery   020 7328 8986
Sherriff Road, West Hampstead, NW6 2AP

Rainbow Montessori School   020 7328 8986
Church Hall, 125 Salisbury Rd, NW6 6RG

Teddies Nurseries   020 7372 3290
2 West End Lane, NW6 4NT

The Learning Tree Nursery   020 7372 7213
Quex Road, Methodist Church, NW6 4PR

Villas Day Nursery   020 7624 2130
78A Brondesbury Villas, NW6 6AD

West Hampstead Day Nursery   020 7328 4787
11 Woodchurch Road, West Hampstead, NW6 3PL

NW7

S Belmont Mill Hill Prep School   020 8906 7270
Mill Hill, NW7 4ED

Busy Bees Day Nursery Mill Hill   020 8906 9123
30 Millway, Mill Hill, NW7 3RB

Fairway Children's Centre   020 8359 3730
1 The Fairway, Mill Hill, NW7 3HS

S Grimsdell Mill Hill   020 8959 6884
Pre-Prep School
Winterstoke House, Wills Grove, NW7 1QR

S Mill Hill School   0208 959 1176
The Ridgeway, Mill Hill, NW7 1QS

S The Mount School   020 8959 3403
Milespit Hill, Mill Hill, NW7 2RX

NW8

S Abercorn School   020 7286 4785
28 Abercorn Place, St John's Wood, NW8 9XP

Al Madina Nursery School   020 7724 7971
Regents Park Mosque, 146 Park Road, NW8 7RG

S American School in London   020 7449 1200
1 Waverley Place, NW8 0NP

S Arnold House   020 7266 6982
1 Loudon Road, St John's Wood, NW8 0LH

Barrow Hill Pre-School   020 7722 5455
Allisten Road, NW8 7AT

Carlton Hill Day Nursery   **020 7641 4491**
`OUTSTANDING OFSTED 2009/10`
86 Carlton Hill, Maida Vale, NW8 0ER
www.leyf.org.uk
6mths-5yrs. 8am-6pm. 51wks. Hoping to return to work,
looking to boost your child's development - or just prepare
them for big school? Award-winning charity LEYF actively
supports lower-income families by helping to reduce the cost
to parents of high quality childcare. Ask our highly qualified &
friendly Nursery staff in Westminster and Camden about
leading childcare you can afford.

Langtry Nursery Centre   020 7624 0963
11-29 Langtry Road, NW8 0AJ

Liberal Jewish Synagogue   020 7432 1286
Nursery School
28 St Johns Wood Road, NW8 7HA

Lisson Green Community   **020 7402 8817**
Nursery
4 Lilestone Street, St John's Wood, NW8 8SU
www.leyf.org.uk
6mths-5yrs. 8.15am-6pm. 51wks.

Luton Street Community   **020 7724 7965**
Nursery
4 Lilestone Street, NW8 8RL
www.leyf.org.uk

Ready Steady Go St Johns Wood   020 7722 0007
21 Alexandra Road, St John's Wood, NW8 0DP

S St Christina's RC   020 7722 8784
Preparatory School
25 St Edmund's Terrace, NW8 7PY

S St John's Wood   020 7722 7149
Pre-Preparatory School
Lord's Roundabout, St John's Wood, NW8 9NE

St John's Wood Early Care   020 7449 6760
and Education Centre
70 Marlborough Hill, NW8 0NH

St John's Wood Synagogue   020 7286 3859
37-41 Grove End Road, NW8 9NA

The Vestry Pre-School   020 7624 2705
St Mark's Church, Abercorn Place, NW8 9YD

Toddler's Inn Nursery School   020 7586 0520
Cicely Davies Hall, Cochrane Street, NW8 7NX

NW9

Beaufort Park Early Care and   020 8732 7940
Education Centre
Heritage Avenue, NW9 5FW

Budding Learners   020 8238 9517
Kingsbury Free Church, Slough Lane, NW9 8QG

Colindale Nursery 020 8327 7816
61 Colindale Avenue, NW9 5EQ

Eton Nursery 020 8358 3632
Hyde Estate Road, The Hyde, Colindale, NW9 6JP

First Steps Daycare 07737 060632
Chandos Lodge, 243 Stag Lane, NW9 0LA

Gower House School and Nursery 020 8205 2509
Gower House, Blackbird Hill, NW9 8RR

Joel Nursery 020 8200 0189
214 Colindeep Lane, Colindale, NW9 6DF

Roe Green Nursery 020 8204 7598
Holy Innocent's Church Hall, Bacon Lane, NW9 0LT

St Andrews Nursery 020 8205 2653
St Andrew's Church Hall, Old Church Ln, NW9 8SX

S St Nicholas School 020 8205 7153
22 Salmon Street, NW9 8PN

The Kindergarten Nursery Schools 020 8202 5687
Marquin Centre, Marsh Dr, West Hendon, NW9 7QE

The Lady House Nursery 020 8905 0485
St Sebastian Church, Hay Lane, NW9 0NG

Tiny Twinkles 07984 908208
1-3 White Cross Hall, 2 Winchester Av, NW9 9SY

Twisty Tales Nursery 020 8617 0422
25 Sheaveshill Avenue, NW9 6SE

NW10

Andrew Memorial Day Nursery 020 8459 2184
Glebe Road, NW10 2JD

Christchurch Nursery School 020 8961 9250
St Albans Road, Harlesden, NW10 8UG

Happy Child Day Nursery 020 8961 3485
15 Longstone Avenue, NW10 3TY

Jubilee Clock Nursery 020 8838 0085
All Souls Church Hall, Station Road, NW10 4UJ

Kindercare Montessori 020 8838 1688
Bridge Park Sports Centre, Harrow Rd, NW10 0RG

Little Acorn Nursery 020 8451 1705
Scout House, Strode Road, Willesden, NW10 2NN

Little Angels Nursery 020 8961 4927
25-27 High Street, NW10 4NE

St Mary's Nursery 020 8459 8578
The Parish Centre, Neasden Lane, NW10 2TS

St Michael's Nursery 020 8961 6399
St Matthews Church, St Marys Road, NW10 4AU

NW11

Clowns 020 8455 7333
153 North End Road, Golders Green, NW11 7HX

Golders Green Day Nursery 020 8458 7389
212 Golders Green Rd, Golders Green, NW11 9AT

S Goldershill School 020 8455 2589
666 Finchley Road, NW11 7NT

Hellenic College Bi-Lingual 020 8455 8511
Montessori Nursery
The Riding, NW11 8HL

Hoop Lane Montessori School 020 8209 0813
31, Unitarian Church Hall, NW11 8BS

Modern Montessori 020 8769 7539
West Heath Drive, Golders Green, NW11 7QG

South postcodes - SE

Coin Street Nursery 020 7021 1600
108 Stamford Street, Southwark, SE1 9NH

Coral Day Nursery 020 7928 0597
Windmill House, Wootton Street, SE1 8LY

Kintore Way Nursery 020 7237 1894
Grange Road, SE1 3BW

Smart Start Nursery 020 7407 5592
55 Tower Bridge Road, Tower Bridge, SE1 4TL

St Patrick's Montessori School 020 7928 5557
91 Cornwall Road, SE1 8TH

Tabard Square EYC 020 7407 2068
10-12 Empire Square, Tabard Street, SE1 4NA

The Arc Childcare Centre 020 7940 8287
39 Crosby Row, SE1 3YD

SE2

Abbey Wood Nursery 020 8311 0619
Dahlia Road, Abbey Wood, SE2 0SX

Croft Day Nursery 01322 431 045
75 Woolwich, SE2 0DY

Mulberry Park Children's Centre 020 8310 0040
Boxgrove Road, Abbey Wood, SE2 9JP

Waterways Nursery 020 8311 5491
Harrow Manor Way, Abbey Wood, SE2 9XH

SE3

Blackheath Day Nursery 020 8305 2526
The Rectory Field, Charlton Road, SE3 8SR

education

S Blackheath High School   020 8852 1537
Wemyss Road, Blackheath, SE3 0TF

Blackheath Montessori Centre   020 8852 6765
Independents Road, Blackheath, SE3 9LF

S Blackheath Nursery and Prep   020 8858 0692
4 St German Place, SE3 0NJ

First Steps Nursery   020 8852 1233
1 Pond Road, Blackheath, SE3 9JL

Greenwich Steiner School   020 8691 9823
Kirkside Road, Greenwich, SE3 7SQ

Kids & Co Nursery   020 8858 6222
41 Westcombe Park Road, Blackheath, SE3 7RE

Lingfield Day Nursery   020 8858 1388
37 Kidbrooke Grove, SE3 0LJ

Lollipops Childcare   020 8305 2014
Orchard House, 69 Charlton Rd, Charlton, SE3 3TH

S Pointers School   020 8293 1331
19 Stratheden Road, Blackheath, SE3 7TH

The Park Nursery   07775 911 601
Vicarage Avenue, St John's Park, SE3 7JT

SE4

Catherine House Day Nursery   020 8692 5015
71 Tressillian Road, Brockley, SE4 1YA

Chelwood Nursery School   020 7639 2514
Chelwood Walk, St Norbert Rd, Brockley, SE4 2QQ

Cherry Li Nursery   020 8691 0497
40 Tyrwhitt Road, Brockley, SE4 1QG

Early Bloomers Pre-School   020 8694 2600
111 Endwell Road, SE4 2PE

Hillyfields Day Nursery   020 8694 1069
41 Harcourt Road, Brockley, SE4 2AJ

Ladywell Early Childhood Centre   020 8314 8275
30 Rushey Mead, Brockley, SE4 1JJ

Lillingtons' Montessori   020 8690 2184
20 Chudleigh Road, Ladywell, SE4 1JW

St Andrews Community Nursery   020 8692 5041
Brockley Road, Brockley, SE4 2SA

SE5

Butterfly Nursery   020 7358 7015
131-139 Camberwell Road, Camberwell, SE5 0HF

Camberwell Grove EYC   020 7274 7245
195e Camberwell Grove, Camberwell, SE5 8JU

Creative Minds Nursery   020 7737 0959
2 Knatchbull Road, Camberwell, SE5 9QS

King's Day Nursery   020 3299 3472
Cutcombe Road, Camberwell, SE5 9RJ

Mini Treasures Day Nursery   020 7252 4452
238 Camberwell Road, Camberwell, SE5 0ET

Ngozi Nursery   020 7701 6031
161 Benhill Road, Camberwell, SE5 7LL

Nicki Day Nursery   020 7708 2738
190 Southampton Way, Camberwell, SE5 7EU

South East Montessori   020 7737 1719
40 Ivanhoe Road, SE5 8DJ

The Nest Pre-School   020 7978 9158
Longfield Hall, 50 Knatchbull Road, SE5 9QY

SE6

ABC Day Nursery   020 8695 0882
1a Melfield Gardens, Beckenham Hill, SE6 3AH

Amimars Nursery   020 8697 5655
142 Broadfield Road, SE6 1TH

Bay Tree House Day Nursery   020 8690 5465
32 Bromley Road, SE6 2TP

Blooming Kidz   020 8695 9959
101 Ardoch Road, SE6 1SL

Pavilion Nursery   020 8698 0878
The Cricket Pavilion, Penerley Road, SE6 2LQ

Rushey Green Children's Centre   020 8314 8275
41 Rushey Green, SE6 4AS

Small Wonders Day Nursery   020 8695 6675
89 Bromley Road, SE6 2UF

S St Dunstan's College   020 8516 7200
Stanstead Road, SE6 4TY

Thornsbeach Day Nursery   020 8697 7699
10 Thornsbeach Road, SE6 1DX

SE7

Charlton Family Centre   020 8856 9906
41-43 Shirley House Drive, Charlton, SE7 7EL

Joyful Gems Day Nursery   020 8319 2007
176 Charlton Road, Charlton, SE7 7DW

Pound Park Nursery School   020 8858 1791
Pound Park Road, Charlton, SE7 8AS

Witty Day Nursery   020 8355 8464
90 Maryon Road, Charlton, SE7 8DJ

SE8

Bunny Hop Day Nursery   020 8691 7171
1 King Fisher Square, Wooton Road, SE8 5TW

Clyde Nursery School   020 8692 3653
Alverton Street, Deptford, SE8 5NH

Grace Day Nursery   020 8694 2299
3 Creekside, Deptford, SE8 4SA

Rachel McMillan Nursery School   020 8692 4041
McMillan Street, Deptford, SE8 3EH

Rainbow Nursery   020 8692 1224
44 Alverton Street, SE8

SE9

Alderwood Childrens Centre   020 8859 7968
Restons Crescent, Eltham, SE9 2JH

Avery Hill Day Nursery   020 8294 2152
41 Alderwood Road, Eltham, SE9 2LR

Elizabeth Terrace Day Nursery   020 8294 0377
18-22 Elizabeth Terrace, Eltham, SE9 5DR

S Eltham College   0208 857 1455
Grove Park Road, Mottingham, SE9 4QF

Eltham Green Nursery   020 8850 4720
Middle Park Avenue, Eltham, SE9 5EQ

Happy Child Montessori   020 8249 2453
36 Grove Park Road, Mottingham, SE9 4QA

Happy Child Montessori   020 8857 9990
35 West Park, Mottingham, SE9 4RZ

Lollipops Childcare   020 8859 5832
88 Southwood Road, New Eltham, SE9 3QT

New Eltham Day Nursery   020 8851 5057
699 Sidcup Road, New Eltham, SE9 3AQ

S St Olave's Prep School   020 8829 8930
106-110 Southwood Road, New Eltham, SE9 3QS

Willow Park Day Nursery Baby Unit   020 8850 8753
13 Glenesk Road, Eltham, SE9 1AG

Willow Park Montessori   020 88508753
19 Glenlyon Road, SE9 1AL

Zoom Nurseries   020 8331 6703
Lionel Road, Eltham, SE9 6DQ

SE10

Little Sponges Montessori   020 8469 9337
38a Hyde Vale, SE10 8QH

education

Robert Owen Early Years Centre   020 8858 0529
43 Commerell Street, SE10 0EA

Sommerville Day Nursery   020 8691 9080
Heathsire Clinic, Sparta Street, SE10 8DQ

Teddies Nurseries Greenwich   020 8858 8266
Chevening Road, SE10 0LB

SE11

Elephant & Castle Day Nursery   020 7735 6317
Longton House, Lambeth Walk, SE11 6LU

Ethelred Nursery School   020 7582 9711
10 Lollard Street, Lambeth, SE11 6UP

James Kane Day Nursery   020 7820 0054
Tyers Terrace, SE11 5LY

Kennington Park Children's Centre   020 7926 8418
Kennington Park Gardens, Kennington, SE11 4AX

Lambeth Walk Day Nursery   020 7735 6317
Longton House, Lambeth Walk, SE11 6LU

Little Starz Nursery   020 7582 8820
14 Whitehart Street, Kennings Way, Kennington,
SE11 4EP

Toad Hall Nursery School   020 7735 5087
37 St Mary's Gardens, SE11 4UF

SE12

S Colfe's Preparatory School   020 8852 0220
Horn Park Lane, Lee, SE12 8AW

Excell Learning Centre   020 8851 3122
59 St Mildreds Road, Lee, SE12 0RE

Grove Park Pre-School   020 8857 8258
353 Baring Road, Grove Park, SE12 0EE

Lingfield Day Nursery   020 8851 7800
155 Baring Road, SE12 0LA

Little Pumpkins Nursery   020 8851 2400
88 Woodyates Road, Lee, SE12 9JH

S Riverston School   020 8318 4327
63-69 Eltham Road, Lee, SE12 8UF

SE13

Baby Lambs Day Nursery   020 8244 4349
322 Lee High Road, Lewisham, SE13 5PJ

Head Start Day Nursery   020 8852 8071
83a Belmont Hill, Lewisham, SE13 5AX

Horizons Day Nursery & Pre-school   020 8318 4125
165 Hither Green Lane, Lewisham, SE13 6QF

Little Stars Nursery   020 8469 1511
56/60 Loampit Hill, Lewisham, SE13 7SX

Scallywags 11   020 8692 7772
120 Lewisham Road, SE13 7NL

Step by Step Day Nursery   020 8297 5070
Bendon House, Monument Garden, Hither Green,
SE13 6TP

Village Nursery   020 8690 6766
St Mary Centre, Ladywell Road, SE13 7HU

Zoom Nurseries   020 8852 0124
71 Beacon Road, SE13 6ED

SE14

Goldsmiths College Nursery   020 7919 7111
Lewisham Way, Lewisham, SE14 6NW

S Haberdashers' Aske's   0207 652 9500
Hatcham College
Pepys Road, New Cross, SE14 5SF

Little Gems Day Nursery   020 8692 0071
Clare Road, Brockley, SE14 6PX

Playhouse Community Nursery   020 8692 9203
Moonshot Centre, Angus St, New Cross, SE14 6LU

Stars of Hope Nursery   020 7639 1777
74 Wildgoose Drive, SE14 5LL

Stepping Stones Montessori   020 7277 6288
Nursery
Church of God of Prophecy, Kitto Road, SE14 5TW

SE15

All Nations Community Nursery   020 7639 1823
The Peckham Settlement, Goldsmiths Road,
Peckham, SE15 5TF

Bellenden Day Nursery   020 7639 4896
198 Bellenden Road, SE15 4BW

Colourbox Day Nursery   020 7277 9662
385 Ivydale Road, SE15 3ED

Goslings Day Nursery   020 7639 5261
106 Evelina Road, SE15 3HL

Little Climbers   020 7564 4597
278 Ivydale Road, Nunhead, SE15 3DF

Little Saints   020 7277 9332
St Andrews Church Hall, 185 Glengall Road, SE15
6RS

Magic Mind Nursery & Pre-School   020 7277 5956
54 Linden Grove, Nunhead, SE15 3LF

Mother Goose Nursery   020 7277 5951

34 Waveney Avenue, Nunhead, SE15 3UE

Nell Gwynn Nursery 020 7252 8265
Meeting House Lane, Peckham, SE15 2TT

Peckham Day Nursery 020 7635 5501
24 Waveney Avenue, Peckham Rye, SE15 3UE

Puddleduck Nursery 020 7252 8448
St Antony with St Silas Community Centre, Merttins Road, Nunhead, SE15 3EB

Sankofa Day Nursery 020 7277 6243
14 Sharratt Street, SE15 1NR

Villa Pre-Prep School & Nursery 020 7703 6216
54 Lyndhurst Grove, SE15 5AH

SE16

5 Steps Community Nursery 020 7237 2376
31-32 Alpine Road, Rotherhithe, SE16 2RE

New Vision Day Nursery 020 7394 0675
Manor Methodist Church, 40 Galleywall Road, Bermondsey, SE16 3PB

Scallywags Day Nursery 020 7252 3225
St Crispin's Church Hall, Southwark Park Road, SE16 2HU

Trinity Childcare 020 7231 5842
Holy Trinity Church Hall, Bryan Road, Rotherhithe, SE16 1HB

SE17

Elephant & Castle Day Nursery 020 7277 4488
15 Hampton Street, SE17 3AN

Magic Roundabout Nursery 020 7277 3643
35 Sutherland House, Sutherland Square, Kennington, SE17 3EE

St Wilfrid's Montessori Pre-School 020 7701 2800
101-105 Lorrimore Road, Kennington, SE17 3LZ

SE18

Bear Hugs Day Nursery 020 8317 8811
110 Sandy Hill Road, SE18 7BA

Cardwell Childrens Centre 020 8854 7342
118 Frances Street, Greenwich, SE18 5LP

Early Years Childcare 020 8855 3716
87 Antelope Road, Woolwich, SE18 5QG

Places for Children 020 8854 0890
130 Brookhill Road, Woolwich, SE18 6UZ

Simba Day Nursery 020 8317 0451
Artillery Place, Woolwich, SE18 4AB

SE19

Colby Road Nursery 020 8761 3482
9B Colby Road, SE19 1HA

First Step Day Nursery 020 8771 7727
11a Harold Road, SE19 3PU

Little Crystals Day Nursery 020 8771 0393
49 Maberley Road, SE19 2JE

St Mary's Family Centre 020 8766 6271
Day Nursery
Our Lady of Fidelity, 147 Central Hill, SE19 1RS

s Virgo Fidelis Prep School 020 8653 2169
Central Hill, SE19 1RS

SE20

Anerley Montessori 020 8778 2810
45 Anerley Park, SE20 8NQ

Archangels Montessori 020 8659 9009
Day Nursery
23 Genoa Road, Penge, SE20 8ES

Community Vision Nursery 020 8659 1972
Community Vision Childrens Centre, Chestnut Grove, SE20 8PD

Kentwood Nursery 020 8659 7976
Kentwood Centre, Kingsdale Road, Penge, SE20 7PR

Norris Day Nursery 020 8778 9152
1 Thornsett Road, Anerley, SE20 7XB

Station House Nursery 020 8659 9477
Station House, Station Road, Penge, SE20 7BE

Stembridge Hall Day Nursery 020 8776 9008
9a Stembridge Road, Anerley, SE20 7UE

SE21

Buds Pre-School 020 8299 2255
Marlborough Cricket Club, Cox's Walk, SE21 7EX

Clive Hall Day Nursery 020 8761 9000
52 Clive Road, West Dulwich, SE21 8BY

Ducks in Dulwich 020 8693 1538
Eller Bank, 87 College Road, Dulwich, SE21 7HH

s Dulwich College Junior School 020 8299 9248
Dulwich Common, Dulwich, SE21 7LD
www.dulwich.org.uk
Boys 8-13yrs. This is the prep school of the large Dulwich College across the road.

s Dulwich College Prep 020 8693 4341
School Nursery
8 Gallery Road, Dulwich, SE21 7AB

education

Dulwich Day Nursery   020 8761 6750
Chancellor Grove, West Dulwich, SE21 8EG

Dulwich Montessori   020 8766 0091
St Stephen's Church, College Road, Dulwich, SE21 7HN

S Dulwich Prep London   020 8670 3217
42 Alleyn Park, Dulwich, SE21 7AA

Dulwich Village Pre-school   020 8693 2402
Old Alleynian Club, Dulwich Common, SE21 7HA

Dulwich Wood Nursery School   020 7525 1192
Lyall Avenue, Dulwich, SE21 8QS

S James Allen Prep School (JAPS)   020 8693 0374
2 Dulwich Village, Dulwich, SE21 7AL

Nelly's Nursery   020 8761 4178
27 Turney Road, SE21 8LX

Nelly's Nursery   020 8761 3535
Rosendale Road, West Dulwich, SE21 8LN

S Oakfield Prep School   020 8670 4206
125-128 Thurlow Park Road, SE21 8HP

S Rosemead Preparatory School   020 8670 5865
70 Thurlow Park Road, SE21 8HZ

Rosemead Early Years   020 8670 5865
70 Thurlow Park Road, Dulwich, SE21 8HZ

Rosendale Children's Centre   020 8761 7411
Rosendale Road, West Dulwich, SE21 8LR

SE22

S Alleyn's School   020 8557 1519
Townley Road, Dulwich, SE22 8SU

Blossoms Montessori   07801 947 404
27 Dunstans Grove, East Dulwich, SE22 0HJ

Dulwich Nursery   020 7738 4007
80 Dog Kennel Hill, Dulwich, SE22 8BD

First Steps Montessori   020 8299 6897
254 Uplands Road, East Dulwich, SE22 0DN

S James Allen's School   020 8693 1181
East Dulwich Grove, SE22 8TE

Mother Goose Nursery   020 8693 9429
248 Upland Road, East Dulwich, SE22 0DN

SE23

Ackroyd Children & Family   020 8291 4933
4 Ackroyd Road, SE23 1DL

Cottage Day Nursery   020 8291 7117
St Hilda's Church Hall, Courtrai Road, SE23 1PL

Faith Montessori Nursery   020 8291 8580
262 Stanstead Road, Forest Hill, SE23 1DE

Pitta Patta Day Nursery   020 8690 4100
48 St German's Road, Forest Hill, SE23 1RX

Rose House Montessori   07968 062 942
Vancouver Road, Forest Hill, SE23 2AG

Rubadubs Nursery   020 8699 0782
17 Davids Road, Forest Hill, SE23 3EP

Seedlings Day Nursery   020 8291 3344
9/11 Firs Close, Forest Hill, SE23 1BB

SE24

2nd Step Nursery & Pre-School   020 7274 9090
St Johns Hall, Heron Road, Herne Hill, SE24 0BJ

Halfmoon Montessori Nursery   020 7326 5300
155 Half Moon Lane, SE24 9HU

S Herne Hill School   020 7274 6336
127 Herne Hill, SE24 9LY

Little Fingers Montessori Nursery   020 7274 4864
83-85 Burbage Road, Herne Hill, SE24 9HD

Ruskin House School   020 7737 4317
48 Herne Hill, Herne Hill, SE24 9QP

The Whitehouse Day Nursery   020 8671 7362
331 Norwood Road, SE24 9AH

SE25

Alpha Day Nursery   020 8656 4725
198 Woodside Green, SE25 5EW

Angel Day Nursery   020 8653 2552
237 Selhurst Road, SE25 6XP

Elizabeth Hammond Day Nursery   020 8916 1184
1 Whitehorse Lane, SE25 6RD

Mulberry Day Nursery   020 8656 4945
10 Howard Road, SE25 5BU

SE26

Cornerstone Day Nursery   020 8676 0478
2 Jews Walk, Sydenham, SE26 6PL

Crystal Day Nursery   020 8659 6417
202 Venner Road, Sydenham, SE26 5HT

Little Cherubs Nursery   020 8778 3232
2a Bell Green Lane, Lower Sydenham, SE26 5TB

S Sydenham High School   020 8768 8000
19 Westwood Hill, Sydenham, SE26 6DL

education

SE27

Dunelm Grove Pre-School   020 8670 2498
23 Dunelm Grove, SE27 9JP

Elmwood Children's Centre   020 7926 8063/64
8 Barston Road, SE27 9HE

Little Starz Children's Centre   020 8761 9020
18 Benton's Lane, SE27 9UD

Nelly's Nursery   020 8761 0770
43 Lancaster Avenue, SE27 9EL

Norwood Manor Nursery   020 8766 0246
48 Chapel Road, SE27 0UR

One World Nursery   020 8761 3308
11 Thurlby Road, SE27 0RL

Teddies Nurseries   020 8761 8827
Gipsy Road Baptist Church, SE27 9RB

SE28

Triangle Day Nursery   020 8312 9456
10 Kellner Road, West Thamesmead, SE28 0AX

South West postcodes

SW1P

Just Learning Day Nursery   020 7222 4459
84a Horseferry Road, SW1P 2AD

Marsham Street Children's Centre   020 7834 8679
121 Marsham Street, Victoria, SW1P 4LX
www.leyf.org.uk
6mths-5yrs. 8am-6pm. 51wks. Hoping to return to work, looking to boost your child's development - or just prepare them for big school..? Award-winning charity WCS actively supports lower-income families by helping to reduce the cost of high quality childcare. Ask our highly qualified & friendly staff about quality childcare you can afford. Nurseries located in Westminster and Camden.

The Little House   020 7592 0195
Napier Hall, 1 Hide Place, Vincent Sq, SW1P 4NJ

S Westminster Abbey Choir School   020 7222 6151
Dean's Yard, Westminster, SW1P 3NY

S Westminster Cathedral Choir School   020 7798 9081
Ambrosden Avenue, Westminster, SW1P 1QH

S Westminster Under School   020 7821 5788
27 Vincent Square, Victoria, SW1P 2NN

SW1V

Pimlico Nursery   020 7931 7978
St James the Less, Moreton Street, SW1V 2PT

Abbots Manor Community Nursery   020 7834 6033
Sutherland Street, Westminster, SW1V 4JP
www.leyf.org.uk
3mths-5yrs. 8.15am-6pm. 51wks. Hoping to return to work, looking to boost your child's development - or just prepare them for big school? Award-winning charity LEYF actively supports lower-income families by helping to reduce the cost to parents of high quality childcare. Ask our highly qualified & friendly Nursery staff in Westminster and Camden about leading childcare you can afford.

Bessborough Nursery   020 7641 6387
1 Bessborough Street, Pimlico, SW1V 2JD
www.leyf.org.uk
6mths-5yrs. 8am-6pm. 51wks.

S Eaton Square Schools   020 7931 9469
79 Eccleston Square, SW1V 1PP
28 & 30 Ecclestone Street, SW1W 9PY
29 Belgrave Road, SW1V 1RB
www.eatonsquareschool.com
Eaton Square School is one of the few co-educational day schools in CentralLondon offering education from 2 to 13 years. With five locations the School offers nursery education (2Ω-4yrs) through Pre-Prep (4-6yrs) to Preparatory (6-13yrs). With small classes and focused teaching the school embraces an extensive curriculum.

Eaton Square Nursery School, Pimlico   020 7931 9469
32a Lupus Street, Pimlico, SW1V 3DZ
www.eatonsquareschool.com
2½-5yrs. 8am-12pm. Term time. They also offer an afterschool club and holiday care. Part of Eaton Square Schools.

Moreton Day Nursery   020 7233 8979
31 Moreton Street, SW1V 2PA

Moreton Day Nursery   020 7821 1979
18 Churton Street, SW1V 2NZ

The Angel Community Nursery   020 7282 1922
St Gabriel, Churchill Gardens, SW1V 3AG
www.leyf.org.uk
6mths-5yrs. 8.15am-5.45pm. 51wks.

SW1W

Eaton House: Belgravia   020 7924 6000
3-5 Eaton Gate, Belgravia, London, SW1W 9BA
www.eatonhouseschools.com
Boys 4-8yrs.

Eaton Square Nursery School, Belgravia   020 7931 9469
28/30 Eccleston Street, Belgravia, SW1W 9PY
www.eatonsquareschool.com
2½-5yrs. 8am-4pm. Term time. Part of Eaton Square Schools.

education

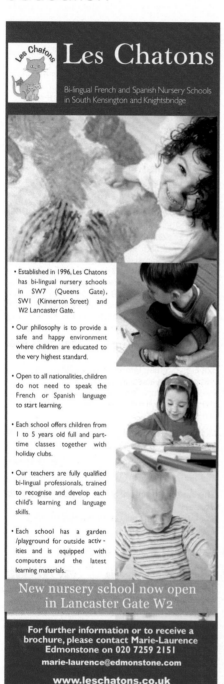

S Francis Holland School   020 7730 2971
39 Graham Terrace, SW1W 8JF

Kidsunlimited   0845 365 2929
30 Gatliff Road, SW1W 8QT

Miss Daisy's Nursery Belgravia   020 7730 5797
Ebury Square, Belgravia, SW1W 9SU

**The Knightsbridge   020 7371 2306
Kindergarten**
St Peter's Church, 119 Eaton Square,
Knightsbridge, SW1W 9AL
2-5yrs. 9am-12pm and 1-3.30pm Termtime. They also run a Wednesday morning toddler group (0-2 years) from 9am-12pm.

Thomas's Kindergarten, Pimlico   020 7730 3596
14 Ranelagh Grove, Pimlico, SW1W 8PD

Young England Kindergarten   020 7834 3171
St Saviour's Hall, St George's Square, SW1V 3QW

Dolphins Nursery   020 7581 5044
67 Pont Street, SW1X 0BD

S Hill House School   020 7584 1331
17 Hans Place, SW1X 0EP

S Knightsbridge School   020 7590 9000
67 Pont Street, Knightsbridge, SW1X 0BD

S More House School   020 7235 2855
22-24 Pont Street, Knightsbridge, SW1X 0AA

S Sussex House   020 7584 1741
68 Cadogan Square, Chelsea, SW1X 0EA

**The Bi-Lingual Belgravia   020 7259 2151
Nursery School**
77-79 Kinnerton Street, SW1X 0ED
www.thefrenchnurseryschool.com
Bi-lingual (English/French) nursery school. 2-5yrs plus a toddler group from 1-2yrs. Sessions are from 9am-12pm. Termtime plus an afternoon club (French or Spanish) all year round.

SW2

Cherubins Day Nursery   020 8671 3256
48 Palace Rd, SW2 3NJ

Lily's Day Nursery   020 8674 8678
Brixton Hill Methodist Church, Elm Park, SW2 2TX

Mini Stars Day Nursery   020 8678 8600
St Margaret's Church, Barcombe Avenue
Streatham Hill, SW2 3HH
www.ministarsltd.com
6mths-5yrs. 8am-6pm. 50wks.

Oak Tree Day Nursery   020 8674 4844
58 Blairderry Road, SW2 4SB

EATON SQUARE SCHOOL

Eaton Square School is an independent, coeducational Nursery, Pre-Preparatory and Preparatory school in the heart of central London

'Every child, every single child, has the capacity to excel'

79 Eccleston Square, London SW1V 1PP
Tel 020 7931 9469 • Fax 020 7828 0164
admissions@eatonsquareschool.com
www.eatonsquareschool.com

Eaton Square Private Schools Limited. Company number 4589393

S Streatham & Clapham High School   020 8674 6912
Wavertree Road, Streatham, SW2 3SR

Streatham Montessori Nursery   020 8674 2208
66 Blairderry Road, SW2 4SB

The Park Kindergarten   **01622 833331**
Telford Park Tennis Club, 35a Killieser Avenue SW2 4NX
2-5yrs. Term time only.

Tinytots Daycare Nursery   020 8671 2220
3 Coburg Crescent, Off Palace Road, SW2 3HS

Holmewood Nursery School   020 8674 3440
66 Upper Tulse Hill, SW2 2RW

SW3

S Cameron House   020 7352 4040
4 The Vale, SW3 6AH

Chelsea Open Air Nursery School   020 7352 8374
51 Glebe Place, Chelsea, SW3 5JE

S Garden House School   020 7730 1652
Turks Row, Chelsea, SW3 4TW

S Hampshire School   020 7352 7077
15 Manresa Road, Chelsea, SW3 6NB

Miss Daisy's Nursery Chelsea   020 7730 5797
St Luke's Church Crypt, Sydney Street, SW3 6NH

Violet Melchett Children's Centre   020 7352 1512
30 Flood Street, SW3 5RR

SW4

Anglo Spanish Nursery School   020 7622 5599
152 Clapham Manor Street, Clapham, SW4 6BX

Ark on the Park Nursery   020 8409 0109
8 Vermont Road, SW4

Baby Room Nursery   020 7498 9450
18 Old Town, Clapham, SW4 0LB

Clapham Manor Children's Centre   020 7627 9917
16 Belmont Close, Clapham, SW4 6AT

Clapham & Clapham Park Montessori   **020 7498 8324**
St Paul's Church Hall, Rectory Grove, SW4 0DX
The Contact Centre, 60 Hambalt Road, Clapham SW4 9EH
www.montessoriclapham.co.uk
Well-established nursery schools in interesting buildings with outdoor provision, offering real Montessori education. Experienced staff. Children 2½ to 6 years. Morning sessions 9.15-12.15 + afternoons to 3.45. ME(UK) registered and accredited.

education

S Eaton House: The Manor   020 7924 6000
58 Clapham Common Northside, Clapham, SW4 9RU
www.eatonhouseschools.com
Co-ed 3-4yrs.

S Eaton House: The Manor   020 7924 6000
Preparatory
58 Clapham Common Northside, Clapham, SW4 9RU
www.eatonhouseschools.com
Boys 8-13yrs.

S Eaton House: The Manor   020 7924 6000
Pre-Preparatory
58 Clapham Common Northside, Clapham, SW4 9RU
www.eatonhouseschools.com
Boys 4-8ys.

S Eaton House: The Manor   020 7924 6000
Girl's School
58 Clapham Common Northside, Clapham, SW4 9RU
www.eatonhouseschools.com
Girls 4-11yrs.

Elm Park Nursery   020 8678 1990
90 Clarence Avenue, Clapham, SW4 8JR

Magic Mind Nursery   020 8674 5544
4 Helby Road, SW4 8BU

Magic Roundabout Nursery   020 7498 1194
Binfield Road, Stockwell, SW4 6TB

Montessori Infant   07795 364 360
Community
The Contact Centre, 60 Hambalt Road, Clapham
SW4 9EH
www.montessoriclapham.co.uk
Part-time Montessori nursery for children aged 1-3 years.

S Oliver House   020 8772 1911
7 Nightingale Lane, Clapham, SW4 9AH

S Parkgate House School   020 7350 2452
80 Clapham Common Northside, SW4 9SD

Stockwell Nursery   020 7738 8606
Stockwell Methodist Church, Jeffrey's Rd, SW4 6QX

SW5

Ladybird Nursery School   020 7244 7771
St Jude's Church, 24 Collingham Road, SW5 0LX

Earl's Court Community   020 7835 1817
Nursery
65 Philbeach Gardens, Earl's Court, SW5 9EE
www.leyf.org.uk
6mths-5yrs. 8am-6pm. 51wks. Hoping to return to work, looking to boost your child's development - or just prepare them for big school? Award-winning charity LEYF actively supports lower-income families by helping to reduce the cost to parents of high quality childcare. Ask our highly qualified & friendly Nursery staff in Westminster and Camden about leading childcare you can afford.

SW6

Active Learning Nursery   020 3031 9095
Grove House, Bagleys Lane, SW6 2QB

Bobby's Playhouse   020 7384 1190
16 Lettice Street, SW6 4EH

Bumpsa Daisies   020 7736 7037
Broomhouse Lane, SW6 3DR

Cranbrook Palace Nursery   020 7381 9523
344-346 Fulham Palace Road, SW6 6HT

Dawmouse Montessori Nursery   020 7381 9385
34 Haldane Road, SW6 7EU

Dawmouse St Peters Montessori   020 7835 5731
St Peters Church Hall, St Peters Terrace, SW6 7JS

S Eridge House Prep   020 7471 4816
1 Fulham Park Road, SW6 4LJ

S Fulham Prep   020 7371 9911
47a Fulham High Street, SW6 3JJ

S Huckleberry House   020 7731 4466
163-165 New Kings Road, Fulham, SW6 4SN

Founded in 1977

L'Ecole des Petits
& L'Ecole de Battersea

Bilingual Nursery and Prep schools leading on to the French Lycee and top London schools

L'Ecole des Petits

10 minutes from Chelsea, offers a unique education to children aged 3-6 years.

- From 3-6 years
- *OFSTED 2009 Report:* "Outstanding school"
- Caring family environment which provides creative and structured learning from the earliest years
- Priority places at L'Ecole de Battersea

L'Ecole de Battersea

5 minutes from Chelsea, offers a unique education to children aged 3-11 years.

- From 3-11 years
- *OFSTED 2011 Report:* "Outstanding quality"
- Top quality facilities and recent total building refurbishment
- Voted one of the top 225 private schools in the country (*Tatler Education Guides 2009–2012*)

At L'Ecole des Petits and L'Ecole de Battersea our highly qualified and motivated teams of bilingual staff teach a curriculum which combines the French National Education and English Education systems.

Small class sizes enable all the children to get the individual attention they need.

As well as academic excellence the schools offer a wide range of sports (including fencing), school outings and events. There are regular dramatic productions and music is popular. The children can also join an abundance of specialist clubs.

The schools provide morning and afternoon bus travel between South Kensington, Battersea and Fulham to help parents with the school run.

L'Ecole des Petits
2 Hazlebury Road, Fulham, London SW6 2NB

L'Ecole de Battersea
Trott Street, Battersea, London SW11 3DS

TEL 020 7371 8350   admin@lecoledespetits.co.uk
www.lecoledespetits.co.uk

education

Imperial Wharf Childcare   020 7731 9130
1 Station Court, Townmead Road, SW6 2PY

S Kensington Prep   020 7731 9300
596 Fulham Road, SW6 5PA

Kiddi Caru Day Nursery   0800 028 4500
2 Piazza Buildings, Lillie Road, SW6 1TR

S L'Ecole des Petits   **020 7371 8350**
`OUTSTANDING OFSTED 2011`
2 Hazlebury Road, Fulham, SW6 2NB
www.lecoledespetits.co.uk
Founded 1977, bilingual school aged 3-6yrs. Warm and
friendly atmosphere, structured curriculum, small classes,
encourages traditional and family values. Continue at L'Ecole
de Battersea, aged 3-11yrs.

Little Lillies   07939 405 635
80 Lillie Road, SW6 1TN

Little People of Fulham   **020 7386 0006**
250a Lillie Road, Fulham, SW6 7PX
www.littlepeople.co.uk
6mths-5yrs. 8am-6pm. 51wks. 80 places. Registration
recommended 1 month in advance.

Peques I Anglo-Spanish   **020 7385 0055**
Nursery School
St John's Church, North End Road, SW6 1PB
www.peques.co.uk
We are a day nursery from three months to five years. We are
open from 8 - 6 for 50 weeks per year. We are a bilingual
nursery delivering the Early Years Foundation Stage
curriculum in English and Spanish; Mandarin is included in
our curriculum and yoga/dance twice a week.

Peques II Anglo-Spanish   **020 7385 5333**
Nursery School
Fulham Baptist Church, Dawes Road, SW6 7EG
www.peques.co.uk
We are a day nursery from three months to five years. We are
open from 8 - 6 for 50 weeks per year. We are a bilingual
nursery delivering the Early Years Foundation Stage
curriculum in English and Spanish; Mandarin is included in
our curriculum and yoga/dance twice a week.

Pippa Pop-ins   020 7610 9900
233 and 165 New Kings Road, SW6 4XE

Pippa Pop-ins   020 7385 2458
430 Fulham Road, SW6 1DU

Puffins Nursery School   020 7736 7442
60 Hugon Road, SW6 3EN

S Queensmill School   020 7384 2330
Clancarty Road, Fulham, SW6 3AA

Rising Star Montessori   020 7381 3511
286 Fulham Palace Road, Fulham, SW6 6HP

S Sinclair House School   020 7736 9182

159 Munster Road, Fulham, SW6 6DA

The Little Tug Boat Day Nursery   020 7731 6648
3 Finlay Street, Fulham, SW6 6HE

The Roche Nursery School   020 7731 8788
70 Fulham High Street, Fulham, SW6 3LG

The Studio Day Nursery   **020 7736 9256**
93 Moore Park Road, Fulham, SW6 2DA
The Studio Day Nursery offers excellent all year round care
combined with strong educational programme including
special needs. Montessori and traditional methods taught by
qualified teachers. Open 52wks. Monday-Friday, 8am-7pm.

S Thomas's Fulham   020 7751 8200
Hugon Road, Fulham, SW6 3ES

Zebedee Nursery School   020 7371 9224
Sullivan Hall, Parsons Green, SW6 4TN

SW7

Eaton House: The Vale   **020 7924 6000**
2 Elvaston Place, South Kensington, SW7 5QH
www.eatonhouseschools.com
Co-ed 3-4yrs.

S Eaton House: The Vale   **020 7924 6000**
2 Elvaston Place, South Kensington, SW7 5QH
www.eatonhouseschools.com
Co-ed 4-11yrs.

Eaton Square Nursery   **020 7931 9469**
School, Knightsbridge
Rutland Gardens, London SW7 1BX
www.eatonsquareschool.com
2½-5yrs. 8am-4pm. Term time. Part of Eaton Square
Schools.

S Falkner House Girls School   020 7373 4501
19 Brechin Place, Knightsbridge, SW7 4QB

S Glendower Preparatory School   020 7370 1927
87 Queen's Gate, South Kensington, SW7 5JX

S Lycée Francais   020 7584 6322
35 Cromwell Road, South Kensington, SW7 2DG

Pooh Corner Kindergarten   **01622 833 331**
St Stephens Church Hall, 48 Emperor's Gate,
London, SW7 4HJ
www.thekindergartens.com
2-5yrs. Term time only.

Queensbury Nursery   **020 7581 0200**
24 Queensbury Place, South Kensington, SW7 2DS
www.queensberrynursery.com
Queensberry Nursery is just 2 mins walk from South
Kensington station. We are open 8am-6pm, 46 weeks per
year and take children from 3mths-5yrs. We are also included
in the NEG Scheme for 3 and 4 year olds.

THE STUDIO DAY NURSERY

"Excellent nursery offering good all-round care, combined with a strong educational programme."
The Good Nursery Guide

A happy stimulating environment for boys and girls aged 2–5 years.
Open all year round Monday to Friday 8am to 7pm.
• **Morning Sessions • Afternoon Sessions • All Day Sessions**
Montessori and traditional teaching methods.
020 7736 9256
Principal and Owner: Jennifer M. R. Williams.
OFSTED Inspected. Early Years Grant available.

RAVENSTONE

PREPARATORY SCHOOL AND NURSERY

A fully co-educational school with a broad range of after-school clubs.
Located close to the parks and museums of South Kensington.

24 ELVASTON PLACE, LONDON SW7 5NL.
FOR FURTHER INFORMATION, PLEASE CALL THE REGISTRAR, MISS LUCY MANKARYOUS,
ON **(020) 7225 3131** OR EMAIL **registrar@ravenstoneschoolslondon.com**

education

S Queen's Gate School 020 7589 3587
133 Queen's Gate, SW7 5LE

Ravenstone Preparatory **020 7225 3131**
School & Nursery
24 Elvaston Place, SW7 5NL
www.ravenstoneschoolslondon.com
From 'Rising 3'. Traditional prep school; wide variety of after
school clubs.

S St Nicholas Preparatory School 020 7225 1277
23 Prince's Gate, SW7 1PT

S St Philip's School 020 7373 3944
6 Wetherby Place, South Kensington, SW7 4NE

The French Nursery School **020 7259 2151**
65-67 Queen's Gate, SW7 5JS
www.thefrenchnurseryschool.com
2-5yrs plus a toddler group from 1-2yrs. 9am-12pm and
1.30-4.30pm. Termtime.

The Willcocks Nursery School 020 7937 2027
Holy Trinity Church, Prince Consort Rd, SW7 2BA

SW8

Bringing Up Baby: 020 7498 3165
3 Peardon Street, Clapham, SW8 3BW

Heath Road Day Nursery 020 7498 9324
119 Heath Road, Lambeth, SW8 3BB

S Newton Prep Preparatory School 020 7720 4091
149 Battersea Park Road, SW8 4BX

Oval Montessori Nursery 020 7735 4816
Stanley Close, SW8 1LA

The Willow Nursery School 020 7498 0319
823-825 Wandsworth Road, SW8 3JL

SW9

Bunnies on the Green 020 7738 4795
60 Stockwell Road, Stockwell, SW9 9JQ

Ferndale Road Day Nursery 020 7733 9779
Ferndale Road, SW9 8AZ

Ladybird Nursery 020 7924 9505
9 Knowle Close, SW9 0TQ

Little Angels Nursery School 020 7274 8333
50 Gresham Road, Brixton, SW9 7NL

St Monica's Nursery 020 7582 0840
83-87 Clapham Road, SW9 0HY

Tia Ana's Nursery 07540 366 935
29 Rhodesia Road, Stockwell, SW9 9DT

Wiltshire Nursery 020 7274 4446
85 Wiltshire Road, SW9 7NZ

SW10

Chelsea Pre-Prep School 020 7352 4856
43 Park Walk, Chelsea, SW10 0AU

Eaton Square Nursery **020 7931 9469**
School, Chelsea
262 Fulham Road, Chelsea, SW10 9EL
www.eatonsquareschool.com
2½-5yrs. 9.15am-4pm. Term time. Part of Eaton Square
Schools.

Home From Home **020 7352 2630**
Cathcart Road, Chelsea, SW10 9JG
6mths-4yrs. 8am-6pm. 47wks. Full or part-time quality
childcare.

Paint Pots Montessori School 020 7376 5780
Chelsea Community Church, Edith Gr, SW10 0LB

S Paint Pots Picasso House Prep 0845 434 411
Slaidburn Street, Chelsea, SW10 0JP

S Redcliffe School 020 7352 9247
47 Redcliffe Gardens, SW10 9JH

Tadpoles Nursery School 020 7352 9757
Park Walk Play Centre, Park Walk, SW10 0AY

"OUTSTANDING"*

- Montessori education

- Open 8am – 6pm
  (50 weeks per annum)

- Extra curricular activities
  including French, Ballet,
  Baby Massage Football
  Coaching, Swimming &
  Gymnastics

Call:

Fulham
020 7386 0006

or

Shepherds Bush
020 8749 2877

www.littlepeople.co.uk

Ofsted
Outstanding
2008|2009

*26/03/09

Little People

DAY NURSERIES
Taking care of Little People since 1978

education

Home from Home
Cathcart Road, SW10

• Personal Homely Childcare
• In a fun interactive learning environment
• Giving complete peace of mind to
  both busy and working parents

8am–6pm Monday – Friday
OFSTED Inspected. From 6 months old

Tel: 0207 352 2630

SW11

S L'Ecole de Battersea   **020 7371 8350**
`OUTSTANDING OFSTED 2011`
Trott Street, Battersea, SW11 3DS
www.lecoledespetits.co.uk
Bilingual school, aged 3-11yrs. Warm and friendly
atmosphere, encourages traditional and family values. High
quality teaching with excellent facilities.

Alphabet Nursery School   020 7924 2678
Chatham Hall, Northcote Road, SW11 6DY

Baby Room Nursery   020 7924 2722
52-54 Webb's Road, SW11 5TB

Battersea Day Nursery   020 7228 4722
18-30 Latchmere Road, SW11 2DX

Bluebells Nursery School   020 7720 2010
All Saints Church, 100 Prince of Wales Drive,
Battersea, SW11 4BD

Bridge Lane Nursery   020 7978 4457
18 Bridge Lane, Battersea, SW11 3AD

S Dolphin School   **020 7924 3472**
106 Northcote Road, SW11 6QP
www.dolphinschool.org.uk
Co-ed 4-11yrs.

S Emanuel School   0208 870 4171
Battersea Rise, SW11 1HS

Lavender Hill Day Nursery   020 7924 1267
204 Lavender Hill, Clapham, SW11 6QP

Mouse Hole Kindergarten   **020 7924 5325**
`OUTSTANDING OFSTED 2008/09`
2a Mallinson Road, Battersea, SW11 1BP
www.thekindergartens.com
2-5yrs. Term time only.

Mouse House Kindergarten   **020 7924 1893**
`OUTSTANDING OFSTED 2008/09`
27 Mallinson Road, SW11 1BW

www.thekindergartens.com
2-5yrs. Term time only.

Noah's Ark Nursery School   **020 7924 3472**
St Michael's Church Hall, Cobham Close, SW11 6SP
www.dolphinschool.org.uk
Co-ed 2¹/₂-5yrs 9am-12.30pm term time. Warm friendly
nursery schools with a Christian foundation. Small classes,
strong home/school partnership, specialist teachers for
music, dance and French. Happy children, dedicated
teachers, parents who are "overwhelmingly positive" about
the nursery.

S Northcote Lodge School   020 8682 8888
26 Bolingbroke Grove, SW11 6EL

Purple Dragon Day Nursery   0844 880 3580
Alexandra Avenue, Battersea Park, SW11 4FN

The Bumble Bee   **020 7350 2970**
Nursery School
Church of the Ascension, Pountney Rd, SW11 5TU
www.thekindergartens.com
2-5yrs. Term time only.

The Marmalade Cat   020 7228 1957
1 Altenburg Gardens, Clapham, SW11 1JH

The Park Kindergarten   **01622 833 331**
`OUTSTANDING OFSTED 2008/09`
St Saviours Church Hall, 351 Battersea Park Road,
Battersea, SW11 4LH
www.thekindergartens.com
2-5yrs. Term time only.

S Thomas's Battersea   020 7978 0900
28-40 Battersea High Street, Battersea, SW11 3JB

S Thomas's Clapham   020 7326 9300
Broomwood Road, Clapham, SW11 6JZ

Thomas's Kindergarten   020 7738 0400
St Mary's Church, Battersea Church Rd, SW11 3NA

SW12

Abacus Early Learning Nursery   020 8675 8093
135 Laitwood Road, Balham, SW12 9QH

Balham Nursery   020 8673 1405
36 Radbourne Road, Balham, SW12 0EF

S Broomwood Hall School   020 8682 8820
Lower School
The Vicarage, 192 Ramsden Road, Balham, SW12
8RQ

S Broomwood Hall School   020 8682 8820
Lower School
50 Nightingale Lane, Balham, SW12 8TE

S Broomwood Hall School   020 8682 8800
Upper School

THE KINDERGARTENS

The Bumble Bee Nursery School SW11
The Crescent Kindergartens SW12 & SW17
The Park Kindergarten SW11
The Park Kindergarten SW2
Pooh Corner Kindergarten SW7
Mouse House Nursery SW11
Mouse House Nursery SW18

We hope you will come and visit us to see how your
child will reach their potential academically,
socially and emotionally whilst having lots of fun
and laughter along the way.

Ballet, Music, French, Drama and Sport are all
taught by specialist staff as part of the curriculum.

Ofsted
Outstanding
2008/2009

For details please contact:
01622 833331
www.thekindergartens.com

68-74 Nightingale Lane, Balham, SW12 8NR

Clapham Park Montessori　　　07757 317 179
St Stephen's Church, Weir Road, SW12 0NU

Crescent Kindergarten III　　**01622 833 331**
OUTSTANDING OFSTED 2008/09
Grafton Tennis Club, 70a Thornton Road, SW12 0LE
www.thekindergartens.com
2-5yrs. Term time only.

Gateway House Nursery School　　020 8675 8258
St Jude's Church Hall, Heslop Road, SW12 8EG

Marmalade Caterpillar　　020 8265 5224
14a Boundaries Road, Balham, SW12 8EX

Nightingale Montessori　　020 8675 8070
St Luke's Church Hall, 194 Ramsden Road,
Balham, SW12 8RQ

Nightingales Nursery　　020 8772 6056
St Francis Xavier College, Malwood Rd, SW12 8EN

Noah's Ark Nursery School　　**020 7924 3472**
Endlesham Church Hall, 48 Endlesham Road,
SW12 8JL
www.dolphinschool.org.uk
Co-ed 2½-5yrs 9am-12.30pm term time. Warm friendly
nursery schools with a Christian foundation. Small classes,

strong home/school partnership, specialist teachers for music,
dance and French. Happy children, dedicated teachers,
parents who are "overwhelmingly positive" about the nursery.

Oaktree Nursery School　　020 8870 8441
21 Ramsden Road, SW12 8QX

Rydevale Day Nursery　　020 8673 6633
33 Little Dimmocks, Rydevale Road, SW12 9JP

Second Step Day Nursery　　020 8673 6817
60 Ravenslea Road, SW12 8RU

Sparkies Nursery　　07939 268 861
St Lukes, Thurleigh Road, Battersea, SW12 8RQ
The Weir Link Nursery　　020 8772 8597
33 Weir Road, Clapham, SW12 0NU

Wainwright Montessori School　　020 8673 8037
102 Chestnut Grove, SW12 8JJ

S Woodentops Kindergarten　　020 8674 9514
& White House Prep
24 Thornton Road, Balham, SW12 0LF

Yukon Day Nursery　　020 8675 8838
Yukon Road, Balham, SW12 9DN

education

SW13

Barnes Montessori   020 8748 2081
Barnes Sports Club, Lonsdale Road, Barnes, SW13 9QL

S Colet Court   020 8748 3461
(St Paul's Prep School)
Lonsdale Road, Barnes, SW13 9JT

Montessori Pavilion   020 8878 9695
Vine Road Recreation Ground, Barnes, SW13 0NE

Nature Kindergarten Nursery   020 8741 1155
Trinity Church Road, Barnes, SW13 8ES

S St Paul's School   0208 748 9162
Lonsdale Road, Barnes, SW13 9JT

The Ark Nursery School   020 8741 4751
Kitson Hall, Kitson Road, Lewisham, SW13 9HJ

S The Harrodian School   020 8748 6117
Lonsdale Road, SW13 9QN

SW14

Kids Inc Day Nursery   020 8876 8144
459b Upper Richmond Road West, East Sheen, SW14 7PR

S Tower House School   020 8876 3323
188 Sheen Lane, East Sheen, SW14 8LF

Working Mums Day Care   020 8392 9969
The Former Mortlake Green School, Lower Richmond Road, SW14 7HJ

SW15

Alton Community Playschool   020 8780 9100
The Putney Vale Youth Centre, Stag House, Stroud Crescent, Putney, SW15 3EJ

Beehive Nursery School   020 8780 5333
Putney Park Lane, SW15

Busy Bee Nursery School   020 8789 0132
19 Lytton Grove, Putney, SW15 2EZ

Eastwood Day Nursery & Creche   020 8788 1444
166 Roehampton Lane, Putney, SW15 4HR

Gwendolen House Nursery School   020 8704 1107
39 Gwendolen Avenue, Putney, SW15 6EP

S Hall School Wimbledon   020 8788 2370
Stroud Crescent, Putney Vale, SW15 3EQ

S Hurlingham School   0208 874 7186
122 Putney Bridge Road, Putney, SW15 2NQ

S Ibstock Place School   020 8876 9991
Clarence Lane, Roehampton, SW15 5PY

S Lion House School   020 8780 9446
The Old Methodist Hall, Gwendolen Avenue, SW15 6EH

Little Fingers Nursery   020 8874 8649
St. Stephen's Church, Manfred Road, Putney, SW15 2RS

S Merlin School   020 8788 2769
4 Carlton Drive, Putney, SW15 2BZ

Noddy's Nursery School   020 8785 9191
2 Gwendolen Avenue, Putney, SW15 6EH

S Prospect House School   020 8780 0456
75 Putney Hill, SW15 3NT

Putney Day Nursery   020 8246 5611
107-109 Norroy Road, Putney, SW15 1PH

S Putney High School   020 8788 4886
35 Putney Hill, SW15 6BH

S Putney Park School   020 8788 8316
11 Woodborough Road, SW15 6PY

Ro's Nursery   020 8788 5704
Putney Leisure Centre, SW15 1BL

Square One Nursery School   020 8788 1546
Lady North Hall, Ravenna Rd, Putney, SW15 6AW

The Roche Nursery School   020 8704 4857
42 Keswick Road, East Putney, SW15 2JE

The Schoolroom   07771 708 513
St Simon's Church Hall, Hazlewell Road, Putney, SW15 6LU

Tiggers Nursery School   020 8874 4668
87 Putney Bridge Road, SW15 2PA

SW16

Abacus Early Learning Nursery   020 8677 9117
7 Drewstead Road, Streatham, SW16 1LY

Allsorts Playgroup   020 8677 5376
Mitcham Lane Baptist Church, 230 Mithcam Lane, Streatham, SW16 6NT

Beechwood School   020 8677 8778
55 Leigham Court Road, Streatham, SW16 2NJ

S Broomwood Hall School   020 8682 8850
Pre Prep
3 Garrard's Road, Balham, SW16 1JZ

Carmena Christian Day Nursery   020 8677 8231
47 Thrale Road, Streatham, SW16 1NT

Caroline's Nursery & Montessori   020 8677 9675
School

27 Aldrington Road, Streatham, SW16 1TU

Cavendish Lodge Nursery School   020 8835 8500
52 Lewin Road, Streatham Common, SW16 6JT

Early Learners Day Nursery   020 8764 8030
162 Eardley Road, SW16 5TG

Heathfield Pre-School   020 8664 6114
39 Estreham Road, Scout Headquarters, SW16 6LS

Hyderi Nursery School   020 8696 9979
26 Estreham Road, Streatham, SW16 5PQ

Kiddi Caru Day Nursery   020 8679 4009
496 Streatham High Road, Streatham, SW16 3QB

Lewin Pre-School   020 8677 9450
Streatham Baptist Church Hall, Natal Road,
Streatham, SW16

Modern Montessori International   020 8769 7539
(MMI) Pre-school
MMI House, 142 Mitcham Lane, Streatham, SW16 6NS

Monti's Day Nursery   020 8764 4115
6 Lilian Road, SW16 5HN

Streatham Vale   020 8764 5092
Holy Redeemer Church Hall, Churchmore Road,

Streatham Vale, SW16

Teddies Nurseries Streatham   020 8835 9898
113 Blegborough Road, SW16 6DL

S **Waldorf School of South-**   020 8769 6587
West London
16-18 Abbotswood Road, Streatham, SW16 1AP

SW17
....

S **Bertrum House School**   020 8767 4051
Pre-prep & Nursery
290 Balham High Road, SW17 7AL

Blackshaw Nursery   020 8672 4789
Blackshaw Road, Tooting, SW17 0QT

Crescent Kindergarten I   **01622 833 331**
OUTSTANDING OFSTED 2008/09
Flat 1, 10 Trinity Crescent, SW17 7AE
www.thekindergartens.com
2-5yrs. Term time only.

Crescent Kindergarten II   **01622 833 331**
OUTSTANDING OFSTED 2008/09
Holy Trinity Church Hall, 74 Trinity Road, SW17 7SQ
www.thekindergartens.com
2-5yrs. Term time only.

Need to Know: be a successful applicant

Prep-Prep entry tips to get your child into London's best independent schools.

- Many schools still accept pupils who are first to sign up so put your child's name down for the school you want as soon as you can after the birth.

- Don't get a tutor. It does no good at 2 or 3 years and looks bad to the school.

- Work on social skills. A 4+ assessment by the school will pick up on children who are interested, engaged, attentive and well behaved.

- Don't hot-house. A four year old doesn't have to be able to read or do maths. Instead a child who has been encouraged to enjoy discovering new things will shine out.

- Don't push. If your child is quiet, as long as he or she is engaged and shows an eagerness to be inspired, a show-off personality is not necessary.

- Who's the best escort? If daddy or nanny usually takes your child to nursery, perhaps they are the best person to drop your child for a session at the Prep-school, otherwise you could have a tearful scene when mummy has to leave.

- Be nice! Be interested and enthusiastic but don't oversell your child or end up being aggressive with the school. Relax and be yourselves, showing that you're ready to support how they do things, and that's why you want your child to go to their school.

education

Eveline Day Nursery School 020 8672 0501
1 Chillerton Road, SW17 9BE

Eveline Day Nursery School 020 8672 7549
30 Ritherdon Road, Tooting, SW17 8QD

S Eveline Day School 020 8672 4673
207 Balham High Road, Balham, SW17 7AE

S Finton House School 020 8682 0921
169-171 Trinity Road, Wandsworth, SW17 7HL

Looking Glass Day Nursery 020 8767 2901
75 Macmillan Way, Tooting Bec, SW17 6AT

Red Balloon Nursery School 020 8672 4711
St Mary Magdalene Church, Trinity Road, Tooting,
SW17 7SD

St Mary's Summerstown 020 8947 7359
Montessori Nursery School
46 Wimbledon Road, SW17 0UQ

Teddies Nurseries Balham 020 8672 4809
272 Balham High Road, SW17 7AJ

Toots Day Nursery 020 8767 7017
214 Totterdown Street, SW17 8TD

Wee Care Day Nursery 020 8767 5501
83 Beechcroft Road, Tooting, SW17 7BN

SW18

3-4-5 and 2 to 3 Nursery School 020 8870 8441
Fitzhugh Community Clubroom, Trinity Road, SW18
3SA

Busy Bees Day Nursery 020 8877 1135
Dolphin House, Riverside West, Smugglers Way,
Wandsworth, SW18 1DE

Eveline Day Nursery School 020 8870 0966
East Hill United Reformed Church Hall, Geraldine
Road, SW18 2NR

Kidsunlimited Nurseries 0845 365 2964
Wandsworth
4 Northside, Wandsworth Common, SW18 2SS

Melrose House Nursery School 020 8874 7769
39 Melrose Road, Wandsworth, SW18 1LX

Mouse House Montessori Nursery
13-15 Barmouth Road SW18
www.thekindergartens.com

Noah's Ark Nursery School 020 7924 3472
West Side Church Hall, Wandsworth Common
Westt side, Melody Road, SW18 2ED
www.dolphinschool.org.uk
Co-ed 2½ -5yrs 9am-12.30pm term time. Warm friendly
nursery schools with a Christian foundation. Small classes,

strong home/school partnership, specialist teachers for
music, dance and French. Happy children, dedicated
teachers, parents who are ''overwhelmingly positive'' about
the nursery.

Riverside Montessori Nursery 020 7078 4098
Ensign House, Juniper Drive, Battersea Reach,
Wandsworth, SW18 1TA

Schoolroom Two 020 8874 9305
Southfields Lawn Tennis Club, Gressenhall Road,
Southfields, SW18 1PQ

S St Michael Steiner School 020 8648 5758
5 Merton Road, Wandsworth, SW18 5ST

Sticky Fingers Montessori 020 8871 9496
Day Nursery
St John the Divine Church Hall, Garratt Lane,
Wandsworth, SW18 4EH

Teddies Nurseries Southfields 020 8870 2009
Duntshill Mill, 21 Riverdale Drive, SW18 4UR

The Colour Box Montessori 020 8874 4969
Nursery School
Magdelen Road, SW18 3NZ

The Gardens Nursery School 020 8871 9478
62 Standen Road, SW18 5TG

The Park Gardens Nursery School 020 8875 1277
Wandle Recreation Centre, Mapleton Road, SW18
4DN

S The Roche School 020 8877 0823
11 Frogmore, Wandsworth, SW18 1HW

**Wee Ones Montessori 020 8870 7729
Nursery**
4 St Ann's Crescent, Wandsworth, SW18 2LR
www.wee-ones.co.uk
Founded in 1992 Wee Ones is a traditional Montessori
Nursery School for children from 1-5 years in a quiet, cosy
environment. Sessions are 9am-12.15pm and 1.15-4.30pm
during termtime with lunch club and holiday activity clubs. Full
day care is available 7.30am-6.30pm.

Wimbledon Park Montessori 020 8944 8584
Nursery School
206 Heythorp Street, SW18 5BU

SW19

Apples and Honey, The Nursery 020 8946 4836
on the Common
1 Queensmere Road, Wimbledon, SW19 5QD

Buffer Bear Nursery 020 8944 5618
Wimbledon Traincare Depot, Durnsford Road,
SW19 8EG

Crown Kindergarten 020 8540 8820

Coronation House, Ashcombe Road, SW19 8JP

Dees Day Nursery   020 8944 0284
2 Mansel Road, SW19 4AA

Dicky Bird's Day Nursery   020 8542 7416
52a Dundonald Road, SW19 3PH

Dicky Birds Day Nursery   020 8942 5779
27 Queens Road, Wimbledon, SW19 8NW

Eveline Day Nursery School   020 8545 0699
89a Quicks Road, SW19 1EX

S Kings College School   020 8255 5300
Southside, Wimbledon Common, SW19 4TT

Little Hall Gardens Day Care   020 8947 7058
49 Durnsford Avenue, SW19 8BH

Noddy's Nursery School   020 8785 9191
Trinity Church Hall, Beaumont Road, SW19 6SP

Oak Tree Pre-School   020 8715 1115
St. Marys Church, 30 St Mary's Road, Wimbledon, SW19 7BP

Playdays Nurseries   **020 8944 8959**
100 Wimbledon Hill Road, Wimbledon, SW19 7PB
www.playdaysnurseries.co.uk
3mths-5yrs. 8am-6pm. 51wks. Wrap around before/after school facility and holiday clubs are also available.

Playdays Nurseries   **020 8946 8139**
58 Queens Road, Wimbledon, SW19 8LR
www.playdaysnurseries.co.uk
3mths-5yrs. 8am-6pm. 51wks. Wrap around before/after school facility and holiday clubs are also available.

St Marks Montessori Nursery   07956 346 938
School
St Marks Church, St Marks Place, Wimbledon, SW19 7ND

St Paul's Playgroup   020 8788 7734
23 Inner Park Road, Wimbledon, SW19 6ED

Sunnyside Nursery   020 8337 0887
192 Merton Road, SW19 1EG

The Castle Kindergarten   020 8544 0089
20 Henfield Road, Wimbledon, SW19 3HU

S The Study Preparatory School   020 8947 6969
Wilberforce House, Camp Road, Wimbledon, SW19 4UN

S Willington Preparatory School   020 8944 7020
Worcester Road, Wimbledon, SW19 7QQ

S Wimbledon High School   020 8971 0902
(Junior School)
Mansel Road, SW19 4AB

SW20

Dicky Birds Pre-School Nursery   020 8942 5779
86 Pepys Road, Raynes Park, SW20 8PF

Eveline Day Nursery Schools   020 8672 7549
Grand Drive, Raynes Park, SW20 9NA

Lollypops Nursery   020 8296 3731
Nelson Hospital, Kingston Road, SW20

Modern Montessori International   020 8947 5453
(MMI) Pre-school
The Pavillion, Cottenham Park, Raynes Park, SW20 0DH

Raynes Park Day Nursery   020 8543 9005
c/o David Lloyd Leisure Club, Bushey Road, Raynes Park, SW20 8TE

Teddies Nurseries Raynes Park   020 8947 2398
St Matthews Church, 3 Spencer Road, Raynes Park, SW20 0QN

S The Rowans   020 8946 8220
19 Drax Avenue, Wimbledon, SW20 0EZ

S Ursuline Preparatory School   020 8947 0859
18 The Downs, Wimbledon, SW20 8HR

education

TW1

St Mary's Day Nursery   020 8744 1885
63 Arragon Road, Twickenham, TW1 3NG

Teddies Nurseries   020 8744 9643
3 March Road, Twickenham, TW1 1BW

Brook House Nursery   020 8892 4853
110 Cole Park Road, Twickenham, TW1 1JA

Twickenham Park Day Nursery   020 8892 0872
Cambridge Road, Twickenham, TW1 2HN

TW2

Teddies Nurseries   0800 980 3801
270 Staines Road, TW2 5AR

Chase Bridge Pre-school   020 8892 1242
Kneller Road, Twickenham, TW2 7DE

Monkey Puzzle Day Nursery   07717 504 709
All Saints Church Hall, Campbell Road, TW2 5BY

Squirrels Day Nursery   020 8893 3645
Nelson School, Nelson Road, Whitton, TW2 7BU

Tic Toc Nursery School   020 8898 4079
298-300 Staines Road, Twickenham, TW2 5AS

TW3

Asquith Nursery Hounslow   020 8570 4409
20 Montague Road, Hounslow, TW3 1LD

TW4

Places for Children   020 8570 5308
Chinchilla Drive, Hounslow, TW4 7NS

TW5

Kinderoos   020 8090 4357
239 Great West Road, TW5 0DG

Old Rectory Nursery School   020 8897 3999
Church Road, Cranford, TW5 9RY3

TW7

9 Months Nursery   020 8847 0303
30a The Grove, TW7 4JU

Buttercups Day Nursery   020 8560 4539
Isleworth Explorers Club, TW7 7EU

Ladybird Lane Day Nursery   020 8232 8839
2 Witham Road, Isleworth, TW7 4AJ

TW8

Bringing Up Baby: 020 8568 7561

Brentford Day Nursery
Half Acre, Brentford, South Middlesex, TW8 8BH
www.bringingupbaby.co.uk
A day nursery for 42 children aged 3mths-5yrs. Open 8am-6.15pm. 50 wks.

Buttercups Day Nursery   020 8568 4355
The Garden House, Syon Park, TW8 8JF

The Little School Daycare   020 8568 4447
44 Boston Park Road, TW8 9JF

TW9

S Kew College   **020 8940 2039**
24-26 Cumberland Road, Kew, TW9 3HQ
www.kewcollege.com
Kew College is a small independent co-educational school for children aged 3-11 years. Our school is described as traditional, yet imaginative and the atmosphere is happy, lively and exciting with a team of enthusiastic, caring and dedicated staff to help fulfil each child's potential. We achieve excellent results for 11+ exams including many scholarships.

Kew Day Nursery   020 8878 9430
Mortlake Road, Kew, TW9 4ES

Grena Road Children's Nursery   020 8334 8720
Grena Road, Richmond, TW9 1XS

TW10

Richmond Day Nursery   020 8332 2085
Marshgate School, Queens Road, TW10 6HY

Ham Nursery School   020 8332 2445
Ham Day Centre, Woodville Road, Ham, TW10 7QW

Maria Grey Nursery School   020 8940 4350
Field House, 18a Friars Stile Road, TW10 6NE

St Elizabeth's Nursery   020 8940 3015
Grove Road, Richmond, TW10 6HN

TW11

Teddington Day Nursery   020 8943 4330
16 Cedar Road, TW11 9AL

Buttons Day Nursery   020 8943 2600
8 Langham Road, TW11 9HQ

TW12

Buttons Day Nursery School   0870 345 9571
51 High Street, TW12 2SX

Greenacres Day Nursery   020 8941 8608
143b High Street, TW12 1NJ

Hollygrove Nursery School   020 8941 1022
The Scout Hall, South Road, TW12 3PE

education

TW13

Once Upon a Time Nursery 020 8751 5810
Blair Atholl, Ashfield Avenue, Feltham, TW13 5BB

Pied Piper Nursery 020 8890 7433
Snakey Lane, Hanworth, TW13 7NB

St George's Day Nursery 020 8831 9980
St George's Church Hall, Feltham, TW13 7QF

TW14

Little Dreams Day Nursery 020 8707 3984
55 Dudley Road, Feltham, TW14 8EJ

TW17

First Learning Nursery 01932 260 600
50 Sheep Walk, TW17 0AJ

Playtime Nursery 01932 246 747
Miles House, Govett Avenue, TW17 8AG

Toad Hall Nursery 01932 572 525
Studios Road, TW17 0QD

TW18

Knowle Green Day Nursery 01784 464 141
Knowle Green, TW18 1AJ

Springtime Nursery 01784 464 316
Thorpe Road, TW18 3HD

St Peter's Nursery School 01784 455 518
Laleham Road, TW18 2DX

Middlesex postcodes (North of M4)

UB1

Grove House Children's Centre 020 85710878
School Passage, North Road, Southall, UB1 2JG

Snowflakes Day Nursery 020 8571 6378
100 Carlyle Avenue, Southall, UB1 2BL

UB2

Nursery on the Green 020 8574 2667
Thorncliffe Road, Southall, UB2 5RN

Pride & Joy Day Nursery 020 8574 2040
Windmill Lane, Osterley, UB2 4NE

St Mary's Day Nursery 020 8574 7402
Norwood Green Road, Southall, UB2 4LA

Toad Hall Nursery 020 8571 6867
Comer Crescent, off Windmill Ave, Southall, UB2 4XD

UB3

Kiddiecare Nursery 020 8813 6000

The Pavillion, 143 Church Road, Hayes, UB3 2LE

MacMillan Nursery School 020 8573 4427
Judge Heath Lane, Hayes, UB3 2PB

Tiny Gems 020 8569 2327
Chrischurch, Waltham Avenue, Hayes, UB3 1TF

UB4

Hungry Caterpillar Day Nursery 020 8842 3003
Ditchfield Road, Yeading, UB4 9BH

Twinkle Tots 020 8561 7272
70 Brookside Road, Hayes, UB4 0PL

Willowtree Marina Day Nursery 020 8841 6555
West Quay Drive, Yealding, UB4 9TB

UB5

Hungry Caterpillar 01895 678 682
Rowdell Road, Northolt, UB5 6AG

Medcliffe Community Nursery 020 8841 1289
41 Woburn Tower, Broomcroft Avenue, UB5 6HT

Pride and Joy Day Nursery 020 8842 4244
Scout Hut, Eskdale Avenue, Northolt, UB5 5DJ

UB6

Busy Bees Day Nursery 020 8810 4207
34-38 Bideford Avenue, Perivale, UB6 8DF

Fairytale Day Nursery 020 8575 6301
Greenford Hall, Ruislip Road, Greenford, UB6 9QN

Busy Bees Day Nursery 020 8422 0122
Greenford Road, Sudbury Hill, Greenford, UB6 0HU

UB7

Bizzy Kids Day Nursery 01895 439 357
Cherry Lane, West Drayton, UB7 9DL

Buffer Bear at Heathrow 020 8759 5457
Inglenook, Sipson Lane, Sipson, Uxbridge, UB7 0JG

Heathrow Day Nursery 020 8754 0659
High Street, Harmondsworth, UB7 0AQ

Littlebrook Nursery 01753 686 029
501 Bath Road, Heathrow Airport, Uxbridge, UB7 0EN

UB8

Once upon a Time Day Nursery 01895 256 335
150 York Road, Uxbridge, UB8 1QW

Premier Nursery 01895 234 455
St John's Road, Uxbridge, UB8 2UR

Young Ones 01895 274 206
2 Gatting Way, Uxbridge, UB8 1ES

education

Childlink Learning Centre   01895 822 129
Hill End Road, Harefield, Uxbridge, UB9 6LQ

Harefield Day Nursery   01895 828 898
Harefield Hospital, Hill End Road, Harefield, UB9 6JH

UB10

Growing Tree Nursery   01895 622 223
Pentland Way, Ickenham, Uxbridge, UB10 8TF

UB11

Busy Bees Day Nursery   020 8573 5723
4 Ironbridge Road, Stockley Park West, UB11 1BF

West postcodes - W1

Beginnings- The Early Childhood   020 7723 0330
Centre
West London Synagogue, 33 Seymour Place, W1H
5AU

Great Beginnings Montessori   020 7258 1066
School
37-39 Brendan Street, Mayfair, W1H 5HD

S Wetherby Preparatory School   020 7535 3520
Bryanston Square, Marylebone, W1H 2EA

Fitzrovia Community Nursery   **020 7580 7632**
54A Whitefield Street, W1T 4ER
www.leyf.org.uk
6mths-5yrs. 8.15am-5.45pm. Hoping to return to work,
looking to boost your child's development - or just prepare
them for big school? Award-winning charity LEYF actively
supports lower-income families by helping to reduce the cost
to parents of high quality childcare. Ask our highly qualified &
friendly Nursery staff in Westminster and Camden about
leading childcare you can afford.

Marylebone Village Nursery   020 7935 2441
Schoo
St James Church Hall, 22 George Street,
Marylebone, W1U 3QY

Holcroft Community Nursery   **020 7636 0419**
10 Carburton Street, W1W 5AL
www.leyf.org.uk
6mths-5yrs. 8.15am-6pm. 51wks.

W2

Cherry Tree Pre-Nursery School   020 8961 2081
26 Artesian Road, W2 5DN

S Connaught House School   020 7262 8830
47 Connaught Square, Bayswater, W2 2HL

Hope Montessori Nursery School   020 3075 0170
Unit 11A West End Quay, South Wharf Road, W2

Hyde Park Nursery   020 7706 8242
St James's Church, Sussex Gardens, Paddington,
W2 3UD

Linden Gardens Pre-School   020 7229 2130
73b Linden Gardens, W2 4HQ

Maria Montessori School   0207 435 3646
Bayswater
St Matthew's Parish Church, 29 St Petersburgh
Place, W2 4LA

Micky Star Children   **020 7262 5590**
58-61 St Michael, W2 1QR
www.leyf.org.uk
6mths-5yrs. 8.15am-6pm. 51wks.

Moorhouse Pre-School   020 7727 7483
Mickleton Lodge, Brunel Estate, Westbourne Park
Road, W2 5UL

Paint Pots Montessori   020 7792 0433
School Bayswater
Bayswater United Reform Church, Newton Road,
Bayswater, W2 5LS

Paint Pots Montessori   020 7402 2529
School Hyde Park
St John's Parish Hall, Hyde Park Crescent, Hyde
Park, W2 2QD

Parkview Lodge Pre-School   020 7289 6714
Parkview Lodge, Senior Street, Westminster, W2
5TE

S Pembridge Hall School   020 7229 0121
for Girls
18 Pembridge Square, W2 4EH

Queensborough Community   **020 7727 9608**
Nursery
5-8 Queensborough Terrace, W2 3TA
www.leyf.org.uk
6mths-5yrs. 8.15am-6pm. 51wks.

Ravenstone Pre Prep   **020 7262 1190**
and Nursery
The Long Garden, St George's Fields, Albion Street,
W2 2AX
www.ravenstoneschoolslondon.com
1-7yrs. 8am-6pm. 48wks.

St James's Pre-School   020 7724 8640
35 Craven Terrace, 170 Gloucester Terrace, South
Kensington, W2 3EL

The Minors Nursery School   020 7727 7253
10 Pembridge Square, W2 4ED

Toddlers & Mums Montessori 020 7243 4227
/07899 908 488
St Stephens Church, Westbourne Park Road, W2 5QT

Warwick Community Nursery 020 7641 4361
Cirencester Street, W2 5SR
www.leyf.org.uk
6mths-5yrs. 8am-6pm. 51wks.

s Wetherby School 020 7727 9581
11 Pembridge Square, W2 4ED

W3

Bizzy Lizzy Day Nursery 020 8993 1664
Priory Community Centre, Acton Lane, W3 8NY

Buffer Bear Nursery 020 8743 7249
10 Stanley Gardens, W3 7SZ

Buttercups Day Nursery 020 8749 9459
27 Old Oak Road, Acton, W3 7HN

Carousel Nursery 020 8993 2009
Acton Hill Church, Woodlands Avenue, W3 9BU

City Mission Nursery 020 8811 2540
St Aidan's Presbytery, 87-89 Old Oak Common Lane, East Acton, W3 7DD

Cybertots 020 8752 0200
1 Avenue Crescent, W3 8ES

Ealing Montessori School 020 8992 4513
St Martin's Church Hall, 5 Hale Gardens, W3 9SQ

Hungry Caterpillar Day Nursery 01895 678 682
John Perryn Primary School, Long Drive, Acton, W3 7PD

s International School of London 020 8992 5823
139 Gunnersbury Avenue, W3 8LG

s King Fahad Academy 020 8743 0131
Bromyard Avenue, W3 7HD

Melrose Nursery 0790 452 3053
St Gabriel's Church Hall, Noel Road, W3 0JE

Park Place Day Nursery 020 8993 8546
Park Place, W3 8JY

South Acton Childrens Centre 020 8992 0724
Castle Close, Acton, W3 8RX

Sunlight Community Nursery 020 8896 3809
and Resource Centre
5/11 Hanbury Road, South Acton Estate, W3 8RX

Village Montessori Nursery 020 8993 3540
All Saints Church, Bollo Bridge Road, W3 8AX

W4

Ark Montessori 020 8932 4766
Rugby Road, W4 1AT

Buttercups Day Nursery 020 8742 8368
38 Grange Road, W4 4DD

Caterpillar Montessori Nursery 020 8747 8531
St Albans Church Hall, South Parade, W4 5JU

s Chiswick and Bedford 020 8994 1804
Park Prep School
Priory House, Priory Avenue, W4 1TX

Chiswick Toddlers World 020 8995 7267
Day Nursery
St Paul's Church Hall, Pyrmont Road, W4 3NR

Devonshire Day Nursery 020 8995 9538
2 Bennett Street, Chiswick, W4 2AH

Elmwood Montessori 020 8994 8177
St Michael's Centre, Elmwood Road, W4 3DY

s Falcons School for Boys 020 8747 8393
2 Burnaby Gardens, W4 3DT

Imaginations 020 8742 1658
Methodist Church Hall, Sutton Court Road, W4 4NL

Leapfrog Day Nursery 020 8742 0011
4 Marlborough Road, Chiswick, W4 4ET

Meadows Montessori School 020 8742 1327
Dukes Meadow Community Hall, Alexandra Gardens, W4 2TD

s Orchard House School 020 8742 8544
16 Newton Grove, Chiswick, W4 1LB

Playdays Nurseries 020 8747 9599
15-19 Chiswick High Road, Chiswick, W4 2ND
www.playdaysnurseries.co.uk
3mths-5yrs. 8am-6pm. 51wks. Wrap around before/after school facility and holiday clubs are also available.

Riverside Children's Centre 020 8995 9299
Back of Cavendish School, Edensor Road, W4 2RG

s The Arts Educational School 0208 987 6600
Cone Ripman House, 14 Bath Road, W4 1LY

Tic Toc Day Nursery 020 8748 5888
11-13 Chiswick High Road, Chiswick, W4 2ND

W5

s Aston House School 020 8566 7300
1 Aston Road, Ealing, W5 2RL

Bumble Bees Day Nursery 020 8992 6263
21 Inglis Road, W5 3RJ

education

Buttercups Day Nursery   020 8840 4838
9 Florence Road, Ealing, W5 3TU

Caterpillar Day Nursery   020 8579 0833
8th Ealing Scout Hall, Popes Lane, Ealing, W5 4NB

S Clifton Lodge Prep School   020 8579 3662
8 Mattock Lane, W5 5BG

S Durston House School   **020 8991 6532**
12 Castlebar Road, W5 2DR
www.durstonhouse.org
An independent day preparatory school for boys aged 4-13, with an average class size of 16. Our aim is to provide an education that allows learning to be an adventure, and where academic excellence is balanced with a wider curriculum including performing arts and team sports.

S Falcons School for Girls   020 8992 5189
15 Gunnersbury Avenue, Ealing, W5 3XD

Happy Child Day Nursery   020 8992 0209
Woodgrange Avenue, W5 3NY

Happy Child Day Nursery   020 8567 2244
283-287 Windmill Road, W5 4DP

Happy Child Montessori   020 8566 1546
2a The Grove, Chiswick, W5 5LH

S Harvington School   020 8997 1583
20 Castlebar Road, W5 2DS

La Chouette   07557 029 255
17 The Mall, Ealing Broadway, W5 2PJ

Maria Montessori Nursery   07850 509 415
Beaufort Road, Ealing, W5 3EB

Mount Park Montessori   07946 624 370
Methodist Church Hall, Pitshanger Lane, W5 1QP

New World Montessori   020 8810 4411
Pitshanger Lane, W5 1QG

Resurrection Day Nursery   020 8998 8954
84 Gordon Road, W5 2AR

Resurrection Day Nursery   020 8810 6241
18 Carlton Road, Ealing, W5 2AW

S St Benedict's School   020 8862 2054
Ealing, W5 2XP

St Matthew's Montessori School   020 8579 2304
North Common Road, W5 2QB

W6

Bayonne Nursery School   020 7385 5366
50 Paynes Walk, W6 8PF

Beanstalk Montessori   020 8563 7508

St Peter's Church, Black Lion Lane, Hammersmith, W6 9BG

Bringing Up Baby   020 8746 1015
50 Richford Gate, 61-69 Richford Street, W6 7HZ

S Bute House School for Girls   020 7603 7381
Luxembourg Gardens, Hammersmith, W6 7EA

Jordans Nursery   020 8741 3230
Paddenswick Road, Hammersmith, W6 0UB

S Latymer Preparatory School   020 8748 0303
36 Upper Mall, W6 9TA

Mace Montessori School   020 8741 5382
30-40 Dalling Road, Hammersmith, W6 0JD

S Ravenscourt Park Prep School   020 8846 9153
16 Ravenscourt Avenue, Hammersmith, W6 0SL

Step By Step Day Nursery   020 8748 1319
1 Bridge Avenue, Hammersmith, W6 9JA

W7

Bunny Park Day Nursery   020 8567 6142
37 Manor Court Road, Hanwell Village, W7 3EJ

Buttons Nursery School   020 8840 3355
99 Oaklands Road, W7 2DT

Playhouse Day Nursery   020 8840 2851
Leighton Hall, Elthorne Park Road, W7 2JJ

W8

S Abingdon House School   0845 230 0426
4-6 Abingdon Road, Kensington, W8 6AF

S Hawkesdown House School   **020 7727 9090**
27 Edge Street, W8 7PN
www.hawkesdown.co.uk
Boys 3-8yrs. First class academic education in a kind and caring school.

Holland Park Pre-School   020 7603 2838
Stable Yard, Holland Park, W8 6LU

Iverna Gardens Montessori   020 7937 0794
Armenian Church Hall, Iverna Gardens, W8 6TP

Little Cherubs Nursery School   020 7376 4460
16a Abingdon Road, W8 6AF

Lloyd Williamson Schools   **020 8962 0345**
112 Palace Gardens Terrace, Kensington, W8 4RT
1-5yrs. 7.30am-6pm. 51wks. The Lloyd Williamson School is a friendly, family run concern with two nurseries near Portobello Road in W8 and W10. They offer a home from home environment, with dedicated staff caring for relaxed, happy and confident children.

RAVENSTONE
PRE-PREP SCHOOL
Nursery ages 1-4, Pre-Prep School ages 4-7

Ravenstone Pre-Prep school is located in its own extensive gardens seconds away from Hyde Park, near Marble Arch.
Open 48 weeks a year, 8am–6pm.
Full range of exciting holiday and after-school activities and clubs.

THE LONG GARDEN, ST GEORGE'S FIELDS, ALBION STREET, LONDON W2 2AX.
TEL (020) 7262 1190 • EMAIL admissions@ravenstoneschools.com • www.ravenstoneschools.com

---

S Thomas's Kensington   020 7937 0583
(Lower School)
39-41 Victoria Road, Kensington, W8 5RJ

S Thomas's Kensington   020 7361 6500
(Prep School)
17-19 Cottesmore Gardens, Kensington, W8 5PR

W9
....
Ashmore Pre-School   020 8968 6225
St Lukes Church Centre, Fernhead Road, W9 3EH

Little Sweethearts Montessori   020 7266 1616
St Saviour's Church Hall, Warwick Avenue, W9 2PT

Queens Park Community   **020 8968 9580**
Nursery
7 Macroom Road, W9 3HY
www.leyf.org.k
6mths-5yrs. 8.15am-6pm. 51wks. Hoping to return to work, looking to boost your child's development - or just prepare them for big school? Award-winning charity LEYF actively supports lower-income families by helping to reduce the cost to parents of high quality childcare. Ask our highly qualified & friendly Nursery staff in Westminster and Camden about leading childcare you can afford.

Windmill Montessori Nursery   020 7289 3410
62 Shirland Road, W9 2EH

HAWKESDOWN HOUSE SCHOOL

An IAPS school for boys aged 3 to 8, in Kensington, W8

For further details please contact the Admissions' Secretary.

Hawkesdown House School,
27, Edge Street, Kensington, W8 7PN.
Telephone: 020 7727 9090.
Facsimile: 020 7727 9988.
Email: admin@hawkesdown.co.uk

education

S Bassett House School 020 8969 0313
60 Bassett Road, Ladbroke Grove, W10 6JP

Dalgarno Pre-School 020 8969 1463
1 Webb Close, W10 5QB

**Katharine Bruce Community 020 7641 5835
Nursery**
Queens Park Court, Ilbert Street, W10 4QA
www.leyf.org.uk
6mths-5yrs. 8am-6pm. 51wks.

S Lloyd Williamson School 020 8962 0345
OUTSTANDING OFSTED 2010
12 Telford Road, W10 5SH
6mths-14yrs. 7.30am-6pm. 51wks. The Lloyd Williamson
School is a friendly, family run concern with two nurseries
near Portobello Road in W8 and W10. They offer a home
from home environment, with dedicated staff caring for
relaxed, happy and confident children. Nursery children
have preferential entry to the school.

New Studio Pre-School 020 8969 5805
Kelfield Mews, Kelfield Gardens, W10 6LS

Spanish Day Nursery 111 020 8960 6661
317a Portobello Road, W10 5SY

Colville Nursery Centre 020 7229 1001
4-5 Colville Square, Notting Hill, W11 2BQ
www.leyf.org.uk
6mths-5yrs. 8am-6pm. 51wks. Hoping to return to work,
looking to boost your child's development - or just prepare
them for big school? Award-winning charity LEYF actively
supports lower-income families by helping to reduce the cost
to parents of high quality childcare. Ask our highly qualified &
friendly Nursery staff in Westminster and Camden about
leading childcare you can afford.

Ilys Booker Under Five's Centre 020 7221 9031
Lower Clarendon Walk, Lancaster West Estate,
Notting Hill, W11 1TZ

Kidsunlimited Nurseries 0845 365 2918
Ladbroke Grove
34 Ladbroke Grove, Notting Hill, W11 3BQ

Ladbroke Square Montessori 020 7229 0125
School
43 Ladbroke Square, Notting Hill, W11 3ND

Maria Montessori School 0207 435 3646
Notting Hill
28 Powis Gardens, Notting Hill, W11 1JG

Miss Delaney's Nursery 020 7603 6095
St James, Norland Church, St James's Gardens,
W11 4RB

Miss Delaney's Too 020 7727 0010
St Clement's Church, 95 Sirdar Road, W11 4EQ

S Norland Place School 020 7603 9103
162 166 Holland Park Av, Notting Hill, W11 4UH

S Notting Hill Prep School 020 7221 0727
95 Lancaster Road, Notting Hill, W11 1QQ

Rolfe's Montessori School 020 7727 8300
206-208 Kensington Park Road, W11 1NR

S Southbank International 020 7229 8230
School Kensington
36-38 Kensington Park Road, Notting Hill, W11
3BU

St Peters Nursery School 020 7243 2617
59a Portobello Road, Notting Hill, W11 3DB

Strawberry Fields Nursery School 020 7727 8363
Nottinghill Community Church, Kensington Park
Road, Notting Hill, W11 2ES

S Tabernacle School 020 7602 6232
32 St Ann's Villas, Holland Park Avenue, Notting
Hill, W11 4RS

The Square School 020 7221 6004
18 Holland Park Avenue, Holland Park, W11 3QU

Acorn Pre-School 020 8740 5522
76 Braybrook Street, W12 0AP

Harmony Neighbourhood Nursery 020 8743 2089
Australia Road, W12 7PT

Ladybird Day Nursery 020 8741 3399
277 & 287 Goldhawk Road, W12 8EU

Happy Child 020 8762 9519
101 Frithville Gardens, Shepherds Bush, W12 7JQ

**Little People of 020 8749 2877
Willow Vale**
OUTSTANDING OFSTED 2008/09
9 Willow Vale, Shepherds Bush, W12 0PA
www.littlepeople.co.uk
4mths-5yrs. 8am-6pm. 51wks.

Newpark Nursery 020 8746 7944
450 Uxbridge Road, Shepherds Bush, W12 0NS

Stepping Stones Nursery School 020 8742 9103
7 Gayford Road, W12 9BY

Vanessa Nursery School 020 8743 8196
14 Cathnor Road, W12 9JA

Corner House Day Nursery

Established 1989

Specialised, professional care and education from fully qualified staff.
For children aged 3 months to 5 years

Tel: 020 8567 2806

W13

S Avenue House School   020 8998 9981
70 The Avenue, W13 8LS

Children's Corner Day Nursery   020 8840 5591
29 Hastings Road, W13 8QH
www.childrenscorner.co.uk
18mths-5yrs. 8am-6pm. 51wks.

Corner House Day Nursery   020 8567 2806
82 Lavington Road, W13 9LR
3mths-5yrs. 8am-6pm. 51wks. Expert care and education
provided by only qualified staff.

Cybertots on the Green   020 8997 3990
2a Drayton Green, West Ealing, W13 0JF

Happy Child Day Nursery   020 8566 5515
Green Man Passage (off Bayham Road), W13 0TG

Home from Home Day Nursery   020 8566 7706
St Luke's Hall, Drayton Grove, Ealing, W13 0LA

Little Angels Day Nursery   020 8566 3349
1a Dudley Gardens, W13 9LU

S Notting Hill and   020 8799 8400
Ealing High School
2 Cleveland Road, Ealing, W13 8AX

www.nhehs.gdst.net
Girls 4-18yrs. Happy, lively atmosphere and real engagement
in learning characterise the Junior Department of this popular
girls' school. Drama, music, sport, clubs and activities help
to provide an environment where your daughter will flourish.
Selective entry at 4+ (Reception) and 7+ (Year 3). Occasional
vacancies in other years. Most progress to successful senior
department at 11+.

W14

Bright Sparks Montessori School   020 7371 4697
25 Minford Gardens, W14 0AP

Holland Park Day Nursery   020 7602 9066
9 Holland Road, W14 8HJ

S Holland Park   020 7602 9266
Preparatory School
5 Holland Road, W14 8HJ
www.hpps.co.uk
Holland Park Pre-Prep School and Day Nursery. Developing
confident and contented children from birth to 8 years. See
our website on www.hpps.co.uk or ring 020 7602 9266 for a
prospectus.

Kensington Day Nursery   020 8529 6101
41a North End Road, Fulham, W14 8SZ

education

Playdays Nurseries   020 7386 9083
13 Barton Road, West Kensington, W14 9HB
www.playdaysnurseries.co.uk
3mths-5yrs. 8am-6pm. 51wks. Wrap around before/after
school facility and holiday clubs are also available.

Playdays Nurseries   020 7385 1955
45 Comeragh Road, West Kensington, W14 9HT
www.playdaysnurseries.co.uk
3mths-5yrs. 8am-6pm. 51wks. Wrap around before/after
school facility and holiday clubs are also available.

S St James Junior School   020 7348 1777
Earsby Street, Olympia, W14 8SH

Holland Park Pre-Prep School and Day Nursery

Developing confident
and contented children
from birth to 8 years.

See our web site on
www.hpps.co.uk or
ring **020 7602 9266**
for a prospectus.

Playdays Nurseries

**Open - 8.00am to 6.00pm, 51 Weeks a Year
For children aged 3 months to 5 Years**

**At Playdays we are dedicated in providing
the finest full-day care and education.
We also offer before/after school programmes
and holiday clubs, for when your child
starts school.**

West Kensington W14
13 Barton Road - Tel: 020 7386 9083
45 Comeragh Road - Tel: 020 7385 1955

Chiswick W4
15-19 Chiswick High Road - Tel: 020 8747 9599

Wimbledon SW19
100-102 Wimbledon Hill Road - Tel: 020 8944 8959
58 Queens Road - Tel: 020 8946 8139

www.playdaysnurseries.co.uk

WC

....

Collingham Gardens Nursery   020 7837 3423
Henrietta Mews, Wakefield Street, WC1N 1PH

Coram Fields Nursery   020 7833 0198
93 Guildford Street, WC1N 1DN

Mace Montessori Nursery School 020 7242 5842
38-42 Millman Street, WC1N 3EW

Thomas Coram   020 7520 0385
49 Mecklenburgh Square, WC1N 2NY

**Turtles Nursery   020 7240 8136
Covent Garden**
47 Dudley Court, 36 Endell Street, WC2H 9RF
www.turtlesdaynurserycoventgarden.co.uk
This newly refurbished nursery accommodating 30 children,
5 minutes from Covent Garden, offers parents wrap-around
care for children aged 0-5yrs. The nursery is open from
8am-6pm, but offers extended care for working parents
before and after these core hours and at weekends. A range
of exciting activities ensures each child is nurtured and
stimulated to enhance their existing skills and championing
new ones.

Do you need Private Tuition
for your children?

*Greycoat Childcare & Education
sources experienced, qualified Private Tutors
to help your child achieve their full potential.
All subjects & levels catered for,
including Common Entrance 11+ and 13+,
GCSE, A Level and more.*

 GREYCOAT
Childcare & Education

To find out more call us on 020 7233 9950
or visit us at www.greycoatchildcare.co.uk

activities

The early years should be all about play. The good news is, that by having fun they are also learning valuable life skills and even taking their first educational steps.

In the first six weeks gazing at faces and enjoying your closeness are about as sophisticated as your child's pastimes get. As the year progresses, trying new fine-motor skills out on soft toys that dangle from a playmat arch evolves into sitting up and playing peek-a-boo and then later, arranging wooden blocks. But as your child reaches his or her first birthday, crawling and perhaps even walking become the new excitement and a whole new level of stimulating fun can be introduced.

12 to 18 months

Being able to stand up is a big deal! Playing with water and sand whilst standing at trays allows your toddler to explore new sensations and observe the behaviour of different materials. Push-along toys will encourage exploring now your child can walk or at least cruise (moving around holding on to things). First words tend to start forming now, too, so silly rhyming play by you will amuse your child - sit face to face so he or she can learn from your expressions, the movement of your lips and your tone of voice. Also play ball rolling games sitting close to each other. Organising skills become more developed than first attempts, so shape sorters and other activities your toddler can sit and explore are a good choice.

18 to 24 months

Language - through stories, music group sing songs and nursery rhymes at home - continues to develop. Moving on from peek-a-boo, slap-stick rolling around together will appeal to an early sense of humour. Now your child is probably more sturdy on his or her legs, ride-on toys and the kind of first bikes he or she can skoot along on are a great idea. Also your child will now enjoy more than just the baby swings at the playground - slides, tunnels and climbing castles appeal when you're at playcentres or the park. Small hands might also enjoy basic jigsaws (ones where a half of an animal has to match another half, for example), and colouring or painting.

2 to 3 years

Skittles - knocking down easy targets with a big enough ball - and kicking a football around are great, more physical activities at this stage. Your child will enjoy creative play - drawing, cutting out shapes with safe scissors, gluing, possibly even making cakes with you. Introduce fun picture books with a joy in language - eg rhyming books by Julia Donaldson like 'A Squash and a Squeeze'. Construction toys go down well now, too.

3 to 5 years

Artistically, your child might be able to start creating pictures rather than scribbles, and by four and half be able to draw a basic self-portrait! Control of pencils gets better and following number and letter shapes might be possible. Activity clubs like early gymnastics, dancing, football and swimming are possible now, and even foreign language lessons.

toddler activities

These classes are where young children can go to experience all types of art media, materials and craft projects with something to take home at the end of the day

Artabugs   0778 959 9931
W4ArtClub, 58 Harvard Road, Chiswick, W4 4ED
www.w4artclub.com
Artabugs offer sensory art painting and making workshops as well as clean/messy parties for children aged 16 months+. Small private group activities, and adult drawing sesions also available.

Arties   07963 952 591
www.arties.co.uk
Energetic and vibrant environment that includes activities like arts and craft, as well as music and movement, for children 18 months to 4 years old. Held at Manor Drive Methodist Church, Barnet, N20 on Mon/Tue/Wed mornings and one session on Mon afternoon. There is also a Fri morning class at Christchurch, Chase Side, Enfield, and in Mill Hill at the Eversfield Center.

Art Start   07811 283 679
Araminta Scarf runs these creative art sessions for children of 18+. Paints, glitter and glue projects themed to seasons and festivals. Mondays 9.15-10.15am or 10.30-11.30am in St Peter's Hall, Portobello Road W11.

Arty Party   020 8675 7055
www.artyparty.co.uk
Arty Party runs holiday workshops and arty birthday parties for children across five locations in London: Balham, Blackheath, Clapham, Wandsworth and Wimbledon. Each session has a different theme and explores materials such as throwing clay pots, screen printing and batik. They look at all sorts of artists, countries and contemporary popular culture for inspiration.

Creative Drawing Studio   07597 169 740
www.creativedrawingstudio.com
Children's art classes in north London held after school, on Sundays, during school holidays and at half terms.

Creative Wiz Kids   020 7794 6797
www.creativewizkids.com
Art, music and movement classes for children aged 1-3 as well as holiday clubs for children aged 3-7yrs. Classes take place in Notting Hill and Hampstead.

Gymboree Play & Music
www.gymboree-uk.com
Award winning classes for 0-5 yrs. Fun for adult and child, with activities based on child development research and over 30 years of experience! Classes include pre-mobile Baby Play & Learn, Play & Learn, Music, Art & Birthday Parties. Cognitive and physical play on purpose-built equipment, and using highest quality props and instruments. Book your **FREE** trial class! Contact your local Gymboree today.

The Life Centre for Children   020 7221 4602
15 Edge Street, W8 7PN
www.thelifecentre.com
Creative classes with inspiring teachers. Morning and afternoon classes weekdays, plus holiday activities. Other classes include cookery, music, baby massage and baby yoga.

Maggie & Rose   020 7371 2200
58 Pembroke Road, W8 6NX
www.maggieandrose.com
The private family member's club Maggie & Rose specialises in cooking, music, dance, art, gardening and language classes for children aged 6mths- 8yrs. Holiday programmes also available for non-members.

Messy Hands   07951 329 447
Sureka Perera runs art and cookery classes for young children in a private room above Jakob's Cafe on Gloucester Road, London. A range of classes are on offer including: toddlers (18m+), pre school and young children's term time art and craft classes, holiday workshops, Saturday classes (3 to 8yrs). She also offers creative or cookery parties for any occasion, or simply a special play date with a few friends. Call for further details.

Paint Pots House   08456434442
www.paintpotshouse.com
Offering a range of creative art classes where children are free to explore through art and music. Creative teachers help build an environment thats fun and nurturing which helps give children more potential. Holidays classes and parties are also available. Venue at St Mary The Boltons, Church Hall, London SW10 9TB.

Ceramic cafés are definitely one of London's great offerings. Children can have great fun decorating some pottery, or you can get a memento plate of your baby's hand or foot print. They make great party venues too.

All Fired Up   020 7732 6688
34 East Dulwich Road, SE22 9AX
www.allfiredupceramics.co.uk
A great place to relax, get creative, have fun with the kids and paint your own ceramics. They run baby and toddler groups and have a café on premises serving home-made food.

Art 4 Fun   020 7794 0800
172 West End Lane, NW6 1SD
www.Art4Fun.com
Make, design and decorate ceramics, wood, glass, mosaic. Great for parties. Open Mon-Sun 10am-6pm.

Biscuit Ceramic Café   020 8853 8588
3-4 Nelson Road, Greenwich, SE10 9JB
www.biscuit-biscuit.com
Choose from a selection of ceramic cups, vases, plates and more to create your own designs. Mon-Sat, 11am-6pm. Sun 11am-5pm.

Ceramics Cafe 020 8810 4422
6 Argyle Road, West Ealing, W13 8AB
www.ceramicscafe.com
The Ceramics Cafe gives you the chance to design your own cup, vase and your baby's footprint on a plate. Open Tues-Sat 10am-6pm, Sun 11am-6pm.

Fired Treasures 020 8371 6709
143 Dollis Road, Mill Hill, NW7 1JX
www.firedtreasures.co.uk
Pottery painting, plaster painting, hand/footprints and casts lots of fun activities.

Paint the Town 020 8920 0868
13 Onslow Parade, Hampden Square, N14 5JN
www.paintthetownpottery.co.uk
Established in 2007 this pottery painting studio is for both children and adults. Workshops for children run throughout the week and there is also a body casting and cafe service as well. Open daily 10am-6pm.

Pottery Café
735 Fulham Road, SW6 5UL 020 7736 2157
332 Richmond Road, TW1 2DU 020 8744 3000
153 Northcote Road, SW11 6QB 020 7223 3388
www.pottery-cafe.com
Decorate your own pottery with your baby's hand or foot (choose from a varity of pottery shapes, including designs from Emma Bridgewater's shop next door to the Fulham branch. Open Mon 11am-6pm, Tues-Sat 10am-6pm (Thurs open until 10pm) and Sun 11am-5pm.

Sammy Duder Ceramics 0870 242 7881
67 Webbs Road, Battersea, SW11 6SD
www.sammyduder.com
This friendly studio in South-West London (just off the North-cote Road) is great for offering a specialist baby handprint and footprint service, using ceramics and clay (or even silver), as well as a range of personalised gifts and commission pieces for special occasions. Open Mon-Sat 10am-6pm, Sun 11am-6pm.

Smarty Paints 020 8772 8702
85 Nightingale Lane, SW12 8NX
www.smartypaints.co.uk
Smarty Paints is a large studio café space and a colourful place to enjoy painting ceramics. Open 10am-6pm Mon-Sat and 11am-6pm Sundays. Parties are also available.

Zebra Ceramics 020 8442 1314
110 Alexandra Park Road, N10 2AE
www.zebraceramics.co.uk
North London's specialist hand/ foot/finger print service for ceramics, clay, silver jewellery and 3D silver & bronze resin. Unique, highest quality mementos. Home visits can be arranged. Commissions taken for personalised, hand painted, beautiful christening gifts, birth plates, birthday presents, giftvouchers and more. Mon-Sat 9am-5.30pm, Sat 10am-5.30pm, Sun 10am-5pm.

> We love **Whippersnappers**. They do really funky songs and everyone is really relaxed. My little boy loves the drums where he can make as much noise as possible. We just go to the drop in on Saturday mornings and no one minds if you turn up half way through.
>
> *Emz, mother of 1, London*

clubs: private

Cupcake 020 3326 4986
11 Heathmans Road, Parsons Green, SW6 4TJ
10 Point Pleasant, Putney, SW18 1GG
www.cupcakemum.com
Cupcake Clubs are members' clubs for mums, mums-to-be and their families. Each venue offers fitness, wellbeing and support for healthy happy parenting. Membership includes access to the spa, café and crèche as well as dozens of FREE classes and seminars each week.

Maggie & Rose 020 7371 2200
58 Pembroke Road, W8 6NX
www.maggieandrose.com
The original Private Family Member's Club Maggie & Rose specialises in cooking, music, dance, art, gardening and language classes for children aged 6 months to 8 years. Holiday programmes also available.

Purple Dragon 020 7801 8688
Grosvenor Waterside, Chelsea, SW1W 8DP
www.purpledragonplay.com
A private members club for families with swimming pool, cooking activities, state of the art recording studio and indoor activities. Open Mon-Sun 10am-5pm, Sun 10am-4:30pm.

dance

Most classes from 2½-3yrs and are great for posture, co-ordination and for graceful confidence. Some children will progress to professional ballet schools, but many more will experience dance for pleasure and a cherished childhood memory.

English National Ballet 020 7376 7076
School
Carlyle Building, Hortensia Road, SW10 0QS
info@enbschool.org.uk
English National Ballet School's Saturday Ballet Classes for children aged from 3 years. ENBS Juniors offers high quality ballet classes; engaging your child's creativity and imagination in a fun learning atmosphere. For a free trial class please call 020 7376 7076.

...gton Ballet School   **01992 813 572**
Creative dance for children from 3 years progressing to classical ballet training with optional examinations. Classes held at Unity Church, 277a Upper Street, N1 2TZ.

St John's Wood Ballet School 01992 813 572
Creative dance for children from 3 years progressing to classical ballet training with optional examinations. Classes held at St Mark's Church Hall, Abercon Place, NW8.

drama

These drama groups offer a small range of activities for the 3yrs+ which are fun, confidence building, and increase co-ordination and concentration.

Allsorts Drama   **020 8969 3249**
www.allsortsdrama.com   **020 8767 5298**
Allsorts Drama for children provide after school, Saturday and holiday courses covering all aspects of drama in a fun and friendly environment developing confidence and other life skills. Ages 4-18 in Hampstead, Kensington & Chelsea, Knightsbridge and Notting Hill. Allsorts also offer drama parties.

Gymboree Play & Music
www.gymboree-uk.com
Award winning classes for 0-5 yrs. Fun for adult and child, with activities based on child development research and over 30 years of experience! Classes include pre-mobile Baby Play & Learn, Play & Learn, Music, Art & Birthday Parties. Cognitive and physical play on purpose-built equipment, and using highest quality props and instruments. Book your **FREE** trial class! Contact your local Gymboree today.

foreign language

Club Petit Pierrot   **020 7385 5565**
www.clubpetitpierrot.co.uk
admincpp@btconnect.com
Established in 1993, London's premier French club offers fun French lessons to children from 8 months to 8 years old, giving them an excellent headstart in French. Their ever popular clubs take place across London. Parent and Toddler groups, mornings, after-school, Saturdays, Holiday clubs and they can also organise private tuition at your home, even during the school holidays. Small groups, excellent results, native French teachers (all CRB checked) all levels. Highly recommended by BBC, Daily Telegraph & Time Out. *FREE trial lesson*.

gym and exercise

The Little Gym   **020 8874 6567**
www.thelittlegym.co.uk
The Little Gym is a place where children can develop their co-ordination, confidence and social skills while just having FUN through its premier developmental gymnastics rogramme. The Little Gym also offers birthday parties and Ofsted registered holiday camps. Branches across London.

Gymboree Play & Music
www.gymboree-uk.com
Award winning classes for 0-5 yrs. Fun for adult and child, with activities based on child development research and over 30 years of experience! Classes include pre-mobile Baby Play & Learn, Play & Learn, Music, Art & Birthday Parties. Cognitive and physical play on purpose-built equipment, and using highest quality props and instruments. Book your **FREE** trial class! Contact your local Gymboree today. Contact your local Gymboree today:

- Bayswater (W2):   020 7229 9294
- Brent Cross (NW4):   020 8201 7778
- Chiswick (W4):   07967 835 059
- Clapham (SW4):   020 7498 2323
- Docklands (E1):   07966 227 583
- Ealing (W5):   07534 953 116
- Hampstead (NW3):   020 7794 8719
- Herne Hill (SE24):   020 8123 8423
- Islington (N1):   07818 153 700
- Kensington (SW7):   020 7581 3511
- Putney (SW15):   020 8780 3831
- Surbiton (KT6):   020 8398 9360
- Wandsworth (SW18):   020 8870 0068
- Wimbledon (SW19):   020 8946 0400

Tumble Tots
www.tumbletots.com
Tumble Tots is designed to develop children's physical skills of agility, balance, climbing and co-ordination through the use of brightly coloured equipment. Each 45 minute weekly session is led by trained staff and is structured according to the different ages and stages of a child's development. Gymbabes from crawling-walking and Tumble Tots for walking-7yrs. Phone for details of classes see overleaf:

- St John's Wood, Muswell Hill and Finchley Central   020 8381 6585
- Battersea, Clapham, Dulwich and Blackheath   020 8464 4433

indoor playcentres

Gymboree Play & Music
www.gymboree-uk.com
Award winning classes for 0-5 yrs. Fun for adult and child, with activities based on child development research and over 30 years of experience! Classes include pre-mobile Baby Play & Learn, Play & Learn, Music, Art & Birthday Parties. Cognitive and physical play on purpose-built equipment, and using highest quality props and instruments. Book your **FREE** trial class! Contact your local Gymboree today. See branches above.

toddler activities

Adventure Kingdom   020 8290 1998
Stockwell Close, Bromley, BR1 3UH
www.bromleymytime.org.uk
Adventure Kingdom has the complete kit to tire out your energetic children with ball ponds, swing bags, climbing frames
and scramble nets. They even have a special play area for
under 4s. It's a great place to have a party and they provide
goodie bags and party food. Their café has a children's menu
which serves everything from pastas to Panini's to chips to
chicken nuggets. Highchairs and baby changing facilities are
available. Open daily 10am-7pm, closing 5pm on Friday.

BR3

Buzz Zone at the The Spa   020 8650 0233
24 Beckenham Road, BR3 4PF
www.bromleymytime.org.uk
This play centre has slides, crawl tubes, scramble nets, cargo
swings and many more features for those aged 5-12. They
have a special play area for toddlers and babies with ball-
ponds, soft see-saws, rockers and slides. They also have a
café with high chairs and baby changing facilities. They host
parties and providing party, balloons, invitations and decorations, within the play frame. Children under 6mths are free,
with prices starting from £4 for members up to £11. Open
9.15am-5.45pm Mon-Sun.

E15

Discover   020 8536 5555
383-387 High Street, Stratford, E15 4QZ
www.discover.org.uk
This Stratford-based activity centre provides a unique sensory
experience for children. On raindy days children can explore
inside the story trail, walking across a wobbly bridge, or stepping on stones across the river to the sound of sploshing.
You can visit the lion's den, make a spoon puppet, or do
some dressing up. Open between 10am-5pm except Mon
during term time, and 11am-5pm Sat-Sun. Entry is £4.50 for
adults and children aged 2yrs+-under 2's are free. It's a 5-10
min walk from Stratford underground (Jubilee/Central lines).

N5

Pyramid Soft Play   020 7226 5982
Highbury Roundhouse, 71 Ronalds Road, N5 1XB
www.highbury-roundhouse.org.uk
Soft play room with large shaped soft cushions and mats for
children to play on, with the focus being a large soft pyramid
that children can climb on. There is also a canteen. Weekly
activities' sessions for chidren, check times and rooms online.

N7

Sobell Safari   020 7609 2166
Hornsey Road, Islington, N7 7NY
www.aquaterra.org
Part of Sobell leisure centre, the Safari soft play centre is for
children up to the age of 10, and up to 4'7 tall. They have

slides, ball pits, tunnels and even a maze, and parties are
available for children under 8yrs. Open 7 days a week,
9.30am-5.30pm Mon-Fri, 9.30am-2.30pm Saturday and
9.30-3.30 Sundays.

N12

Clown Town   020 8361 6600
The Coppetts Centre, Colney Hatch Lane, Finchley,
N12 0SH
www.clowntown.co.uk
This long-established play centre has soft play areas for
under 5's and ball pits, swings and slides, as well as a baby
area. The café serves hot food such as chips and chicken
nuggets. Birthday parties are also available. Open daily
9.30am-6.30pm.

N19

Highgate Newtown Centre   020 7272 7201
25 Bertram Street, N19 5DQ
www.hncc.co.uk
This centre offers a wide range of activities; preschool soft
play centre, trikes and bikes, parent and toddler groups,
creche, music and movement, story sessions. 4-12s' holiday
playschemes, gymnastics, trapeze, football, yoga, pottery,
Woodcraft Folk and guitar. Open Mon-Fri 9am-10pm.

N22

Little Dinosaurs   020 8444 1338
The Grove, Alexandra Park, N22 7AY
www.littledinosaurs.co.uk
Little Dinosaurs is a purpose built indoor playcentre and cafe
set within the grounds of Alexandra Park. There's a great cafe
serving hot and cold drinks, cakes and a breakfast/lunch
menu. They also host Little Dinosaur children's parties, which
includes 45 mins play, sole use of the Dinosaur party area,
tea, themed party packs and invitations. Open Mon-Fri
9.30am-5.30pm, Sat 10am-5.30pm, Sun 10am-5pm.

NW6

Adventure Soft Room   020 7625 6260
150 Brassey Road, West Hampstead, NW6 2BA
www.sidings.org.uk
Sidings Adventure Soft Room runs during termtime on Tuesday and Thursday mornings from 10.30am. They have
bouncy castle, soft play equipment and a baby corner. Plenty
of room to run around and let off steam. Ideal for children just
starting to crawl or walk.

SE10

Toddlers World Greenwich   020 8317 5020
80 Trafalgar Road, Greenwich, SE10 9UX
www.gll.org
This indoor playcentre has soft mats, ball pond, bouncy castle, slides and swings, suitable for babies and toddlers aged
6mths-4yrs. They have a café with seating in the leisure club.
Highchairs and baby changing facilities are available. Ses-

sions run either morning or afternoon, and usually last around 2 hours. Children must be supervised at all times. For current session times either call or visit the GLL leisure website. Other Greenwich Leisure centres also have a Toddler's World including: Plumstead, Thamesmere, Coldharbour and Eltham.

SE16

Discovery Planet　　　　　**020 7237 2388**
Redriff Road, Surrey Quays, SE16 7LL
www.surreyquaysshoppingcentre.co.uk
A large indoor area full of mostly feral children who terrorise the centre on Saturday mornings. But that's not to say your children wont love it and it's cheap at £3.99. There's a party room with a Shrek theme but you'll have to opt for Burger King just outside the centre (or you can slope off to Frankie and Bennys locally). Open Mon-Fri 12-4pm, Sat 10am-6pm, Sun 11-5pm.

SW1

Purple Dragon Play Chelsea　　**0844 880 3580**
Ground Floor, Bramah House, Grosvenor Waterside, 30 Gatliffe Road, Chelsea, SW1W 8DP
www.purpledragonplay.com/chelsea
A private members club for families with swimming pool, cooking activities, state of the art recording studio and indoor activities to suit all tastes. During school holidays they do offer day passes for non-members, which can be helpful if you need a base for the day in London. Open Mon-Sat 10am-5pm, Sun 10am-4:30pm.

SW6

Gambado Chelsea　　　　　**0207 384 1635**
7 Station Court, Townmead Road, SW6 2PY
www.gambado.com
Giant play frame, dodgems, carousel, climbing wall, week day activities and fantastic birthday parties. Yum Yum café selling a selection of tasty treats. Open Mon-Sun 9.30am-5.30pm.

SW15

Eddie Catz　　　　　　　**0845 201 1268**
68-70 Putney High Street, SW15 1SF
www.eddiecatz.com
Playframe, games, kiddie rides, padded toddler area. TV lounge, internet access, café restaurant. Daily morning classes for under 5s. Holiday camps and workshops. Children's parties. Open Mon-Sat 9.30am-6pm, Sun 10am-6pm.

SW18

It's a Kids Thing　　　　　**020 8739 0909**
279 Magdalen Road, Earlsfield, SW18 3NZ
www.itsakidsthing.co.uk
Award-winning indoor play centre and café offering a full children's menu of healthy options. The centre is also a location for term time classes for both, sports and arts. It's also a great place to hold birthday parties.

SW19

Eddie Catz - Wimbledon　　　**0845 201 1268**
42 Station Road, SW19 2LP
www.eddiecatz.com
Playframe, games, kiddie rides, padded toddler area. TV lounge, internet access, café restaurant. Daily morning classes for under 5s. Holiday camps and workshops. Children's parties. Open Mon-Sun 9.30am-6pm.

TW7

Kidzone Soft Play　　　　　**07857 897 535**
Woodlane, Isleworth, TW7 5ED
www.kidzoneuk.net
Bouncy castle, ball pool, soft play, ride-on-toys, party hire £90 for 2hrs. Open Mon-Fri 9.30am-3pm.

W3

West London Health　　　　**0845 130 9111**
and Racquets Club
36 Bromyard Avenue, Acton, W3 7AU
www.virginactive.co.uk/en/clubs/west-london
This family-orientated sports, health and fitness club has an on site day nursery and creche offering care from 6 weeks to 5yrs, as well as running Club-V, a full programme of children's activities from 4-11yrs after school and during half terms and holidays, including: swimming lessons, tennis, football, arts and crafts and an indoor soft play area.

W4

Piccolo Playcentre　　　　　**07525 773 659**
Hogarth Youth & Community Centre, Duke Road, Chiswick, W4 2JR
piccolocaffe.co.uk
Formally known as Childs Play Cafe, Piccolo Caffe has become a popular local hub for parents looking for a cafe and play space. In addition to the play area there are art and craft workshops and holiday play schemes. Open Mon-Fri 9am-5pm.

W10

Bramley's Big Adventure　　　**020 8960 1515**
136 Bramley Road, Ladbroke Grove, W10 6TJ
www.bramleysbig.co.uk
Tucked under London's Westway flyover this London indoor playcentre offers unlimited play for children aged 0-11yrs. There are no specific sessions so children can actually play all day. There's a three-tier play frame with slides, giant ball ponds and a special area for children under 5, who would otherwise find it too chaotic. Parents can take advantage of free wifi in the cafe, which offers organic and fair trade food. Great venue for children's parties with food and party bags provided. Open Mon-Fri 10am-6pm, Sat-Sun and bank holidays 10am-6.30pm.

oddler activities

music

Bea's Baby Music School   020 8670 9378
www.babymusic.co.uk
Groups for 0 - 6yrs. Not a franchise. Professional musicians provide accompaniment to Bea for a genuine musical start leading to Bea's acclaimed early beginner piano course. Puppets bubbles instruments, and brilliant live music. Join in and SING SING SING. Our customers said: "after 24 years of nanny jobs this is the first time I haven't been bored by music groups - I've recommended you to everyone".

Blueberry Playsongs   020 8677 6871
www.blueberryplaysongs.co.uk
Fun with live music for 6mths-3+yrs. Barnes, Chelsea, Clapham, Hammersmith, Notting Hill, Queen's Park, Wandsworth, Wimbledon. Talented group leaders, guitar-accompanied action songs, nursery rhymes, instruments, games and dancing. Stimulating, social and really good fun. Blueberry parties available too! Contact us for your trial class.

Gymboree Play & Music
www.gymboree-uk.com
Award winning classes for 0-5 yrs. Fun for adult and child, with activities based on child development research and over 30 years of experience! Classes include pre-mobile Baby Play & Learn, Play & Learn, Music, Art & Birthday Parties. Cognitive and physical play on purpose-built equipment, and using highest quality props and instruments. Book your **FREE** trial class! Contact your local Gymboree today.

Need to Know: Apps

There are a raft of educational apps aimed at preschool children. Although Angry Birds and Fruit Ninja may be universally popular here are a few ideas to sneak in a bit of early education.

 Dr Seuss interactive story books - £2.49

 The Story Mouse Talking Books - Free

 Peppa Pig's Party Time - £2.99

 In the Night Garden - £1.49

All apps available from **itunes.apple.com**

Monkey Music   01582 766 464
www.monkeymusic.co.uk
Educational and entertaining music classes for children across the UK, led by specialist teachers in an imaginative and social environment. Classes are small and carefully structured, with children from 3 months-4 years grouped according to age. For classes in London please see advert.

- Putney, Barnes and Fulham   020 8480 6064
- Blackheath, Greenwich,   020 8764 5185
  Dulwich and Herne Hill
- Twickenham, Teddington,   020 8847 4031
  Kew, Richmond and Chiswick
- Muswell Hill, Crouch End,   020 8889 0114
  Highgate, Finchley Central and East Finchley
- Clapham, Battersea, Forest Hill,   020 8699 0977
  Balham (SW12), Crystal Palace and Sydenham
- Chelsea, Knightsbridge,   020 8767 9827
  Belgravia and Gloucester Road
- Hampstead, West Hampstead,   020 8438 0189
  Notting Hill, Swiss Cottage, Primrose Hill, Queen's Park, Belsize Park, Holland Park, Kensington High St & Finchley Road.
- Southfields, Wandsworth,   020 8764 5185
  Earlsfield, Tooting, Balham and Streatham
- Southfields, Wimbledon   020 8704 1852
  and Raynes Park

Mini Music Makers   020 7207 5501
www.mini-musicmakers.org
Music groups in central Pimlico for babies and toddlers aged 0-3yrs. The classes are run by Jeremy de Satgé, a professional and classically trained barritone. So alongside the nursery rhymes, action songs, bell shaking and other percussion instruments children will have direct access to a first-class musician.

Sing and Sign   01273 550 587
www.singandsign.co.uk
This was the first baby signing business to launch in the UK over 10 years ago, and it now has a remarkable 170 franchises across the UK. These award-winning music classes for parents and babies are designed to teach baby signing and help communication before speech. Toys, props and instruments add to the fun. Age-range 6mths-2yrs.

Whippersnappers   020 7738 6633
Brockwell Lido, Dulwich Road, SE24 0PA
www.whippersnappers.org
Whippersnappers have been running zany and zestful interactive musical workshops for babies and toddlers for 15 years. Their classes are multi-cultural and very welcoming. Classes feature African drumming, musical instruments from around the world, theatrical props, puppets, dressing up and bubbles. Branches also in Holland Park and Kensington, W11.

toddler activities

rugby

Ruggerbeez Limited   0844 544 6784
www.ruggerbeez.com
Ruggerbeez classes are designed for ages 2-7 yrs. Boys and girls enjoy weekly non-contact play sessions under the guidance of experienced coaches. Key benefits include development of balance, core motor and social skills and most importantly fun.

The Nature Bug   07521 778 136
www.thenaturebug.co.uk
Nature-inspired activity classes for pre-school aged children aged 2-5yrs. Come along, make friends, have fun & learn about the natural world on your doorstep. Games & stories, art & crafts, movement & music, outdoor fun & wildlife encounters! FREE taster sessions available. Venues in Blackheath, New Cross and Lewisham. A new venue in East Dulwich coming soon.

swimming classes

Aquakiddies/Babies   01273 833 101
www.aquababies-uk.com
The original and best specialist provider of baby and toddler swimming classes. We encourage early development of children's natural swimming skills and teach you how to teach your child to swim safely. Fun and social! Pools in Westminster, Regents Park, Marble Arch, Kensington, Willesden, Islington, Heathrow and nationally.

Little Acorns Music

My son and daughter both loved David's music group as toddlers and used to look forward to Thursday mornings - especially loved the weekly themes!

Karen74, Surrey, Mother of 2

parties for under-5s

Avoid being too ambitious and everyone will have lots of fun without too many tears. Even you!

Children's parties with tantrums and plastic tiaras aren't solely the preserve of TV sitcom scripts, but it can be easy to end up stressing out on what should be a jolly day for everyone. Here are a few tips to guide you through the early years.

Your baby's first birthday

While you might gather with a few mums and babies to have a celebratory slice of cake, you don't need to go to town on a huge first birthday party. Traditionally, this is instead a celebration of parenthood – you made it to year one! So plan a gathering of close friends and family at home.

Second and third birthdays

For a second birthday, a tea party at home with small tables and chairs will ensure that the catering aspect of the party contains itself to one room and not your carpet. A ball pond or a few tunnels will provide enough excitement - but remember to put away toys that you don't want to be played with (favourites or new presents). Leave organised party games (even pass the parcel) until your child's third birthday, when three or four simple games spread out across a two-hour party is plenty. The children will require a lot of organising so make sure you take parents up on their offer to stay for the duration! (Put out a plate or two of nibbles and pizza for them to graze on while the children are eating.)

From three you can book an entertainer - the children will be amused and should be fairly well-behaved - but keep games to simple ideas like musical bumps.

Toddler parties are fairly tame so older siblings - unless they have a flare for helping - are best packed off to a friend's house so they don't get bored.

Fourth and fifth birthdays

If your child attends a nursery or playgroup this party could be a whole class event. Parents won't always expect to stay so ask them to if you are unhappy about supervising all the children alone (and if they go, make sure you have a mobile number just in case).

For big parties, if you are hiring a play space, check out what party food they serve or choose somewhere you can bring your own food if the fish finger and fries option doesn't appeal. Themed parties with dressing up are very popular. You can also play traditional party games. Party entertainers are again in their element with this age group. Magic, silly songs, puppets, balloon modelling, bubble machines, face painting, white rabbits, doves, and even snakes with all delight. However, good entertainers are popular so you need to book around six weeks ahead, particularly during festive seasons.

Christening and
first birthday gifts

Three hearts bracelet
Molly Brown £154
A sterling silver charm bracelet with three love hearts in silver, pink and red enamel with heart shaped links to make the length adjustable as the wrist grows.
www.mollybrownlondon.com

Little Miss Sunshine charm
Links of London £40
Put a smile on a little face with this iconic Mr Men sterling silver charm for a necklace or bracelet.
www.linksoflondon.com

Stretch silver charm bracelet
Merci Maman £30
Personalised name on a charm (clover, star or girl) with four sterling silver beads on a stretchy elastic (blue, silver or pink).
www.mercimaman.co.uk

Bon-Bon bracelet
Kit Heath £149.95
Beautiful enamel and silver beads threaded on to simple silver bracelet.
www.kitheath.com

parties & celebrations

party catering

Cake Dreams　　　　　　　　020 8889 2376
www.cakedreams.co.uk
Tracey Bush, a north London mum, has been making delicious hand-crafted fantasy cakes in any shape, size or design for over 10 years. She's a true cake artist and can compile anything you want to dream up. Think big, even if that means a cupcake tower.

Cakes4Fun　　　　　　　　020 8785 9039
100 Lower Richmond Road, Putney, SW15 1LN
www.cakes4fun.co.uk
Wonderful 2D and 3D cake sculptures and or cakes with edible photo icing. They have a large selection of styles to choose from on their website, and some to view in their showroom. Cake courses also on offer for keen mums.

The Cake Kit Company　　　　01635 203 884
www.partypieces.co.uk
If you like the idea of cooking your own novelty cake, try this cake kit company, set up by Kate Middleton's brother. All the ingredients for the cake, ready-to-roll fondant icing and a step-by-step guide are provided (including the candles).

Jane Asher Party Cakes　　　020 7584 6177
22-24 Cale Street, SW3 3QU
www.jane-asher.co.uk
Dip into the queen of cake's catalogue for a selection of over 3000 children's novelty cakes. Delivered by courier anywhere in the UK you can choose seasonal styles (ie bunnies at Easter) as well as buy cake moulds (ladybirds/lions). Choice of vanilla, chocolate or fruit with a double layer of butter icing for filling. Yum!

London Cake Company　　　020 8523 8283
97 Station Road, Chingford, E4 7BU
www.londoncake.com
The London Cake Company is a celebration cake specialist. They cater for common childhood allergies and can make egg free and gluten free cakes. Cakes can be collected from their store or delivered by courier. If you need a cake in hurry you can also pick up a standard cake base from their store and have your message piped while you wait.

Love to Cake　　　　　　　07779 790 822
www.lovetocake.co.uk
Amazingly lifelike cake masterpieces and cake pops created by Louise Hill - a master cake sculptor. Although on maternity leave as we go to press, just looking at her blog and website may inspire you to attend one of her masterclasses at the Make Lounge in Islington (www.themakelounge.com).

The Cake Store　　　　　　08000 520 058
111 Sydenham Road, London, SE26 5EZ
www.thecakestore.co.uk
Beautifully hand-crafted cakes with many TV and film themes including Cars 2, In the Night Garden, Cat in the Hat, Alvin and the Chipmunks, Captain Jack Sparrow and many more. They also make amazing cup-cake towers which create perfect portions to take home. Delivery London wide.

www.thecakestore.co.uk

parties & celebrations

party entertainers

Peter Pinner's Parties　　　020 8863 1528
www.funandmagic.co.uk
This family-run business has been providing children's entertainers for over 40 years. Parents can choose a number of different acts including magic, balloon modelling, ventriloquism, puppet shows, discos, games and face painting. Parties are tailored to suit the age of the children (3yrs-teens).

Blueberry Playsongs　　　**020 8677 6871**
www.blueberryplaysongs.co.uk
Blueberry parties are wonderfully fun musical parties for 1 to 5 year olds. Our talented entertainer will play and sing guitar-accompanied songs with actions, joining in, jumping, circle games and dancing. They also bring along a puppet, shaky eggs and a colourful parachute if space permits. Costs £105 in central London and £115 in outer London. Costs include 20 balloons, sticker labels for each child and a gift for the birthday child. Book at least 3 weeks in advance. London wide.

Fizzie Lizzie　　　020 7723 3877
www.fizzielizzie.co.uk
Elizabeth Morgan is friendly and funny - and perfect for the 2-8yr old agegroup. She's a master of children's magic, balloonery, puppets, slapstick, singing, bubbles, storytelling, games, plate-spinning, juggling and other circus skills. She will also delve deep into her artists box for face painting, tattoos, arts and crafts workshops.

Pepper Pot Parties　　　07971 145 589
www.pepperpotparties.co.uk
A team of entertainers from Pepper Pot Parties provides fun-filled children's entertainment for ages 2-12yrs, including dance parties, face-painting, balloon modeling, magic, competitions and games. London and home counties.

party ideas/themes

Blueberry Playsongs　　　**020 8677 6871**
www.blueberryplaysongs.co.uk
Blueberry parties are wonderfully fun musical parties for 1 to 5 year olds. Our talented entertainer will play and sing guitar-accompanied songs with actions, joining in, jumping, circle games and dancing. They also bring along a puppet, shaky eggs and a colourful parachute if space permits. Costs £105 in central London and £115 in outer London. Costs include 20 balloons, sticker labels for each child and a gift for the birthday child. Book at least 3 weeks in advance. London wide.

The Little Gym
www.thelittlegym.co.uk
Fully supervised private parties with music, games and obstacle courses that kids love. Plus they can take care of everything from invitations to clean-up. Parties are held on Saturday and Sunday afternoons in Chiswick (020 8994 3729), Hampton & Teddington (020 8977 0099), Wandsworth (020 8874 6567) and Westfield (020 8735 0817).

YogaBugs　　　020 8772 1800
www.yogabugs.com
Gentle yoga based parties for children aged 3yrs+. Children follow an adventure story which incorporates yoga techniques to relax children, followed by games. Classes are nationwide with London and south east classes in the following areas. Please check your nearest class for details, as not all teachers offer parties.

party shops

N3

Surprises　　　020 8343 4200
82 Ballards Lane, Finchley, N3 2DL
www.surprisesltd.co.uk
A one-stop-party-shop selling party decorations, balloons and other party paraphernalia. You can also hire children's tables, chairs, crockery and cutlery. Open 10am-6pm Mon. 9.30-6pm Tue-Sat.

NW5

Party Party　　　020 7267 9084
3 & 11 Southampton Road, Gospel Oak, NW5 4JS
www.partypartyuk.com
Party decorations, balloons, party bag fillers, tableware are all available from this party shop, as well as direct from their website. They also have a small range of toddler fancy dress. Open 9.30am-5.30pm Mon-Sat

NW6

Oscar's Den　　　020 7328 6683
127-129 Abbey Road, St John's Wood, NW6 4SL
www.oscarsden.com
Oscar's Den is a popular party shop for north west London families. From special themed goody bags to balloons, they provide a complete party planning service including the booking of a children's entertainer or cake maker. Just drop off your details and they'll take care of it. Open 9.30am-6pm Mon-Fri, 9.30am-5.30pm Sat and 10am-2pm Sun.

NW7

Balloonland　　　020 8906 3302
12 Hale Lane, Mill Hill, NW7 3NX
www.balloonland.co.uk
This store originally only sold ballons, but due to their success they now offer a range of party wares including decorations, tablewares and childrens fancy dress. They also stock a wide selection of balloons including latex, foil, character, Disney, walker and personalised. Open 9am-5:30pm Mon-Fri and 9:30am-5:30pm Sat, closed Sundays.

SW1

Semmalina Starbags　　　020 7730 9333
225 Ebury Street, Pimlico, SW1W 8UT
www.starbags.info
Set up by showbiz sisters Emma Forbes and Sarah Standing,

Semmalina Starbags offers a quirky mix of fun contemporary and vintage clothing for 0-8yrs, as well as enchanting toys, sweets and Starbag party bags. Open Mon-Sat 9.30am-5.30pm.

SW4

Lyntes Balloon Services **020 7622 4818**
1 Ascot Parade, Acre Lane, Clapham, SW4 7EY
www.lyntes.co.uk
The most inexpensive balloon shop we know in London offering personalised and themed balloons, as well as party decorations and banners. Order helium balloons in advance and pick them up on the day of your party. Open Mon-Fri 10am-6pm. Sat 9pm-7pm. Closed on Sun.

SW6

Circus Circus **020 7731 4128**
176 Wandsworth Bridge Road, Fulham, SW6 2UQ
www.circuscircus.co.uk
This is a real gem of a party shop where the staff are so knowledgeable they end up organising the party for you with their list of recommended entertainers, caterers and bouncy castle contacts. They have a great dressing up range with outfits for newborns upwards, decorations, games and pinatas. Open Mon-Sat 10am-6pm. sun 10am-1pm.

SW11

Party Superstores **020 7924 3210**
268 Lavender Hill, Clapham Junction, SW11 1LJ
www.partysuperstores.co.uk
Although one half of this store suffered during the summer riots of 2011 (and transferred to the department store opposite), in this section they still sell a huge range of tableware, balloons, streamers, party decorations and cake decorations. Open Mon, Tue, Wed, Sat 9am-6pm, Thurs-Fri 9am-7pm. Sun 10.30am-4.30pm.

SW13

The Treat Garden **020 8878 4525**
17 Station Road, Barnes, SW13 0LF
www.thetreatgarden.co.uk
Set up by passionate Barnes resident Elizabeth Haselgrove the Treat Garden offers a party bag service (sweets and pocket money toys), and can host small parties for up to 12 children in the shop. Open Mon-Fri 9.30am-6.30pm, Sat 10am-6pm and Sun 11am-4.30pm.

SW18

Balloon & Kite Company **020 8946 5962**
613 Garratt Lane, SW18 4SU
www.balloonshop.com
Balloons are arranged in pic n' mix style bins in all colours, shapes, sizes and materials - and can be pre-filled with helium if you order in advance. They also stock party products and kites. A delivery service is also available. Open Mon-Fri 9am-6pm. Sat 9.30am-5.30pm.

SW19

Party Party Wimbledon **020 8944 9495**
23 High Street Wimbledon, SW19 5DX
Party Party sell a wide range of party goods and novelty items such as poppers, masks and decorations. Open Mon-Sat 10am-5.30pm. Sun 11am-5pm.

Wimbledon Party Shop **020 8543 8519**
270A The Broadway, Wimbledon, SW19 1SB
www.wimbledonpartyshop.co.uk
Set up in 2010 by Angelo Menegotto, this family run party shop in Wimbledon has everything you'll need to get your party going. From decorations and tableware, balloons (including giant dummy balloons for baby showers), fancy dress costumes and animal masks, plus a whole range of small toys for party bags. You'll also find contacts for local face painters or entertainers. Mon-Fri 9am-6pm, Sat 8am-6pm.

Need to Know: Expert party tips

We asked professional party organisers for their best advice for throwing a successful children's party.

- Book your entertainer well ahead. If you haven't found a venue locally then many party organisers, such as Twizzle (twizzle-parties.com) have a whole range at their fingertips for every post code.

- Plan your party around your child's natural mealtimes so everyone has a good appetite.

- Liaise with other parents if children's birthdays in the same class clash across one weekend.

- Make sure the sweet things aren't on the table before the savoury – and decide whether to put the cake in the party bag or serve it at the table.

- Ask parents to mention allergies when they RSVP so you can cater accordingly.

- Party bags are becoming ever more sophisticated, but stick to your budget and you'll be surprised how much you can find that delights the under 5s.

parties & celebrations

W8

Non Stop Party Shop   **020 7937 7200**
214-216 Kensington High Street, W8 7RG
www.nonstopparty.co.uk
As the name implies this shop is all about year-long fun. They offer everything you could possibly need for any themed party including personalised balloons, themed tableware, pinatas, dressing up masks, streamers and more. Delivery service available. Open Mon-Sat 9.30-6pm. Sun 11am-5pm.

W13

Bouncing Kids Party Shop   **020 8840 0110**
127 Northfield Avenue, W13 9QR
www.bouncing-kids.com
A dedicated party store that has everything you need for your

Bigoodi, New Kings Road

party including fancy dress, face-painting make up, personalised balloons, tableware, pinatas and recommended party entertainers. Products can be viewed on their website. Open 9am-5.30pm Mon, Fri, Sat and 6pm on Tue, Wed, Thurs. 10am-9pm Sun.

party supplies

Ethical Party Bags   **07948 343 653**
www.ethicalpartybags.com
Ethical and fairtrade party bags for children with cloth bags and innovate treats - many under £1.

Frog in the Field   **08451 702 010**
www.froginthefield.co.uk
Offering pre-filled party bags made from hand printed cotton.

Party Pieces   **01635 201844**
www.partypieces.co.uk
Founded by Carol Middleton in the late 1980s (long before Kate met Wills) this quintessential online party shop offers next day delivery on party tableware, cake making equipment, balloons, party bag treats and activity ideas. Baby's 1st birthdays are a speciality. Register too for Pippa Middleton's online blog, The Party Times.

party venues

Also see Ceramic Cafè's, Indoor Playcentres, Days Out locations and Farms.

Animal Magic Parties   **01235 816 947**
www.animalmagicponyparties.co.uk
Unusual animal and reptile parties for private children's parties. Animal Magic Pony Parties comes to you with their travelling zoo incorporating ponies to ride, fluffies to pet as well as their de-scented skunks, chinchillas, giant rabbits, African pygmy goats and new to their menagerie in 2012 - meerkats. Book early to avoid disappointment.

Battersea Zoo   **0845 601 6679**
Battersea Park, SW11 4NJ
www.batterseaparkzoo.co.uk
For animal loving children Battersea Park Zoo offers great party packages for children aged 3yrs+ 7 days a week. It costs £25 per child and this includes everything from room hire, food, party bags, zoo tour and the chance to meet animals in the farm. There is also a special 'Birthday Brick' for the birthday child, which has their name painted on it and remains at the zoo for them to see on future visits.

Bigoodi   **020 7471 8730**
52 New Kings Road, Fulham, SW6 4LS
www.mybigoodi.com
A new beauty and nail boutique, shop and party venue for children aged 0-10yrs (Bigoodi is a French hair roller). Located in the heart of Fulham, this Parsons Green beauty salon offers a sophisticated range of party packages to suit all tastes and hairstyles (party packages offered on Sat/Sun). Open Tues-Sat 10am-6pm, Sun 10am-2pm.

parties & celebrations

Bramley's Big Adventure   020 8960 1515
136 Bramley Road, Ladbroke Grove, W10 6TJ
www.bramleysbig.co.uk
All-inclusive children's parties including 75 minutes play and
45 minutes in the private party room including a birthday tea.
Bronze, silver, gold, themed and private hire party packages
available. Parties can be booked during weekdays and weekends.

Coram Fields   020 7837 6138
98 Guilford Street, Camden, WC1N 1DN
www.coramsfields.org
Two rooms are available to hire (£80 for 3 hours max. 25
children). Facilities include a small kitchenette for parents to
prepare food, tables and chairs. Parent's should bring their
own music (and sound system), games and an entertainer if
they wish. They also have a playground, sandpit and the pets
corner.

Cupcake   020 3326 4986
11 Heathmans Road, Parsons Green, SW6 4TJ
10 Point Pleasant, Putney, SW18 1GG
www.cupcakemum.com
The Cupcake private members clubs are the perfect venues
to host your children's party. Whether you're simply looking
for a friendly, open space to let your children play freely, or
want a fully catered event with a music or dance theme, they
have a number of packages to suit all tastes and budgets.

Gymboree
www.gymboree-uk.com/children-baby-kids-parties
Custom-made and fully interactive parties for babies and
children from newborn to 5 years at selected locations.
Choose from a range of themes and let Gymboree create a
wonderfully unique day for your little one, and a stress-free
experience for you!

- Bayswater (W2):   020 7229 9294
- Brent Cross (NW4):   020 8201 7778
- Chiswick (W4):   07967 835 059
- Clapham (SW4):   020 7498 2323
- Docklands (E1):   07966 227 583
- Ealing (W5):   07534 953 116
- Hampstead (NW3):   020 7794 8719
- Herne Hill (SE24):   020 8123 8423
- Islington (N1):   07818 153 700
- Kensington (SW7):   020 7581 3511
- Putney (SW15):   020 8780 3831
- Surbiton (KT6):   020 8398 9360
- Wandsworth (SW18):   020 8870 0068
- Wimbledon (SW19):   020 8946 0400

Gambado   0870 027 3705
www.gambado.com
London's leading family indoor play centre. Giant play frame,
dodgems, carousel, climbing wall, week day activities and
fantastic birthday parties. Yum Yum café selling a selection of

Make-your-own pizza parties at
Pizza Express

tasty treats. Centres in Chelsea, Beckenham and Watford.

- 7 Station Court, Townmead   **020 7384 1635**
  Road, Chelsea, SW6 2PY
- Natwest Sports Ground,   **020 8662 6910**
  Copers Cope Road, Beckenham, BR3 1NZ
- Woodside Leisure Park,   **01923 892 140**
  North Orbital Road, Watford, WD25 7JZ

It's A Kids Thing   020 8739 0909
www.itsakidsthing.co.uk
London's original and award winning activity centre; we specialise in exclusive party hire. Beautiful venue with 2 tier soft play; climb, slide and hide. Our fantastic team will cater for all your needs; children and adults. Legendary parties – including Laser DJ/Disco, Funky Feet and Costume Party! Parties for 10 children up to 40. Available 7 days a week. Ages 1-8 years.

Paradise Wildlife Park   01992 470 490
White Stubbs Lane, Broxbourne, Herts, EN10 7QA
www.pwpark.com
Paradise offers two fantastic fun-filled packages for kids in the Tumble Jungle and the Safari Sam's Restaurant.

The Golden Hinde   020 7403 0123
St Mary Overie Dock, Cathedral Street, SE1 9DG
www.goldenhinde.com
Ahoy there for pirate parties on board this Tudor ship! Led by two jolly sailors (in pirate costume), party goers will learn to raise the anchor, play pirate games and fire the cannons before settling down to a sumptuous banqueting tea. It's a 2

hour romp, suitable from 5-12 years, maximum 30 children and available after school or on Sundays. Or you could keep it a family affair and book a History tour sleepover available for children aged 6yrs+.

Pizza Express   08453 899 489
www.pizzaexpress.com
Selected restaurants offer children's parties during the day at selected times. Children will make a Margherita pizza with 2 toppings of their choice, a side salad, desert and drink. For larger parties certain restaurants have a separate room that can be hired, with prices around £200 which includes your personal waiter and helium balloons.

Puppet Barge   020 7249 6876
Little Venice, W9 2PF
Richmond TW10 6UT
www.puppetbarge.com
The Puppet Barge is a unique venue for children's parties. Moored along the river Thames at Little Venice during the winter and spring months parents can hire the whole barge or book tickets for one of their great shows, and hire their birthday tea room after the show.

The V&A Museum of Childhood   020 8983 5200
Cambridge Heath Road, Bethnal Green, E2 9PA
www.vam.ac.uk/moc
A variety of different options are available when booking a party at the Museum of Childhood; just room hire or party food and entertainment included. Prices range accordingly from £100-£200+. Ideally for children 4yrs+ if they wish to take part in the activities (up to 25 children).

West London Stables   020 8964 2140
20 Stable Way, Latimer Road, London W11 6QX
www.westlondonstables.co.uk
Situated just below the A40 flyover in west London is a thriving riding stables with about 20 ponies which are made available for pony-heaven parties from around 5yrs+. Children of any ability can play gymkana style games (ie around the world) as well as spend time grooming and learning about their care before tea.

WWT London Wetland Centre   020 8409 4400
Queen Elizabeth Walk, Barnes, SW13 9WT
www.wwt.org.uk/london
The 42 hectare London Wetland Centre is an unusual party venue with a wildlife encounter theme. Your party group will be led on various outdoor activities depending on the season before retiring to the tower room for party tea. The party price includes entry fees, the activities, goody bags and special party invitations. Available on Saturday/Sunday 10.30am-1pm, suitable from 5-12yrs.

Whippersnappers   020 7738 6633
Brockwell Lido, Brockwell Park, Dulwich Road, SE24 0PA
www.whippersnappers.org
Fun and interactive parties for babies, toddlers and their parents. In your own home or at a venue of your choice. Songs, props, drumming, dressing up, dancing and bubbles. Funky fun for everyone.

Party time fun at Whippersnappers

days out

From arts and history to theatre and music, London's best venues aren't just for grown-ups. There are some splendid attractions to keep toddlers, under-5s and even babies amused.

Beyond local baby massage groups, parks and indoor soft play centres for rainy days, it can sometimes feel like all the most exciting things to do are aimed at over-5s. However, the greatest places have great facilities for even the smallest children.

Things to do with babies and under-3s

Many museums have kids' trails and touch-screen games for older children, but a few have really made an effort to give over more than just one small corner to well-designed activities that amuse and delight small children.

At the **V&A Museum of Childhood** in Bethnal Green *(see p170)* the Creativity Gallery includes a 'Sensory Pod' with lights, colourful, textured surfaces and reflective walls for babies and small children to marvel at, and dressing up clothes to encourage 'make believe' games. On the first floor there is also a sandpit!

Similarly, **Mudlarks** at the **Museum of London Docklands** *(see p168)* is a children's gallery which not only has a Docklands-themed soft play section but a water-play area where little hands can create dams and watch how the river flow changes – a proven way to keep under-5s amused for hours! They also hold weekly group sessions for babies and toddlers.

Discover Children's Story Centre in Stratford *(see p167)* is a colourful playcentre inspired by stories and books. There are lots of things to crawl or clamber over, and age-specific crafts and activities as well as storytelling sessions for less boisterous little ones.

Theatre for babies, toddlers and under-5s

Theatre spaces where children should be seen and heard might be rare, but the regular Tales from the Shed musical shows at the **Chickenshed Theatre** in Southgate *(see p170)* are specially designed to be bright, funny and lively for babies and under-3s - toddling onto the stage area is positively encouraged! The **Polka Theatre** in Wimbledon and the **Unicorn** at London Bridge are both dedicated to children's shows, some of which appeal to the very young *(see p171)*, and at the **Puppet Theatre Barge**, which is moored most of the year at Little Venice *(see p171)*, they carefully arrange the seating so smaller children get the best view.

Day trips with under-5s

Once your child is toddling they will love places like the charmingly old-fashioned **Bekonscot Model Village** where everything is best explored from their height. Additionally, **Legoland** *(see p171)* is particularly good for under-5s, with dedicated play and water areas, sedate rides for little ones, puppet shows and of course, its own model village, Miniland. Older toddlers and pre-schoolers who want to get more physical will enjoy **Diggerland** in Kent or running about on a Winnie-the-Pooh walk in **Ashdown Forest**. At this age, a steam train ride will delight, too. Try the **Bluebell Railway** in East Sussex or **Buckinghamshire Railway Centre**, where there are special days through the year when the train is pulled by Thomas the Tank engine.

New & re-launched places for days out in London 2012

London Pleasure Gardens. Launching this summer, this park on the north side of the Thames just east of the Isle of Docks aims to be a South Bank-style cultural destination with events and attractions, including family activities.
www.londonpleasuregardens.com

Emirates Air Line. From this summer, pedestrians, wheelchair users and cyclists can board the brand new cable car that crosses the Thames from Greenwich Peninsula (near The O2) to the Royal Docks.
www.tfl.gov.uk

The Cutty Sark. Re-opened in June 2012 after extensive renovations showing seafaring life in a tea clipper.
www.rmg.co.uk/cuttysark

HMS Belfast. Re-opened in May 2012, HMS Belfast offers a fantastic glimpse into the world on board a WWII warship.
www.iwm.org.uk

Proud Camden. A popular bar, restaurant and gallery for grown-ups, Proud Camden now has a lunchtime club on Saturdays and Sundays where you can eat while the kids get merry with face-painting, magic, stories and other activities.
www.proudcamden.com

London Aquarium. A new underwater tunnel was re-opened in the Pacific Reef shark tank - and new sharks have been introduced.
www.visitsealife.com/london

London Wetlands Centre. See the new Asian short-clawed otter sanctuary opened in June 2012.
www.wwt.org.uk/visit-us/london

Find more days out ideas and reviews at www.babydirectory.com/whats_on

aeroplanes, trains and ships

Cutty Sark   020 8312 6608
King William Walk, Greenwich, SE10 9HT
The beautifully restored Cutty Sark is the world's only surviving tea clipper and one of Britain's greatest maritime treasures. The ship has been raised 3 meters in the air and for the first time visitors can walk underneath the shining copper hull to admire its streamlined shape. Special family weekends (1st weekend of the month) and half term and holiday events offer a number of craft workshops, sea-themed stories and roleplay games (eg Meet the captain). And a special children's trail tells the story of the ship's cargoes with interactive touch screens on board and in the dry dock below. Not suitable for pushchairs on board although there is wheelchair access. Cafe serving drinks, snacks and sophisticated sandwiches (so we suggest you bring your own). Open Tues-Sun 10am-5pm (last admission 4.30pm). Admission: £12 adult, 5-16yrs £6.50 and under 5s free.

Golden Hinde   020 7403 0123
Pickfords Wharf, Clink Street, SE1 9DG
www.goldenhinde.com
This full-size replica of Sir Francis Drake's Tudor ship is great fun to visit. There are guided tours and pirate fun days as well as a chance for the whole family to do a sleepover and live as shipmates for a few hours (sleeping on the cannon deck)! Open daily 10am-5.30pm.

HMS Belfast   020 7940 6300
Morgan's Lane, Tooley Street, SE1 2JH
hmsbelfast.iwm.org.uk
Active in World War II, HMS Belfast is an evocative day out for young and old. It's important to wear sensible shoes to safely scramble around inside and out, but themed activity days help bring this ship, moored near London Bridge, back to life for little historians. Under-16s go free. Open daily 10am-6pm (10am-5pm winter).

London Canal Museum   020 7713 0836
12-13 New Wharf Road, N1 9RT
www.canalmuseum.org.uk
Here you can see inside an original narrowboat, peer into a Victorian ice well, and find out how people lived and worked on the canals in their heyday in centuries gone by. Open Tue-Sun 10am-4.30pm.

Royal Air Force Museum   020 8205 2266
Grahame Park Way, Hendon, NW9 5LL
www.rafmuseum.org.uk
Even little ones enjoy getting close to the huge aircraft on display at this very family-friendly museum. There is a wealth of history for older kids to explore and free fun activities to keep everyone amused. There are also themed events around the year, especially during school holidays. You can book birthday parties here for children aged 5 and over. Open daily 10am-6pm, some exhibits close earlier (closed Christmas Day, Boxing Day and early January).

aquariums and river life

Sea Life London Aquarium   0871 663 1678
Westminster Bridge Rd, SE1 7PB
www.visitsealife.com/london
Choose an off-peak period to visit this aquarium to get the best out of your visit as many preschoolers find it hard to cope with the dark and mysterious atmosphere combined with the large tourist crowds during holidays. But there are plenty of hands-on experiences such as touch pools, live feeding demos and new in 2012 the Pacific Shark Reef Encounter with walk-through tunnels. Or try the Penguins in the Antarctic Ice adventure section. Try playing underwater I Spy, identifying colours and the diferent types of fish faces to engage their curiosioty. Open daily Mon-Thur 10am-6pm; Fri-Sun 10am-7pm (Christmas holiday times vary).

Horniman Museum   020 8699 1872
100 London Road, Forest Hill, SE23 3PQ
www.horniman.ac.uk
This small scale aquarium has low viewing windows and an abundance of "Nemos" which preschoolers love spotting. There's a tank of pulsating jellyfish, complete with tentacles entangled, which is mesmerising to watch. There's an aquarium quiz for slightly older children, with weekend storytelling and other activities to get involved in. Café and restaurant is open with highchairs, changing facilities and shop. Good buggy storage. Access free. Open 10.30am-5.30pm daily.

The London Eye   0871 781 3000
Jubilee Gardens, South Bank, SE1 7PB
www.londoneye.com
Although really small children won't be able to appreciate this big wheel ride above the Thames, even toddlers can appreciate the light, height and scale of a half-hour 'flight' in a pod. Pushchairs need to be folded flat to carry on board, or there is an area where you can leave fixed prams (limited availability). Open daily from 10am, last evening flight times vary depending on the season.

London Duck Tours   020 7928 3132
Chicheley Street, SE1 7PY
www.londonducktours.co.uk
Can't decide between a bus tour and a boat cruise? Do both, with London Duck Tours, who use amphibious landing craft first used on World War II to travel around London's roads before heading onto the River Thames itself! Duck Tours aren't cheap, but they are very safe for children and the guides on board offer a really thorough tour of the central London landmarks these bright yellow trucks go past.

Thames Clippers   020 7001 2222
www.thamesclippers.com
Thames Clippers with their large windows allow children to see a completely different view of London. In addition to using an Oyster card for single journeys, you can also buy a River Roamer ticket which allows you to get on and off at various piers, and children under 5 travel free.

The Cutty Sark has been renovated for 2012

days out

Pirate fun aboard the Golden Hinde

art centres and galleries

Barbican Centre   020 7638 4141
Silk Street, EC2Y 8DS
www.barbican.org.uk
Although there are not always children's events on stage here, look out for occasional shows as well as checking out the regular Saturday workshops with the Family Film Club. There are also a number of free family events in the Barbican Children's Library featuring storytellers, poets and magicians. School holidays and bank holiday weekends see art and craft workshops, puppet-making activities and storytelling workshops as well as special events during Children's Bookweek. Open Mon-Sat 9am-11pm, Sun and public holidays 12-11pm.

Camden Arts Centre   020 7472 5500
Arkwright Road, Camden, NW3 6DG
www.camdenartscentre.org
Expect to find galleries, landscaped gardens and a well-organised programme of workshops and creative activities. Check the web for the what's on calendar and look out for the "Make and Do" craft workshops taking place every Sunday between 2-4.30pm, which is free for families to drop in to at any time. There is a family-friendly café with lots of buggy space. Open 10am-6pm.

Design Museum   0870 833 9955
28 Shad Thames, SE1 2YD
www.designmuseum.org
This modern museum on the river near Tower Bridge is a wonderful place to inspire little designers and artists. During the holidays there are lots of special events and throughout the year there are Design Museum Family Days, Children's Gallery Tours and creative workshops (from 5yrs+). Open daily 10am-5.45pm (closed Christmas Day and Boxing Day).

Dulwich Picture Gallery   020 8693 5254
Gallery Road, SE21 7AD
www.dulwichpicturegallery.org.uk
As well as an excellent place for school visits, this airy art gallery also welcomes families on their weekend gallery tours (3pm Sat and Sun). They have drop-in art and craft sessions for all ages on the first and last Sunday or each month, art in the garden during summer months, and other regular drop-in events in school holidays. Good café with highchairs. Open Tues-Fri 10am-5pm, Sat, Sun and Bank Holidays 11am-5pm.

Jackson's Lane Centre   020 8340 5226
269a Archway Road, Highgate, N6 5AA
www.jacksonslane.org.uk
This busy arts centre has been refurbished in recent years but still thrives on a mix of grown-up and children's arts. As well as booking shows suitable for children in their regular programme, there are ongoing dance, music and drama sessions for under-5s including Diddi Dance, Rucksack Music and Crazee Kids), termtime parent and toddler groups for drop-in, and holiday workshops.

National Gallery   020 7747 2885
Trafalgar Square, WC2N 5DN
www.nationalgallery.co.uk
There are free family sessions every Sunday, with Magic Carpet Storytelling in the mornings for under-5s, where children can sit in front of a painting while the narrator brings it to life with a story. On Sundays there are also free hands-on art sessions for children 5 to 11 (11am-1pm), and in the holidays there is a busy programme of activities and events through the week. You can't book ahead but they are popular so go early. Open daily 10am-6pm (Fri until 9pm), closed Christmas Day, Boxing Day and New Year's Day.

National Portrait Gallery   020 7312 2463
2 St Martin's Place, WC2H 0HE
www.npg.org.uk
The National Portrait Gallery organises free family activities at weekends and in school holidays with artist-led workshops and family drop-in sessions. Every third Saturday of the month there are Family Art Workshops suitable for adults and children 5+ at 11.30am and 2.30pm where you can explore the gallery and then take part in an art activity. Get free tickets one hour before the event from the Information Desk. On the same day there are drop-in 30-minute storytelling sessions for 3+ and adults. No ticket required. Open daily 10am-6pm.

OSO Arts Centre　　　　　020 8876 9885
19-21 Station Road, Barnes, SW13 0LF
www.osoarts.org.uk
Set on Barnes common by the pond, this community arts
centre includes Blueberry Playsongs music sessions for little
ones as well as yoga and Pilates classes for mums.

Royal Academy　　　　　020 7300 8000
Burlington House, Piccadilly, W1J 0BD
www.royalacademy.org.uk
Lots of regular family workshops based on current exhibitions
in the main galleries. If you go on a hot day, be prepared with
a change of clothes to let the little ones play in the fountain
jets in the main courtyard. Open 10am-6pm.

Somerset House　　　　　020 7845 4600
The Strand, WC2R 1LA
www.somersethouse.org.uk
Somerset House host regular Saturday family workshops as
well as ice-skating in the winter and free creative drop-ins
during the holidays. Somerset House also hosts the London
Craft Fair bringing together over 300 of the most innovative
and influential international designer-makers and is a rare opportunity to meet the makers and buy their work.

Southbank Centre　　　　　020 7960 5226
Belvedere Road, SE1 8XX
www.southbankcentre.co.uk
There are great family events in the various Southbank
spaces all year round - from classical concerts for young
ones to free performances and art installations such as the
ever-popular 'Appearing Rooms' fountains by Jeppe Hein
that children love to run around in every summer.

Tate Britain & Tate Modern　　　　　020 7887 8888
www.tate.org.uk/families
There are lots of free family things to do at the Tate galleries.
At Tate Britain the art trolley is available for creative sessions
on Saturday and Sunday, 11am-5pm and at anytime you can
access the Family Reading Area or go on one of the family
trails. Every weekend Tate Modern runs Start art sessions for
families, Saturday and Sunday, 12-4pm and special family
trails, guides and the Family Zone area are available to enjoy
when you visit at anytime. There are special sessions during
the weeks in holidays. Make a day of it and take the Thames
Clipper boat along the Thames, from piers just outside either
gallery (under-5s sail free).

baby shows

The Baby Show　　　　　0871 231 0844
www.thebabyshow.co.uk
These are the UK's biggest baby shows for mums, dads, babies, toddlers and grandparents too. Taking place four times
a year in London's Excel Centre (February), at the NEC in
Birmingham (May), Manchester's EventCity (Aug/Sept) and
London's Earls Court (October). In addition to hundreds of
exhibitors there are advice workshops on money matters,
breastfeeding, nutrition with Annabel Karmel and much more.
Ticket prices vary dependent upon time of booking, save by
booking in advance online or by calling 0871 231 0844.

Need to Know: Free activities

When you're out and about, small
children might spend hours in a museum
or get bored in 10 minutes flat, so places
that are free to visit are a Godsend.

- Many of London's best galleries and
  museums are free for all.
- Most others will allow under-12s or
  under-2s in free.
- Watch out for special family days when
  a venue has extra, free entertainment.
- Ask for free trails and activity packs –
  many venues have them at their infor
  mation desk.
- During school holidays places like the
  National Maritime Museum offer daily
  free crafts and activities suited to a
  range of ages.
- For babies and under-5s, venues like the
  Museum of London Docklands run free
  drop-in story and music sessions during
  school hours in term-time.

days out

castles

Buckingham Palace
020 7766 7300
Buckingham Palace Road, SW1A 1AA
www.royalcollection.org.uk
Although most people visit for the art, there is plenty for children (especially aged 5 to 11 years) to do and to get inside the Queen's home is a pretty special thrill. There are family audio tours and garden activities. You will need to check any pushchairs in before touring State Rooms, but there are baby carriers on loan if you need them. Open between Mar-Oct.

Changing the Guard
Buckingham Palace/The Mall, SW1A 1AA
www.changing-the-guard.com
There are two different ceremonies you can catch to see the Queen's red-coated, black fluffy-hatted soldiers. The changing of the Queen's Guard takes place at Buckingham Palace daily at 11.30am in summer and every other day in winter. The Queen's Life Guard changing ceremony takes place each weekday at 11am and 10am and on Sundays at Horse Guards (about five minutes' walk away, in Whitehall).

Hampton Court Palace
0844 482 7777
East Molesey, Surrey, KT8 9AU
www.hrp.org.uk
Even if your children are too young to appreciate the grandeur and evocative space within the Palace (great for children six-plus), the Maze is a hoot that should keep everyone busy for a while. There is also a soft play room for under-5s, audio guides for older children and in rooms like the Tudor kitchens sights and smells have been conjured up to take you all back in time. Open daily Mar-Oct 10am-6pm, Oct-Mar 10am-4.30pm (grounds open longer hours all year round). There is also the annual Hampton Court Flower Show (July) to which children are welcome.

Tower of London
020 7709 0765
Tower Hill, EC3N 4AB
www.hrp.org.uk
Tales of treachery, torture, some of Britain's most dramatic historic moments and the amazing collection of Crown Jewels - there's lots to see but mostly for older children. Newer attractions here include Fortress where you can get a taste of defending a castle under siege and a look at the exotic animals sent as gifts to the Monarchy. There are regular family trails and events, and during school holidays there are wonderful extra activities and re-enactments. Open Mar-Oct Tue-Sat 9am-5.30pm (Sun and Mon from 10am); Nov-Feb Tue-Sat 9am-4.30pm (Sun and Mon from 10am).

Windsor Castle
01753 868 286
Windsor, Berkshire, SL4 1NJ
www.royalcollection.org.uk
There are family trails to follow at this royal residence, and in the holidays there are lovely activities like Christmas crafts. Open daily 9.45am-5.15pm from March-Oct and until 4.15pm Nov-Feb. Children will be fascinated by watching the Changing of the Guard which takes place on alternate days at 11am (Call 020 7321 2233 to double check).

cinemas

Odeon Cinemas
0871 224 4007
www.odeon.co.uk
ODEON Kids screenings are every Saturday and Sunday mornings at pocket money prices. What's more with every child ticket you get a free adult ticket. ODEON Newbies is exclusively for parents with new babies with screenings held on weekday mornings. Branches are in; Barnet, Camden, Covent Garden, Greenwich, Holloway, Kensington, Leicester Square, Putney, Richmond, South Woodford, Streatham, Surrey Quays, Swiss Cottage, Uxbridge and Wimbledon.

Barbican Centre Family Film Club
020 7382 7000
Silk Street, EC2Y 8DS
www.barbican.org.uk/familyfilmclub/membership.htm
Becoming a member of the Barbican Family Film Club brings children a whole host of things to do, see and make. Every Saturday there are family films, as well as access to their activity trolley, and special workshops once a month. For an annual membership, you get discounted film tickets, goody bags and a special invitation to their Christmas party.

BFI London IMAX Cinema
0870 787 2525
1 Charlie Chaplin Walk, Waterloo, SE1 8XR
www.bfi.org.uk/imax
"Image Maximum" refers to the 20m high x 26m wide screen which encompasses your peripheral vision to such an extent that you feel as if you are "in" the movie not merely watching. Added to that you also get a 3D projection making the flat images appear round and totally touchable. So if it's big impact experience you want then you are going to the right place. Lots of great kids movies for the 4yrs+ age group Child standard ticket £5.25, under-4s free.

The Picturehouses
www.picturehouses.co.uk
This independent chain of cinemas offer art-house and foreign-language films alongside more mainstream blockbusters. For new parents check their special 'Big Scream' screenings for mothers and babies; or Autism-friendly screenings for children with particular sound and light sensitivities. A regular kids club on Saturdays shows films for £1 (plus free coffee for parents). Branches are in Clapham, Notting Hill (The Gate), Greenwich, Ritzy Brixton, Stratford East and Hackney.

Phoenix Cinema
020 8442 0442
52 High Road, East Finchley, N2 9PJ
www.phoenixcinema.co.uk
The Phoenix offers regular 'Bringing up Baby' screenings and a Saturday kids club. They also offer bottle warming facilities and have a lift which is convenient for pushchairs.

Rio Cinema
020 7241 9410
103-7 Kingsland High Street, E8 2PB
www.riocinema.co.uk
The Rio offers specially priced tickets - £2 children and £3 accompanying adults - for the Saturday Morning Picture Club and Tuesday afternoon Playcentre Matinees, to help children to enjoy great films at an affordable price.

farms

Brooks Farm   **020 8539 4278**
Skeltons Lane Park, Leyton, E10 5BS
www.walthamforest.gov.uk/brooks-farm-leyton.htm
Because this farm is a semi-working farm the life of the place
changes through the seasons, though there is always a
chance to get close to farm animals, pets and Merlin the
llama. There is a chance to stroke some of the animals and
get a picture of working farm life, as well as gardens to explore. They have a social room with a kitchen which is suitable for parties. Open Tue-Sun 10.30am-5.30pm (winter
10.30am-4.30pm).

Coram's Fields   **020 7837 6138**
93 Guilford Street, WC1N 1DN
www.coramsfields.org
This delightful little park near Russell Square offers a rare
chance to hear sheep and hens making their farmyard
noises in central London. Adults aren't allowed into the
park unless they are accompanied by children and in addition to the handful of animals, there is a vegetarian café, a
huge sandpit and playgrounds suitable for toddlers and
older children, a paddling pool that is shaded by huge
trees in summer, and lots of space to run around. Open
daily except Christmas Day and Boxing Day, 9am-7pm
(winter 9am-dusk).

Featherdown Farms, see Travel pg 174

Need to Know: Animal visit safety

In recent years there have been a handful of incidents regarding hygiene and child
safety at farms around London, with E.coli being a particularly dangerous hazard.
Here are some useful tips to make your day out a happy one.

- Cover existing grazes and cuts before visiting.

- Take any inhalers as farms can be dusty and leafy.

- Pregnant visitors should avoid contact with animals, especially sheep at lambing time.

- There will be lots of hand-washing stations – USE THEM!

- Before having food and drink, wash hands again.

- Try to discourage your children from walking in animal droppings and wash

- down wellies when you get home.

- Don't give back dropped toys and dummies before thoroughly washing them.

- Monitor any contact your child has with the animals, including feeding and petting.

- To avoid bites or other injuries, remind your child animals should be treated with respect and that some won't enjoy being touched.

- Follow the advice and instructions at the farm or zoo you are visiting.

...arm   **020 8543 5300**
and Riding School (from 8yrs+)
39 Windsor Avenue, Merton Abbey, SW19 2RR
www.deencityfarm.co.uk
See geese, ducks, ponies, horses, cows, pigs and other farm animals and pets along with a couple of alpacas and explore the community garden at this lively farm set on a part of the National Trust's Modern Hall Park Estate. The farm is very child-focused with plenty of opportunities for little ones to get a real feel for farming. They run regular special events and you can book children's parties here. Tue-Sun 10am-4.30pm.

Freightliners Farm   **020 7609 0467**
Sheringham Road, Islington, N7 8PF
www.freightlinersfarm.org.uk
A small but wonderful city farm in Islington, Freightliners has pigs, lambs, hens and other animals as well as an ornamental garden for chilling out. This community-led project often has special events in holidays, a café and a farm shop, too. Open 10am-4.45pm Tues-Sun (open until 4pm autumn/winter).

Hackney City Farm   **020 7729 6381**
1a Goldsmiths Row, off Hackney Road, E2 8QA
www.hackneycityfarm.co.uk
See pigs, cows, sheep, birds and other cute farm and pet animals, find out how to grow a fruit and veg patch or join in the many craft activities on offer regularly through the year. They also run several green farm projects and have a fab Italian/Mediterranean café. Open Tue-Sun 10am-4.30pm.

Trips out of town

When you're making a day of it, you need somewhere that will entertain the oldest and the youngest in your party. These ideas are within a day's visit of London, or you could make a weekend of it.

Butterfly World Hertfordshire
www.butterflyworldproject.com

Hever Castle Kent
www.hevercastle.co.uk

Chessington World of Adventures
www.chessington.com

Peppa Pig World New Forest
www.peppapigworld.co.uk

Woburn Safari Park Bedfordshire
www.woburn.co.uk

Hounslow Urban Farm   **020 8831 9658**
Faggs Road. Feltham. TW14 0LZ
www.hounslow.info/urbanfarm
A recent amalgamation of this farm with the Tropical Zoo at Syon Park has secured the future of both these animal sanctuaries. They've got micro-pigs, lambs, peacocks, owls and baby pygmy goats. Every weekend and through holidays there are family-friendly events including pig racing and animal-handling. Open daily 10am-5pm (5.30pm summer, 4pm winter).

Golder's Hill Park   **020 8455 5183**
West Heath Avenue, Golders Green, NW11 7QP
Wander down to the lower part of Golder's Hill Park and you'll find a small 'zoo' to wander round for free as part of your visit. There are deer and small mammals and birds from other parts of the world. It's not huge but it's a lovely way to spend your morning on the way to the playground.

Kentish Town City Farm   **020 7916 5421**
1 Cressfield Close, Kentish Town, NW5 4BN
www.ktcityfarm.org.uk
This is very much a city farm aimed at giving local socially disadvantaged children and those with special needs the chance to experience a farm setting and real animals close-up. Visitors are encouraged to get involved with all aspects of animal care. There are regular activities including low-cost pony riding for children resident in Camden. Open daily 9am-5pm. Free admission.

Mudchute Farm & Park   **020 7515 5901**
Pier Street, Isle of Dogs, E14 3HP
www.mudchute.org
Set in rolling parkland on the Isle of Dogs, Mudchute Farm is a free to visit unexpected animal haven in the shadow of the new corporate centre, Canary Wharf. There are over 200 animals and birds to look at including rare breed farm beasts, a pets corner, and their very popular llamas. The riding school and park café (Mudchute Kitchen) are worth checking out too. Party options available. Open Tue-Sun 9am-5pm.

Newham City Farm   **020 7474 4960**
Stansfeld Road, Beckton, E16 3HR
Pigs, sheep, pygmy goats, beehives and a duck pond - Newham City Farm has a real country feel to it and is a great escape for a morning with the animals. Plus it's free to wander around (donations welcome). Open Tue-Sun 10am-5pm (winter 10am-4pm).

Spitalfields City Farm   **020 7247 8762**
Buxton Street, E1 5AR
www.spitalfieldscityfarm.org
There are lots of great activities at this city farm throughout each week, but a real highlight for children aged 8 to 13 is the Young Farmers Club on Saturdays, 10.30am-3.30pm, which gives children a chance to really get stuck into the running of the farm and take part in creative activities. Open daily 10am-4pm. Closed Mon.

Stepping Stones Farm

020 7790 8204

Stepney Way, Stepney High Street, E1 3DG
www.steppingstonesfarm.net

Giving people a chance to sample rural life and crafts for over 30 years, Stepping Stones is completely volunteer-run. Schools are welcome during the week and the public can look around on weekends and Bank Holidays. Open Tues-Sun, 10am-4pm and bank holiday Mondays. Admission is free, donations are very welcome!

Surrey Docks City Farm

020 7231 1010

South Wharf, Rotherhithe Street, SE16 5ET
www.surreydocksfarm.org.uk

Complete range of animals including donkeys, pigs, sheep, goats, rabbits and ponies. You can buy fresh produce from the farm on Saturdays and find out more about their animal welfare as you get close to their herds and flocks. They also host birthday parties and you can take your own food. Open 10am-5pm. Closed Mon.

Vauxhall City Farm

020 7582 4204

24 St Oswalds Place, entrance (Tyers Street), SE11 5HS
www.vauxhallcityfarm.info

See the horses, cows, rabbits and hens at this busy city farm, along with a chance to enjoy your picnic in the ecology space or discover how natural dyes are used by the farm's spinning group. Open Wed-Sun 10.30am-4pm (closed Christmas Day and Boxing Day).

museums

British Museum

020 7323 8000

Great Russell Street, WC1B 3DG
www.thebritishmuseum.ac.uk

For younger children, the vibrant, light space of the Great Court is the real draw, but as children begin to find out about the many key periods in British and world history they become fascinated by the many artefacts in the galleries dedicated to periods like Ancient Greece and Rome, Ancient Egypt and Asia. There are special handling sessions where children can get close to these historic pieces with a museum guide, there is a children's trail, and every weekend there are free activities for families. During special exhibitions and holidays there is often free live entertainment too. Open 10am-5pm daily and 8.30pm on Thurs and Fri. Admission free.

Discover

020 8536 5555

383-387 High Street, Stratford, E15 4QZ
www.discover.org.uk

This Stratford-based activity centre provides a unique sensory experience for children, based on and around children's story books. On rainy days children can explore inside the story trail, walking across a wobbly bridge, or stepping on stones across the river to the sound of sploshing. You can visit the lion's den, make a spoon puppet or have fun dressing up. Outside there is a wooden pirate ship in a small garden, where you can walk up a chain, jump from a gang plank, and peep through portholes. This year's exhibition is Superheroes

The Kid's Zone at the National Army Museum

Took my 2 boys aged 5 and 3 to **Disney on Ice**. The older one really enjoyed it, and appreciated the skating skills. He got restless after an hour and half. The youngest was bored after about 45 minutes. 1 hr 45 is a bit too long.

Dragon stole the show. Too be expected I suppose, but definitely merchandising overkill.

Busy Lizzie, mother of 2

(running until 4th November). Open between 10am-5pm except Mon during term time, and 11am-5pm Sat-Sun. Entry is £4 for adults and children aged 2yrs+ - under 2's are free.

Geffrye Museum   020 7739 9893
136 Kingsland Road, E2 8EA
www.geffrye-museum.org.uk
Although this museum is dedicated to British home interiors and gardens through the ages, children will love a visit here as much as the grown-ups. There are always wonderful activities inside and out, such as Saturday Specials (first Sat of each month) with quizzes, crafts and other workshops. In the holidays other special family events in the gardens are great fun. Open 10am-5pm Tues-Sat, 12pm-5pm Sun. Admission free.

Horniman Museum and Gardens   020 8699 1872
100 London Road, Forest Hill, SE23 3PQ
www.horniman.ac.uk
This museum has both permanent museum-style exhibits (music and musical instruments from all around the world, as well as stuffed animals/birds in glass cabinets) combined with temporary exhibitions, children's workshops and a small but perfectly stocked aquarium which caters well for toddlers. There's a good café/restaurant with highchairs which extends into a large Victoria glasshouse and the shop has a good selection of museum related toys and crafts. Open 10.30am-5.30pm daily. Admission free (apart from temporary exhibitions).

Imperial War Museum   020 7416 5320
Lambeth Road, SE1 6HZ
www.iwm.org.uk
More suitable for over-5s, this excellent museum does not flinch from reflecting the reality of war, but it does so in a positive and forward-looking way that inspires children. See tanks, rockets and planes, walk through a recreated trench and get stuck into the regular family events. Café, restaurant and shop. Open 10am-6pm daily. Admission free.

London Transport Museum   020 7565 7299
The Piazza, Covent Garden, WC2E 7BB
www.ltmuseum.co.uk
Children can get a real feel for what it's like to drive buses, trams and trains old and new at this lively museum. There are always themed events around school holidays and special

exhibitions, and there are hands-on galleries where children can explore London life through the sounds, texture and experiences of bygone times. There are free, downloadable trails and for smaller children there is a miniature London for them to take over! As well as the Upper Deck cafeteria and bar, there is an indoor picnic area space if you want to bring your own food. Open daily 10am-7pm (11am-7pm Fri, 10am-6pm Sun).

Museum of London Docklands   020 7001 9844
1 Warehouse, West India Quay, Hertsmere Rd, E14 4AL
www.museumindocklands.org.uk
Set in an old warehouse, this museum tells the story of the Thames, the docks and the world beyond which was brought to London in cargo clippers, and sailors who arrived on ships in ancient times. Displays in the main galleries appeal to older children though even toddlers will love the dark alleyways created as 'Sailortown', the lawless docklands of the Victorian era. The highlight of this visit for preschoolrs has to be Mudlarks - an indoor sensory play area with beachcombing activites and more. There are special free activities and storytelling sessions through the year. Free. Open daily 10am-6pm.

Museum of London   020 7001 9844
150 London Wall, EC2Y 5HN
www.museumoflondon.org.uk
Children of school age will love the evocative Fire of London exhibition, and junior school age children will be able to lead you through the Roman galleries with ease, but even smaller ones can enjoy the free activities that are on offer through trails and weekend events. Open 10am-5.30 Mon-Sat, 12pm-5.50pm Sun. Admission free.

National Army Museum   020 7881 2455
Royal Hospital Road, Chelsea, SW3 4HT
www.national-army-museum.ac.uk
Life-sized models of soldiers, model battlefields and other artefacts tell the story of 1000 years of British military history. Make a b-line for the Kids' Zone where there is a free interactive learning and play space including a forest and castle. There are also construction, reading, art activity and board-game areas. It's especially good for under-10s and there is a soft-play area for babies and toddlers. There are baby changing units available in the male and female toilets and if you've taken a picnic you can eat it in the Lunchroom area of the café. Open 10am-5.30pm daily.

National Maritime Museum   020 8312 6565
Romney Road, Greenwich, SE10 9NF
www.nmm.ac.uk
Find out about boats and ships and Britain's seafaring glory days. For little fighters the Nelson section is full of fascination, including a peek at the uniform he died in (the blood on the stockings is from one of his fellow seamen, who died a few hours before he fell himself at the Battle of Trafalgar). At weekends and in the holidays there are lots of free performances and children's workshops to enjoy. In the rear grounds of the museum there is a jolly playground, too. Open daily 10am-5pm.

Natural History Museum   020 7942 5000
Cromwell Road, SW7 5BD
www.nhm.ac.uk
This popular museum has been loved by generations, though it's best suited to children who are fascinated by dinosaurs and older children who enjoy the study of nature rather than those expecting to see lots of cute animals (most appear here as bones or pinned up behind glass). The dinosaur exhibitions (special events are paid for but the rest are free) are wonderful but do expect to queue to go round unless you get here very early. For older children (over-7s) The Cocoon is a state-of-the-art interactive space where you can even see the Museum's scientists at work. There are free explorer backpacks for under-7s, and if you bring your own picnic you can eat it on the lawns outside or in the basement family area. Children aged 8-11 can be booked onto sleepover 'Dino Snores'. Café/restaurant, nappy changing and shop. Open 10-6pm Mon-Sat, 11am-5.50pm Sun. Admission is free.

Pollock's Toy Museum   020 7636 3452
1 Scala Street, W1P 1LT
www.pollockstoymuseum.com
Set in a tiny-looking shop on a backstreet in central London, Pollock's is a treasure trove just waiting to be discovered. A collection of Victorian toy theatres, Edwardian tin toys and many other bygone delights will capture your child's imagination. If the old dolls and teddies inspire, there's a charming toy shop on the ground floor. Open Mon-Sat 10am-5pm.

Ragged School Museum   020 8980 6405
46-50 Copperfield Road, E3 4RR
www.raggedschoolmuseum.org.uk
This is a curious museum where children can really get an idea for just how lucky they are today! In costume and with recreated school rooms, this museum tells the tale of what life was like for children going to school in the Victorian times. A Ragged School was a basic educational place for poor children so you can imagine how hard life was for the young pupils. Go on one of the Sundays when children can sample a lesson themselves.

Royal Observatory   O20 8312 6565
and Planetarium
Blackheath Avenue, Greenwich Park, SE10 8XJ
www.nmm.ac.uk
Sitting at the top of Greenwich Park, this is to spot from which Greenwich Meantime is set - a line on the ground in the courtyard marks out where 'east' and 'west' begin. The buildings here show how time has been measured and how the science of the stars has shaped out view of the world and beyond. Just behind the Observatory you'll find the Peter Harrison Planetarium which costs a small fee to enter. They have regular films and the Space Safari is suitable for children under 7 (under-3s admitted free). All other shows are recommended for ages 5+. The Royal Observatory is free and open daily 10am-5pm.

River & Rowing Museum   01491 415 600
Mill Meadows, Henley on Thames, RG9 1BF
www.rrm.co.uk
Explore the magical story of Wind in the Willows in this

Top 5: Family-friendly chains

Many restaurants provide kids' menus or smaller portions, but these places offer a special welcome to children, with table activities and great food. All these restaurants have locations across London so check their websites for your nearest branch.

....

Carluccio's *www.carluccios.com* Simple but delicious Italian food served quickly for restless diners. The children's menu is broad enough for all tastes and milder dishes from that menu can be served in adult portions for bigger kids.

Giraffe *www.giraffe.net* The huge family-friendly menu here means that children aren't just expected to settle for sausage and chips if they fancy a small portion of steak. Indeed, the menu takes into account different sized appetites for little ones and older kids, without hiking up to adult prices.

Nando's www.nandos.co.uk Portugese peri-peri chicken might seem a bit exotic for some children but the Nandinos menu includes a milder version of grown-ups' favourites. This restaurant's friendly atmosphere has established it as a firm favourite for birthday parties, too.

Pizza Express www.pizzaexpress.com Whoever thought of dough balls with Nutella a couple of years back was a genius. The Piccolo Menu covers a range of meaty and veggie choices and service is fairly snappy.

Pizza Hut www.pizzahut.co.uk Not the poshest pizza place in town but their kids' parties offering includes making your own pizza and unlimited visits to the Ice Cream Factory (ice cream plus buckets of sprinkles). The staff are patient and friendly, even if some of your guests behave like it's the last days of Rome…

enchanting walk-through exhibition. E.H. Sheppard's famous illustrations are brought to life with beautiful 3D models of their adventures. See Ratty and Mole's picnic on the riverbank, get lost in the Wild Wood or watch the weasels at Toad Hall. The Museum also has free backpacks full of puzzles, stories and games for children, as well as a Museum trail and colouring and crafts in the galleries. There is a fantastic programme of workshops and fun days for families during school holidays, full details are on the website. There is a great café serving home-cooked food and lovely Wind in the Willows lunchboxes for children. The Museum is a member of the Family Friendly Museum scheme and a signatory of the Kids in Museums manifesto.

Science Museum   020 7942 4454
Exhibition Road, South Kensington, SW7 2DD
www.sciencemuseum.org.uk

There are exhibits and activities to fire all imaginations here. The best bet is to visit their website, which organises visit suggestions by age group from under-5s to adults, but generally, there are interesting things to explore for all ages. New galleries include 'Who Am I?' where you can see how your body is put together, try a new look or even hear what your voice would sound like if you were the opposite sex. The IMAX 3D cinema shows films better suited to older children (there is a charge for these, and the fabulous Fly Zone interactive flight simulators). Special events include workshops, storytelling and science displays.

V & A Museum of Childhood   020 8980 2415
Cambridge Heath Road, Bethnal Green, E2 9PA
www.museumofchildhood.org.uk

Refurbished a couple of years ago, this is a light and airy space that's welcoming for children and adults. Exhibits include glass cases full of toys and other artefacts from young life through the ages, but there are also plenty of things children can touch and play with. Dressing up, DIY punch and judy puppet shows, a sandpit for little ones, and an amazing sensory corner for babies will charm, as will the rocking horses. There are daily and weekly activities for all ages (0-12), most are drop-in and free to attend. During holidays there are extra themed events organised.

theatres

Arts Depot   020 8369 5455
Nether Street, Tally Ho Corner, North Finchley, N12 0GA
www.artsdepot.co.uk

There's music, comedy and theatre for all here, but their busy children's theatre programme, music sessions and other activities make this North Finchley arts centre a wonderful hub for families.

Chicken Shed Theatre   020 8351 6161
Chase Side, Southgate, N14 4PE
www.chickenshed.org.uk

So much of what is on offer for children isn't suitable until they are 3 years old, but at the morning Tales from the Shed

The Legoland Hotel, new for 2012

shows at this theatre you'll see babes in laps smiling away to the colourful, musical antics of the performers and their fluffly cuddly friends. Toddlers are encouraged to get up and wander around the live performance or swamp the stage area when one of their favourite furry characters appears from behind a curtain. An absolute joy for any child pre-school and there are many youth theatre projects to get involved in.

Colour House Children's Theatre 020 8542 5511
Merton Abbey Mills, Watermill Way, SW19 2RD
www.colourhousetheatre.co.uk
Although there is comedy and theatre for adults here, the Children's Theatre is a real draw. The lively weekend shows (when in season) appeal to pre-schoolers, and it's possible to book a party here where the performers even join your children after the show for food, games and a mini disco.

Little Angel Theatre 020 7226 1787
14 Dagmar Passage, off Cross Street, Islington, N1
www.littleangeltheatre.com
London's first and only permanent puppet theatre, the shows here are magical and can be enjoyed by children and parents. The setting of a proper theatre is a wonderful experience for children and the programme changes through the year, including classic stories retold, such as 'Fantastic Mr Fox' and 'Handa's Surprise'. There are regular puppet clubs and fun days for children aged 2 to 16, and for children 11 to 15 there is the Little Angel Youth Theatre.

Lyric Theatre Hammersmith 08700 500 511
King Street, Hammersmith, W6 0QL
www.lyrictheatre.co.uk
This is more of a great theatre with Children's shows than a children's theatre. But they have a comprehensive programme of events and shows for pre-school children. Their website includes a section "Lyric Children" with shows highlighted in blue for the Under 5s. There's also a café, nappy changing facilities and a great picnic place round the corner on the riverside.

New Wimbledon Theatre 0870 060 6646
The Broadway, Wimbledon, SW19 1QG
www.theambassadors.com/newwimbledon
This theatre regularly stages shows for children. Call or visit website for upcoming shows and times.

Polka Theatre for Children 020 8543 4888
240 The Broadway, Wimbledon, SW19 1SB
www.polkatheatre.com
Standing proud for decades, this south-west London theatre is dedicated to theatre, workshops and other shows specifically for children. As well as puppet shows there are live comedy shows and lively ways for children to get involved themselves. Events are suitable for pre-schoolers all the way up to teens.

Puppet Theatre Barge 020 7249 6876
opposite 35 Blomfield Road, W9 2PF
www.puppetbarge.com
When in London, the Barge is moored at Little Venice. Even in winter, a puppet show in this compact and cosy floating theatre is a magical experience. Rows only take about six people at a time and children are seated in spots where they won't have their view blocked by a grown-up. Shows include fables, musical comedies and other simple child-friendly puppet theatre. Check the website for their programme; it clearly states what age groups each show is suitable for and many are suited to the very young.

Tricycle Theatre 020 7328 1000
269 Kilburn High Road, NW6 7JR
www.tricycle.co.uk
There are special youth programmes and children's activities at this Kilburn theatre. Saturday Theatre and Family Films are just two of their regular sessions and in term time there are courses available for young people.

Unicorn Theatre 020 7645 0560
147 Tooley Street, More London, Southwark, SE1 2HZ
www.unicorntheatre.com
This dynamic theatre presents shows and workshops to suit all ages of children.

theme parks

Chessington World of Adventures 01372 729 560
Leatherhead Road, Chessington, Surrey, KT9 2NE
www.chessington.co.uk
Although the theme park rides take centre stage, there are still a wide range of beasts from zebras and monkeys to tigers and penguins to gaze upon in what for decades was simply a zoo with a few slides! There are rides for little children and some toddler shows for when you need to sit back and chill out. Older children will no doubt love the late opening hours every Halloween… Open daily March-October. The zoo remains open for selected weekends through the winter with seasonal activities taking place.

Legoland 0870 504 0404
Winklfield Road, Windsor, Berkshire, SL4 4AY
www.legoland.co.uk
Legoland Windsor, just 40 minutes from Central London, is a mecca for children and adults alike, who come to pay homage to the primary-coloured bricks. While it's suitable for all ages (particularly the 5-12yrs), the lengthy queues during school holidays and half terms are testing (including getting into and out of the car park), and toddler tantrums are par for the course. Despite these challenges, this much-loved park offers exciting rides for young children including the Dragon rollercoaster and Pirate Falls. Miniland and Duplo Land are a few of the places to make a beeline for with under 5's, and many recommend starting at the far end of the park to avoid the queues, which can also be avoided by the purchase of a Q-bot. The latest ride to open, the Atlantis Submarine Voyage, is a submarine voyage through a 1 million litre tank, complete with reef-tip sharks, parrot fish and cownose rays swimming between Lego figures such as King Neptune. The enormous Lego shop is definitely a highlight. Open mid-March to early November - check website for opening times. New for 2012 is the Legoland Hotel helping families to make the most of their visit with pre-opening access times.

Thorpe Park　　　　　　　　0870 444 4466
Staines Road, Chertsey, Surrey, KT16 8PN
www.thorpepark.com
There is lots to do for little ones at Thorpe Park while the big kids swoosh along on daring rides in the sky. Indeed, Neptune's Beach is a sand a water space for families to paddle and play that is exclusive to visitors with young children. Small children will also love the scenic railway and gentle rides in the Octopus Garden.

zoos and wetlands

Battersea Park Children's Zoo　　020 7924 5826
Battersea Park, Battersea, SW11 4NJ
www.batterseaparkzoo.co.uk
This zoo is very child-focused, with cute ring-tailed lemurs and otters to watch, animal encounters to enjoy and a playground for letting off steam. From monkeys to mice, rabbits to exotic birds, there is plenty to see. Birthday party options include guided tours. Open 10am-5.30pm (winter 10am-4pm).

London Wildlife Trust　　　　020 7252 9186
28 Marden Road, East Dulwich, SE15 4EE
www.wildlondon.org.uk
There are 57 nature reserves dotted around London, including many in central parts of the city. These are wonderful spots in which to get close to mini-beasts or just to run around outdoors. These include the Centre for Wildlife Gardening (28 Marsden Road SE15 4EE, 020 7252 9186) which is open Tue-Thur, and Sun 10.30am-4.30pm. Also, just behind Kings Cross and St Pancras stations you'll find Camley Street Nature Reserve (12 Camley Street N1C 4PW, 020 7833 2311) which is open daily 10am-5pm.

Paradise Wildlife Park　　　　01992 470 490
White Stubbs Lane, Broxbourne, Herts, EN10 7QA
www.pwpark.com
Paradise is a fantastic place to get up close and personal with tigers, lions, monkeys, zebras, reptiles, birds and camels. What makes Paradise unique is the fact you can touch and feed many of the animals. Paradise is widely regarded as the most interactive zoo in the UK.

WWT London Wetland Centre　　020 8409 4400
Queen Elizabeth Walk, Barnes, SW13 9WT
www.wwt.org.uk/visit-us/london/
In south west London, this vast wetland area is a great place from which to escape the city's bustle. Spot feathered friends have fun pond dipping, explore the designer Bat House, and allow the children to let off steam in the adventure playground. At weekends there are family activities including art and craft workshops and storytelling sessions and at Christmas there are free husky rides and a Santa's Grotto. New to the centre in 2012 are 4 Asian short-clawed otters in a purpose built hide. Open daily 9.30am-6pm.

ZSL London Zoo　　　　　　020 7722 3333
Regent's Park, London, NW1 4RY
www.zsl.org
Regent's Park zoo has delighted generations of children and continues to innovate in animal welfare as well as a better visiting experience, so parents in fear of sad-looking animals hopefully will be pleasantly surprised. In the last couple of years the new Gorilla Kingdom walk-through experience, the swampy indoor Rainforest Life areas and Penguin Beach have given a fresh vitality to the place. Birthday parties catered for. Open 10am (closing times vary - from 4pm in winter to 6pm in summer).

Visit the new otter sanctuary at WWT London Wetland Centre

Travel with babies and toddlers

Many luxury holiday companies specialise in family packages so you don't have to be less adventurous or settle for cheap and cheerful options now you've got children. However, whether you're booking a self-catering or hotel holiday, there are a few things to bear in mind.

What to consider first

With babies and children, your family timetable is likely to be less predictable than a hotel's restaurant opening hours. Consider going self-catering (or at least in a self-contained flat or villa within a hotel complex) so you have your own space to make noise, eat and be busy at the hours that suit you.

If you are booking a place with a pool, consider what access your child might have to it, unattended. Many villas offer gated pool areas even if the pool is for your use only.

What else does the property offer? Pre-kids, a shower room might have sufficed but if bathtime is a valuable and loved part of your baby's evening routine, make sure you book somewhere with a bath. Also check what staircases are like at the property, and if there are stairgates. Do you need a cot? Travelcots are heavy, but if you don't feel confident about what is offered by the holiday company, take your own.

Destinations

Consider flight distances and the likely weather where you want to go. Do these suit your child? And will your baby or child need to get vaccinations? Check this out in good time and consult your doctor about their suitability before you book anything.

Travel

Make sure all passports are up to date before you book any travel and find out if the place you are going to requires a visa for entry.

If you are flying, check facilities at the airport you'll be using on your way out and on your return as you will have to amuse your child during check-in and security queuing times. Ideally, if your child still needs a pushchair, you will be able to keep yours until you board the plane, or at least borrow something similar from the airline when you check your buggy in.

Find out exactly what carry-on items you will be allowed to board the plane with. Don't forget you can carry most of your baby essentials, including food for use while you're away, in your checked-in luggage, so you don't need to lug it all through security anyway.

Think also about what food is likely to be available on board your flight. If it's not included in the price of your flight ticket you might as well buy something you know your child likes to eat from the departure lounge cafés rather than making do with the expensive, limited choice on the plane.

travel

camping

Canvas Holidays
0845 268 0827
www.canvasholidays.co.uk
A independent family camping holiday company with 39 years experience of providing self-drive camping and mobile home holidays in France and the rest of Europe, including Spain, Italy, Luxembourg, Germany, Austria, Switzerland and Holland.

Eurocamp
0844 406 0402
www.eurocamp.co.uk
Eurocamp is the market-leader in self catering holidays to Europe. Their superbly equipped holiday parks are located in 12 European countries and now the USA and Canada too and offer a range of accommodation. A number of the sites offer free swimming lessons.

Feather Down Farms
01420 80804
www.featherdown.co.uk
Feather Down Farms are essentially camping holidays without having to assemble a tent. Each farm location (across the UK, Holland and France) hosts a few rather up-market canvas structures and gives visitors access to washing/laundry facilities as well as selling farm produce via an on-site store. Each tent has a traditional oven, provides fluffy duvets and a cold water tap. Surrouding you are paddocks of friendly animals with a dawn chorus to match. Some have bike rental facilities, so you and can get out and about a bit to see the surrounding countryside too. Exactly the right balance of "roughing it" and "home comforts".

Keycamp
0844 406 0200
www.keycamp.co.uk
Stay in a fully equipped 'Supertent' with 4 bedrooms, chalet or a luxury mobile home with shower and toilet. Camping sites across 9 countries including France, Spain, Italy, Croatia, Austria, Switzerland and the USA. Kids clubs are also available at most of the sites.

Siblu Holidays
0871 911 2288
www.siblu.com
With 6 Siblu selection parcs in France and an additional 19 across France, Spain and Italy, these family orientated holidays offer specific children's activities between May and September. Bubbles for 1-4yr olds and the Pirate Club for 5-9yr olds, with some parcs offering pony riding lessons.

hotels: child friendly

Armathwaite Hall Hotel
01768 776 551
Bassenthwaite Lake, Keswick, Cumbria, CA12 4RE
www.armathwaite-hall.com
This Luxury 4 star Lake District Country House Hotel is privately owned by the resident Graves family. They have many excellent facilities for families including an indoor swimming pool (and Spa), with 'Trotters World of Animals' within the grounds and children's summer holiday activities. They offer baby listening if you are dining in the hotel, or they can arrange for a baby sitter to come in if you are going out.

Babington House
01373 812 266
Babington, Frome, Somerset, BA11 3RW
www.babingtonhouse.co.uk
This is a small boutique hotel with 32 bedrooms, located in the Main House, Coach House, Stable Block and Lodge. The family bedrooms are really mini-apartments with adjoining bedrooms, en suite bathrooms, terrace and equipped with the latest technology from plasma screens and DVD players to wireless internet access as well as baby products. They provide a free crèche service in The Little House from 1yr+ where entertainment, games and other activities are provided for all ages. An indoor and outdoor swimming pool provides special children's sessions.

Bedruthan Steps Hotel
01637 860 555
Mawgan Porth, Cornwall, TR8 4BU
www.bedruthan.com
Family run hotel perfect for all the family with Ofsted registered clubs, and even a 'Teenage Room' for older siblings. Great indoor soft play area including separate toddler section with ride on toys. Themed art and craft workshops supervised by trained nursery assistants. Good outdoor activities including a shallow paddling/learners' swimming pool and activity playground. Also for children who find sitting down to a meal with grown ups a little boring, there is a Supper Club from 7pm.

Calcot Manor
01666 890 391
Tetbury, Gloucestershire, GL8 8YJ
www.calcotmanor.co.uk
The charming country house hotel, set in peaceful gardens, is renowned for the excellence of its restaurant and the informality of its Gumstool Inn. It offers 35 beautifully furnished bedrooms, with several options for families including Deluxe Family Suite with a twin bed children's room. The Playzone is a converted barn soft play area, and also on offer is a superb health and beauty spa, which children are aslo able to use at specific times.

Crieff Hydro Hotel
01764 655 555
Crieff, Perthshire, Scotland, PH7 3LQ
www.crieffhydro.co.uk
This is one of Scotland leading hotel resorts with a contemporary four star hotel and self-catering lodges and cottages. They have excellent childcare facilities with a dedicated "Big Country" nursery/playroom which offers daily creche periods for 2-12yr olds. There are two swimming pools, bikes to hire and a dedicated hair and beauty salon for the spa-minded.

Dunblane Hydro
01786 822 551
Perth Road, Dunblane, Scotland, FK15 0HG
www.dunblanehydrohotel.com
Luxurious Victorian Hotel set in over 10 acres of landscaped grounds, ideal location to explore the Central Highlands, Stirling and Loch Lomond National Park. Playroom, Board Games Library, Baby sitting, Children's High Teas offer youngsters a mouth-watering selection of their favourite foods and are served daily from 5pm-6pm. A crèche is available during the school holidays.

Knoll House   01929 450 450
Studland Bay, Dorset, BH19 3AQ
www.knollhouse.co.uk
Gardens, pools, tennis and golf for all ages, health spa, playroom, separate children's restaurant, adventure playground. Easy access to 3 miles of golden beach. Connecting rooms for families with children.

Fowey Hall   01726 833 866
Hanson Drive, Fowey, Cornwall, PL23 1ET
www.foweyhallhotel.co.uk
One of the most impressive family hotels in Cornwall, Fowey Hall overlooks the pretty sailing town of Fowey as well as enjoying spectacular views over the estuary and far out to sea. The perfect place to unwind, relax and enjoy some memorable times with your family.

Moonfleet Manor   01305 786 948
Fleet Road, Weymouth, Dorset, DT3 4EH
www.moonfleetmanorhotel.co.uk
Moonfleet Manor, overlooking the world famous Chesil Beach and the Fleet Lagoon, is set in the heart of some of England's least discovered, yet most beautiful countryside. This handsome Georgian manor presides over an inspirational location of World Heritage status.

New Park Manor   01590 623 467
New Park Manor, Lyndhurst Road, New Forest, SO42 7QH
www.newparkmanorhotel.co.uk
In 1666, King Charles II designated New Park Manor as his favourite hunting lodge on his return from exile in France. Today, New Park Manor provides guests with an array of family friendly facilities - including an award winning Spa, extensive gardens and a complimentary crèche for children up to eight years old.

Polurrian Bay Hotel   01326 240 421
Polurrian Road, Mullion, Cornwall, TR12 7EN
www.polurrianhotel.com
Perched on the cliffs amongst 12 acres of gardens, this luxury family seaside hotel offers stunning views across Mounts Bay and the Atlantic Ocean beyond. All of our public rooms have a sunny, welcoming feel, whilst our bedrooms feature fluffy towels, comfy beds and spectacular views.

Priory Bay Hotel   01983 613 146
Priory Drive, Seaview, Isle of Wight PO34 5BU
www.priorybay.co.uk
If you're after a pampering break on the Isle of Wight then check out the Priory Bay Hotel. They have family rooms (with a seperate sleeping area or twin bedroom) in the hotel as well as self-catering cottage suites for larger families and dogs. No onsite creche facilities - but they offer a Saturday and Sunday lunch nanny service. You can also hire a therapist for massages etc in your room.

The Club Hotel and Spa   01534 876 500
Green Street, St. Helier, Jersey, JE2 4UH
Chic townhouse 5 star hotel with marine-based spa and Michelin-starred Bohemia restaurant to pamper mum and dad.

travel

The Elms   **01299 896 666**
Stockton Road, Abberley, Worcestershire, WR6 6AT
www.theelmshotel.co.uk
The Elms Hotel is much loved by children and parents alike. Located in beautiful rural Worcestershire, this Queen Anne mansion boasts a family friendly spa with adjacent brasserie, fine dining restaurant and complimentary crèche.

The Elmfield   **01271 863 377**
Torrs Park, Ilfracombe, EX34 8AZ
www.theelmfield.com
The Elmfield is a small boutique style hotel with a friendly home from home atmosphere. Children of all ages are welcome, and well catered for. Access to the Coastal path and lovely views combine with the heated swimming pool, play room, movie-lounge and cosy bar, to provide a perfect get away.

The Evesham Hotel   **01386 765 566**
Coppers Lane, Evesham, Worcestershire, WR11 1DA
www.eveshamhotel.com
Situated on the edge of Evesham, this hotel is run with humour and a little eccentricity. They claim well-behaved children are as welcome as well-behaved grown ups. No specific crèche or children's clubs but baby listening/sitting is available. Indoor and outdoor play areas and an indoor swimming pool.

The Grove   **01923 807 807**
Chandler's Cross, Hertfordshire, WD3 4TG
www.thegrove.co.uk
Fabulous designer hotel in stately home and grounds with state-of-the-art spa and golf course. Anouska's crèche and play area will occupy your children all day if required. Little extras to keep the children happy and occupied include child sized bathrobes, a box of toys for children up to 10yrs and children's DVD's.

The Ickworth Hotel   **01284 735 350**
& Apartments
Horringer, Bury St Edmunds, Suffolk, IP29 5QE
www.ickworthhotel.co.uk
The East Wing at Ickworth was home to the Hervey family for almost 200 years. It has now been transformed into one of the most remarkable luxury family-friendly hotels in the UK.

The Woolacombe Bay Hotel   **01271 870 388**
Woolacombe, Devon, EX34 7BN
www.woolacombe-bay-hotel.co.uk
This family-friendly hotel in Woolacombe Bay offers a beachy holiday for families. Facilities include an indoor and outdoor pool, adventure playground, swings, morning crèche for the under 5's and a children's club for the over 5's. Children's tea is between 5-5.30pm.

Trefeddian Hotel   **01654 767 213**
Aberdyfi, Wales, LL35 0SB
www.trefwales.com
A family friendly 3 star hotel with spectacular views overlooking Cardigan Bay. A well established family run hotel with an indoor heated swimming pool and only minutes away

from 4 miles of award winning sandy beach. Indoor playroom, baby listening and babysitting available as well as children's menu and early suppers. Dogs are welcome.

Watergate Bay Hotel   **01637 860 543**
Watergate Bay, Newquay, Cornwall, TR8 4AA
www.watergate.co.uk
Great supervised indoor playroom, so parents can enjoy time on their own. There is also an outdoor playground, a warm paddling pool, sandpits and trampolines. A children's tea is between 5-6pm for children under 7yrs and a free baby listening service in the evenings. Jamie Oliver's Fifteen Cornwall restaurant is within walking distance.

Woolley Grange   **01225 864 705**
Woolley Green, Bradford on Avon, Wiltshire, BA15 1TX
www.woolleygrangehotel.co.uk
A beautiful Jacobean Manor House standing in 14 acres of grounds on the outskirts of the medieval wool town of Bradford-on-Avon in Wiltshire, Woolley Grange was a family home for 400 years before being converted into the first Luxury Family Hotel in 1989.

resorts

Bluestone Resorts   **01834 888 599**
www.bluestonewales.com
Bluestone National Park Resort in Pembrokeshire is set within 500 acres of natural splendour it comprises luxury lodges set around a traditional village. Awarded "five star" status by Visit Wales, our superb family friendly facilities mean that family holidays have never been this good.

SANI RESORT.
The Mediterranean Destination

Sani Resort   **0800 949 6809**
www.saniresort.com   crs@saniresort.gr
Set on the Kassandra peninsula in Halkidiki, Greece, Sani Resort is a family-run, privately-owned luxury haven, consisting of four five-star hotels in unspoiled and peaceful surroundings. In this 1000-acre ecological reserve you'll find shallow crystal-clear waters ideal for children, five miles of white soft sands, an exclusive yacht marina, three spas, over thirty bars and restaurants, Ofsted-standard childcare and a wide range of sporting, leisure and entertainment activities. Call or e-mail us quoting "LBD2012" to claim your special treat.

Center Parcs   **08448 267 723**
www.centerparcs.co.uk
Centres at Longleat, Elveden, Whinfell Forest and Sherwood Forest with more centres across Europe. Great outdoor activities and huge indoor pools with slides etc.

travel

Club Med
0871 424 4044
www.clubmed.co.uk
All inclusive holiday villages located all over the world. A number of them offer childcare facilities for babies and young children during the day with good family discount packages.

self catering

Amazing Holidays
01460 30609
www.amazing-holidayhomes.co.uk
A family run business providing three luxurious holiday homes to rent in Cornwall, Spain and Switzerland. Big family groups can taken on a sea-view house in Cornwall which sleeps up to 10, or you can opt for a Swiss chalet in Haute Nendaz.

Bosinver Farm Cottages
01726 72128
St Austell, Cornwall
A delightful selection of farm cottages that have been converted from old farm buildings, surrounded by lovely gardens. Cottages come equipped with high quality nursery equipment. A heated swimming pool, all-weather tennis court, sauna, games room, BBQ area, cycle hire, fishing lake, nature trails and a full farmyard.

The Rosevine
01872 580 206
Rosevine, Nr Portscatho, Truro, Cornwall, TR2 5EW
www.rosevine.co.uk
The Rosevine is perfect for chic family holidays by the sea on the Roseland Peninsula in Cornwall. Apartment-style family suites include mini-kitchens, ideal for looking after the needs of little ones. There is also a restaurant serving fabulous food, and an indoor pool.

Treworgey Cottages
01503 262 730
Cornwall
www.cornishdreamcottages.co.uk
Paradise for parents and children. Eighteenth Century cottages at the head of the Looe Valley with views to the river below. Each Five Star cottage has its own private garden, log fire, antiques, dishwasher, DVD, and fresh flowers. 150 acres with sea views to roam. Homemade food. WiFi. On site horse riding, tennis, swimming, play and friendly animals.

ski companies

Meriski
01285 648 518
www.meriski.co.uk
No one knows Meribel like Meriski! Whether you are skiing as a couple with a group of friends or as a family, Meriski offers the perfect balance of accommodation. With 10 authentic, luxury chalets in Meribel, sleeping 6 - 17+ guests there is something for everyone. Visit our website www.meriski.co.uk.

Ski Famille
08456 443 764
www.skifamille.co.uk
Ski Famille offers quality catered chalets in the Three Valleys and Les Gets. All holidays include free in-house childcare provided by a team of qualified and experienced carers. Ski Famille make skiing with young children fun and stress free.

Ski Magic
0151 677 2317
www.skimagic.co.uk
Family friendly, company, based in La Tania in the 3 Valleys, France. Fully catered chalets, in enviable positions either on or very close to the piste, offering high standard cuisine. In house childcare with fun loving, highly trained nannies on a full or part time basis. Rest assured that your children will have as much, if not more, than you! FREE child places are on offer most weeks.

travel companies

Blue Chip Holidays
0844 273 3989
www.bluechipholidays.co.uk
Luxury 4 & 5* self-catering holidays in some of the finest locations in the South West. The new Fabulous for Families collection introduces wonderfully stylish Baby Friendly properties perfect for even the tiniest of travellers and Star Family houses, cottages and barns - each with a little extra something to make a family holiday to remember.

Martinhal
+351 282 240 200
www.martinhal.com
Martinhal Beach Resort & Hotel is ideal for families of all ages to relax and unwind in a stunning beach front setting. Located on the unspoiled Western Algarve, Martinhal boasts a wide selection of family houses and a five star hotel. Please visit the Martinhal website for the latest family offers.

Powder Byrne International
020 8246 5300
www.powderbyrne.com
Leading luxury holiday specialist with over 27 year's experience providing a seamless service for families for skiing, sunshine and adventure holidays. Their qualified staff deliver award winning childcare and active kids programmes, with crèches from 4 months to 3 years across a range of hand-picked destinations, with dedicated support for parents to enjoy.

Sunsail Clubs
0844 463 2395
www.sunsail.co.uk/babydir
Sunsail Club Vounaki is not only perfect for adults, but is great for kids too! The Kids' Clubs cater for children aged 4 mths - 17 yrs and offer a full programme of on and off water activities. Please call 0844 463 2395 or visit www.sunsail.co.uk/babydir for more information.

Family Holidays Company
01920 733007
www.familyholidayscompany.com
With oodles of experience this expert team have hand-picked the best family friendly resorts abroad. The website is jam packed with family relevant info, has online prices for all family room options and the knowledgeable team are always on hand to assist. Competitively priced and ABTA bonded. Great for Lapland too.

Travel Matters
020 8675 7878
www.travelmatters.co.uk
A long-established family-focused travel agency based in South West London, founded on the principle of good travel advice.

good advice

As a pregnant woman you have key rights in your favour to protect your job and conditions of employment. As parents you also have important rights after the baby is born.

Pregnancy and your workplace

These are the key points. When you take time out of work to attend antenatal appointments you should still get paid. You are also protected in law against unfair treatment or dismissal, and working entitles to you maternity leave and maternity leave benefits. Your employer must ensure your workplace is a safe and healthy place for you and your baby. If you are ill during pregnancy, your sickness pay should be the same as at any other time.

However, to get paid time off for appointments, you do need to tell your employer you are pregnant. Don't feel you need to do this immediately, but you do need to notify them at least 15 weeks before the baby is due. You also need to give your employer fair warning of when you plan to start your maternity leave. You are entitled to take your maternity leave any time from up to 11 weeks before the due date, though most women prefer to take as much time off as possible after the baby arrives.

The rules around taking leave are quite clear regarding when you might have to take the leave earlier (due to illness, for example), so it is worth reading up on the specifics so you are clear.

Maternity leave

You are entitled to take up to 52 weeks' maternity leave and during this time you continue to be an employee with the same rights (eg to holiday leave) as if you were doing your job. If you have worked continuously for at least 26 weeks by the time you are 25 weeks pregnant you qualify for Statutory Maternity Pay (90% of your regular earnings for six weeks, then a statutory sum or 90% of your earnings if that is lower). If you return to work after 26 weeks you are entitled to your old job back on the same terms. After 26 weeks your employer is entitled to offer a suitable job at the same level with terms at least as good as your previous role. While you are on leave you can do up to 10 days' work for your employer (eg for training). However you can choose NOT to do these 'Keeping in Touch Days' and your employer cannot penalise you.

Paternity leave

Men can now claim up to 26 weeks' additional paternity leave if they are employed and meet certain criteria. This allows a father to claim a statutory sum or 90 per cent of his weekly average earnings during this period (whichever is lower). He must provide eight weeks' notice to his employer that he intends to take the time off, and can only take APL once his partner has returned to work.

A man taking APL continues to be employed under the same conditions as if he were at work, and is entitled to return to the same job on the same terms as if he hadn't been away, as long as he returns within 26 weeks.

There are many important details attached to working and maternity rights. For more information, go to **www.hse.gov.uk/mothers**

good advice

councils

Your local council is an excellent source of information. For enquiries about parks, play centres etc ask for the Children's Information Service. The Early Years department deals with childcare and early education. Some produce booklets about what's on offer for children in the borough - although they can sometimes be out of date. Here are the main switchboard numbers as the individual departments do get moved around during the year.

Barnet CIS   0800 389 8312
www.barnet.gov uk

Bromley CIS   020 8464 0276
www.bromley.gov.uk

Camden CIS   020 7278 4444
www.camden.gov.uk

City of Westminster CIS   020 7641 7929
www.westminster.gov.uk

Ealing CIS   020 8825 5588
www.ealing.gov.uk
Directory of Day Care and Related Services for Children under 8.

Enfield CIS   020 8482 1066
www.enfield.gov.uk

Greenwich CIS   020 8921 6921
www.greenwich.gov.uk

Hackney Learning Trust   020 8820 7000
www.hackney.gov.uk

Hammersmith & Fulham CIS   020 8735 5868
www.lbhf.gov.uk

Haringey Childcare Information Service   020 8801 1234
www.haringey.gov.uk

Hounslow CIS   020 8583 2000
www.hounslow.gov.uk
A-Z Guide for 0-12s.

Islington CIS   020 7527 5959
www.islington.gov.uk

Kensington & Chelsea CIS   020 7361 3302
www.rbkc.gov.uk

Lambeth CIS   0845 601 5317
www.lambeth.gov.uk

Lewisham CIS   0800 085 0606
www.lewisham.gov.uk

Newham CIS   020 8430 2000
www.newham.gov.uk

Richmond upon Thames CIS   020 8891 7554
www.richmond.gov.uk

Southwark CIS   020 7525 5000
www.southwark.gov.uk

Tower Hamlets CIS   020 7364 5000
www.towerhamlets.gov.uk

Waltham Forest CIS   020 8539 0864
www.lbwf.gov.uk

Wandsworth CIS   020 8871 6000
www.wandsworth.gov.uk

working/franchise opportunities

We list many businesses and franchises that are looking to expand, such as Monkey Music and Jo Jingles. So register with us online at www.babydirectory.com to hear about businesses for sale.

Gymboree-uk.com
www.gymboree-uk.com
Gymboree is the longest running and most successful child development programme in the world. Curriculum-based classes (including birthday parties) offer a highly flexible franchise opportunity, enabling you to organise the business to your personal requirements and in tune with the local market. There are almost 400 worldwide franchisees with over 30 years of experience, and a dedicated UK support system. Please visit www.gymboree-uk.com/gymboree-working-with-children-franchise/ or email us directly at franchise@gymboree-uk.com for an information pack.

Tatty Bumpkin   0845 680 0480
www.tattybumpkin.com
"I stood by the Giggle Tree and laughed out loud..." Tatty Bumpkin offers an established, ethical and profitable country-wide children's franchise. Our unique concept is dual-income; with award winning yoga-inspired classes and a range of organic clothing and fair trade class related products for babies and children 0-7 years.

helplines

Abuse/Domestic Violence
Organisation that advise on how to protect yourself or your children and support given to victims.

Kidscape 020 7730 3300
www.kidscape.org.uk
Support and advice on bullying and sexual abuse.

Women's Domestic 0161 839 8574
Violence Helpline
www.wdvh.org.uk

Adoption
To adopt you need to be approved by the British authorities (at least 6mths). The first step is to contact your local authority where a social worker will conduct a Home Study to assess your suitability to adopt. To adopt from overseas the government has to formalise the paperwork (6-9mths) and send the papers to the British Embassy in your chosen country.

Adoption UK 0870 770 0450
www.adoptionuk.org.uk

After Adoption 0161 839 4930
www.afteradoption.org.uk

BAAF 020 7593 2000
www.baaf.org.uk
British Association for Adoption and Fostering. Information and advice for prospective parents; list of UK children looking for families [normally 5yrs+].

OASIS 0870 241 7069
www.adoptionoverseas.org.uk

Intercountry Adoption Centre 020 8449 2562
www.icacentre.org.uk
Advice and information and workshops for parents wanting to adopt from overseas.

Post-Adoption Centre 0870 777 2197
www.postadoptioncentre.org.uk
Daily advice line which offers advice, information and support to all affected by adoption.

Bereavement and loss
Support and information for parents whose pregnancies fail or whose baby or child dies.

Baby Loss
www.babyloss.com
Online information and support for women who have experienced the loss of their baby.

Child Bereavement Trust 01494 446 648
www.childbereavement.org.uk

Child Death Helpline 0800 282 986
www.childdeathhelpline.org.uk
Open daily 7pm-10pm, 10am-1pm Mon-Fri and Wed 10am-4pm.

Cot Death Society 0845 601 0234
www.cotdeathsociety.org.uk

Cruse Bereavement Care 0870 167 1677
www.crusebereavementcare.org.uk
Support and advice when someone you know has died.

FSID Helpline 020 7233 2090
Foundation for the Study of Infant Deaths

Miscarriage Association 01924 200 799
www.miscarriageassociation.org.uk

Stillbirth & Neonatal Death 020 7436 7940
www.uk-sands.org

Charities, campaigns and appeals
Charities funding research into pregnancy and birth complications as well as diseases affecting babies.

ChildLine 0800 1111
www.childline.org.uk

CLIC Sargent 0845 301 0031
www.clicsargent.com
Care and support for families with cancer and leukaemia.

NSPCC 0800 800 500
www.nspcc.org.uk

Tommy's 0870 777 3060
www.tommys.org
Information for parents-to-be to ensure a healthy pregnancy.

good advice

Education

Organisations that help parents whose children have a learning difficulty or find reading/writing difficult as well as home-educating groups.

British Association for   020 7539 5400
Early Childhood Education
www.early-education.org.uk
Promoting good education for all families.

British Dyslexia Association   01189 668 271
www.bdadyslexia.org.uk
www.dyslexia-inst.org.uk

Barrington Stoke   0131 225 4113
www.barringtonstoke.co.uk
Publishers of books that entice the most reluctant readers.

British Institute for Learning   01562 723 010

Difficulties
www.bild.org.uk

British Stammering Association   020 8983 1003
www.stammering.org

Children's Information Service   0800 960 296
www.childcarelink.go.uk
Split into regional councils you can find details about childminders, pre-schools and nurseries in your area.

Daycare Trust   020 7840 3350
www.daycaretrust.org.uk
Help and support in finding and paying for high quality childcare.

Dyspraxia Foundation   01462 454 986
www.dyspraxiafoundation.org.uk

Home Education   01707 371 854
Advisory Service
www.heas.co.uk

Environmental Campaigns

Organisations that care and campaign on environmental issues.

Real Nappy Network   020 8299 4519
www.realnappy.com

Womens Environmental Network   020 7481 9004
www.wen.org.uk
Campaigns on issues that link women, health and the environment. Campaigns promote positive alternatives to polluting practices and consumer items.

Families and relationships

Help for step-families, foster, single and adopting parents.

National Council for   0800 185 026
One-Parent Families
www.oneparentfamilies.org.uk

National Family Mediation   020 7383 5993
www.nfm.org.uk

Parentline Plus   0808 800 2222
www.parentlineplus.org.uk
Information, advice and workshops for parents on a range of parenting topics such as coping with a new baby. Excellent website and message board.

Relate   020 8367 7712
www.relate.org.uk

Gingerbread   0800 018 4318
www.gingerbread.org.uk
Leading support group for single parents.

Single Parent Travel Club   0870 241 621
www.sptc.org.uk
Network of mums and dads joining up on holidays and days out.

Grandparents' Federation   01279 444 964
www.grandparents-federation.org.uk

Fatherhood

Information and support for fathers.

Fathers Direct   020 7920 9491
www.fathersdirect.com
Support and information for expectant, new, solo and unmarried dads.

Families Need Fathers   020 7613 5060
www.fnf.org.uk
Produces booklets and regular newsletters from its informative website.

Fertility, preconception pregnancy and women's health

Support and information if you are trying to get pregnant or have health problems during pregnancy.

Action for ME Pregnancy
Network
www.afme.org.uk
0845 123 2314

Action on Pre-Eclampsia
www.apec.org.uk
020 8427 4217

Association for Improvements
in the Maternity Services
www.aims.org.uk
0870 765 1433

Ante-natal Results and Choices
www.arc-uk.org
020 7631 0285
For people having ante-natal tests where there is a risk of abnormality.

Continence Foundation
www.continence-foundation.org.uk
0845 345 0165

Ectopic Pregnancy Trust
www.ectopic.org
01895 238 025

Group B Strep Support
www.gbss.org.uk
01444 416 176

Endometriosis Society
www.endo.org.uk
020 7222 2781

Infertility Network UK
www.infertilitynetworkuk.com
0870 118 8088
Confidential advice on interfility and reproductive health.

Women's Health Concern
www.womens-health-concern.org
0845 123 2319
Giving confidential advice to women on all heath matters.

Food and nutrition

Organisations that guide parents on healthy eating during pregnancy and for babies and children.

Baby Milk Action
www.babymilkaction.org
01223 464 420

British Allergy Foundation
www.allergyfoundation.com
01322 619 898
Dealing with food intolerance, allergies and chemical sensitivity.

Nut Allergy Sufferers:
Anaphylaxis Campaign
www.anaphylaxis.org.uk
01252 542 029

Allergy Testing Direct
01489 581 968
Diagnostic allergy testing service and advice for parents.

Coeliac UK
www.coeliac.co.uk
01494 437 278
Information about gluten and wheat intolerances.

Diabetes UK
www.diabetes.org.uk
020 7323 1531

Food Standards Agency
www.eatwell.gov.uk
020 7276 8000
Provides the latest information on food safety.

Vegetarian Society
www.vegsoc.org
0161 925 2000
Advice and information about feeding a vegetarian diet to babies and children.

Illness and disability help

Organisations that help with disabilities and conditions affecting children. Also organisations that help parents with a disability.

Action for Sick Children
www.actionforsickchildren.org
0800 074 4519

Birth Defects Foundation
www.birthdefects.co.uk
08700 707 020
For parents whose child has a birth defect.

Birthmark Support Group
www.birthmarksupportgroup.org.uk
01202 257 703
Support and information for anyone who has a birthmark.

BLISS
www.bliss.org.uk
0870 7700 337
Support for parents of special care babies.

Brain Injured Children
www.bibic.org.uk
01278 684 060

Cerebral Palsy Helpline
www.scope.org.uk
0808 800 3333

good advice

Illness and disability help cont.

Children's Heart Federation — 0808 808 5000
www.childrens-heart-fed.org.uk
Information on all aspects of bringing up a child with a heart condition.

Cleft Lip and Palate Assoc — 020 7833 4883
www.clapa.com

Contact a Family — 0808 808 3555
www.cafamily.org.uk
Links families of children with special needs through contact lines with local parent support groups.

Cystic Fibrosis Trust — 020 8464 7211
www.cftrust.org.uk

Disability Alliance — 020 7247 8763
www.disabilityalliance.org

Down's Syndrome Assoc — 020 8682 4001
www.dsa.uk.com

Epilepsy Association — 01132 108 800
www.epilepsy.org.uk

Fragile X Society — 01371 875 100
www.fragilex.org.uk
For those with inherited learning disabilities.

Hyperactive Childrens Support Group — 01903 725 182
www.hacsg.org.uk

LOOK — 0121 428 5038
www.look-uk.org
Advice and support for parents with visually impaired children.

Meningitis Trust — 0845 600 0800
www.meningitis.org

National Autistic Society — 020 7833 2299
www.nas.org.uk

Deaf Parenting UK — 07789 027 186
www.deafparent.org.uk

Parents for Inclusion — 020 7735 7735
www.parentsforinclusion.org
A network of parents of disabled children and children with special needs.

Money and benefits

Government agencies, information and tax advice about employment, maternity benefits/leave and tax credits.

Citizen's Advice Bureau.
www.nacab.org.uk
Free and confidential advice on a wide range of issues such as debt management.

Inland Revenue Tax Credits — 0845 300 3900
www.taxcredits.inlandrevenue.gov.uk

Stressed, depressed and lonely parenting

Organisations providing help if you have had a bad birth experience or trauma, if your baby cries constantly, or if you children's behaviour is out of control. Also if you are feeling low and unhappy.

Association for Post-natal Illness — 020 7386 0868
www.apni.org

Birth Crisis Network — 01865 300 266
www.sheilakitzinger.com/birthcrisis.htm
Was set up to offer a listening service for mothers who have experienced a bad or traumatic birth.

Meet A Mum Association — 0845 120 3746
www.mama.co.uk
Open 7pm-10pm Mon-Fri. Helping mothers who feel depressed or lonely.

Working parents

Information and advice on how to find the right childcare when you go back to work and information for parents trying to balance career and family.

Working Families — 020 7628 2128
www.workingfamilies.org.uk

Mother @ Work — 01273 670 003
www.motheratwork.co.uk
A monthly webzine dedicated to working mothers.

© The Baby Directory